CentOS 6 Linux Server Cookbook

A practical guide to installing, configuring, and administering the CentOS community-based enterprise server

Jonathan Hobson

[PACKT] PUBLISHING

open source ✲
community experience distilled

BIRMINGHAM - MUMBAI

CentOS 6 Linux Server Cookbook

First published: April 2013

Production Reference: 1090413

Published by Packt Publishing Ltd.
Livery Place
35 Livery Street
Birmingham B3 2PB, UK.

ISBN 978-1-84951-902-1

www.packtpub.com

Cover Image by Jasmine Doremus (jasdoremus@gmail.com)

Credits

Author
Jonathan Hobson

Reviewers
Ugo Bellavance

Benoît Benedetti

Frank Lemmon

Acquisition Editor
Joanne Fitzpatrick

Lead Technical Editor
Dayan Hyames

Technical Editors
Dominic Pereira

Saijul Shah

Project Coordinator
Abhishek Kori

Proofreader
Mario Cecere

Indexer
Hemangini Bari

Production Coordinator
Shantanu Zagade

Cover Work
Shantanu Zagade

About the Author

Jonathan Hobson is a Web Developer, Systems Engineer, and Applications Programmer, who, for more than 20 years has been working behind the scenes to support companies, organizations, and individuals around the world to realize their digital ambitions. With an honors degree in both English and History and as a respected practitioner of many computer languages, Jonathan enjoys writing code, publishing articles, building computers, playing video games, and getting "out and about" in the big outdoors. He has been using CentOS since its inception and over the years, it has not only earned his trust, but it has become his first-choice server solution. CentOS is a first class community-based enterprise class operating system, it is a pleasure to work with, and because of this, Jonathan has written this book in order that his knowledge and experience can be passed on to others.

About the Reviewers

Ugo Bellavance, who has done most of his studies in e-commerce, started using Linux at Red Hat 5.2, got Linux training from Savoir-Faire-Linux at age 20, and got his RHCE on RHEL 6 in 2011. He's been a consultant in the past, but he's now an employee for a provincial government agency for which he manages the infrastructure (servers, workstations, network, security, virtualization, SAN/NAS, PBX). He's a big fan of open source software and its underlying philosophy. He's worked with Debian, Ubuntu, SUSE, but what he knows best is RHEL-based distributions. He's known for his contributions to the MailScanner project (he has been a technical reviewer for the *MailScanner* book), but also dedicated his time to different open source projects such as Mondo Rescue, OTRS, SpamAssassin, pfSense, and a few others.

I thank my lover, Lysanne, who accepted to allow me some free time slots for this review even with a two year-old and a six month-old to take care of. The presence of these three human beings in my life is simply invaluable.

I must also thank my friend Sébastien, whose generosity is only matched by his knowledge and kindness. I would never have reached that high in my career if it wasn't for him.

Benoît Benedetti works as a Linux System Administrator, for the University of Nice Sophia Antipolis, where he graduated with a degree in computer science.

He is always interested in resolving new problems, as it's an opportunity to work with new technologies. Benoît loves helping users, teaching students, and writing technical articles for *GNU/Linux Magazine* and *GNU/Linux Pratique*—the historical monthly magazines about Linux in France.

He would like to thank every person who dedicates their time developing free and open source software, and making them available for us to play with.

Frank Lemmon is a Senior Software QA Professional with seven years of CentOS experience. His past work experience includes working at Yahoo!, Qualys, Hewlett-Packard, and various other start-ups.

He worked as a reviewer on the first edition of the book, *OWASP Developer's Guide*.

In memory of my father, who valued the importance of education and was an inspiration to me.

www.PacktPub.com

Support files, eBooks, discount offers and more

You might want to visit www.PacktPub.com for support files and downloads related to your book.

Did you know that Packt offers eBook versions of every book published, with PDF and ePub files available? You can upgrade to the eBook version at www.PacktPub.com and as a print book customer, you are entitled to a discount on the eBook copy. Get in touch with us at service@packtpub.com for more details.

At www.PacktPub.com, you can also read a collection of free technical articles, sign up for a range of free newsletters and receive exclusive discounts and offers on Packt books and eBooks.

http://PacktLib.PacktPub.com

Do you need instant solutions to your IT questions? PacktLib is Packt's online digital book library. Here, you can access, read and search across Packt's entire library of books.

Why Subscribe?

- ▶ Fully searchable across every book published by Packt
- ▶ Copy and paste, print and bookmark content
- ▶ On demand and accessible via web browser

Free Access for Packt account holders

If you have an account with Packt at www.PacktPub.com, you can use this to access PacktLib today and view nine entirely free books. Simply use your login credentials for immediate access.

This book is dedicated to my family. I couldn't have done it without you.

Table of Contents

Preface

Building a server can present a challenge. It is often difficult at the best of times and frustrating at the worst of times. They can represent the biggest of problems or give you a great sense of pride and achievement. Where the word "server" can describe many things, it is the intention of this book to lift the lid and expose the inner workings of this enterprise-class computing system with the intention of enabling you to build the professional server solution of choice.

CentOS is a community-based enterprise class operating system. It is available free of charge, and as a fully compatible derivative of Red Hat Enterprise Linux (RHEL) it represents the first choice operating system for organizations, companies, professionals, and home users all over the world who intend to run a server. It's widely respected as a very powerful and flexible Linux distribution and regardless as to whether you intend to run a web server, file server, FTP server, domain server, or a multi-role solution, it is the purpose of this book to deliver a series of turn-key solutions that will show you how quickly you can build a fully capable and comprehensive server system using the CentOS 6 operating system.

So with this in mind, you could say that this book represents more than just another introduction to yet another server-based operating system. This is a cookbook about an enterprise-class operating system that provides a step-by-step approach to making it work. So, regardless as to whether you are a new or an experienced user, there is something inside these pages for everyone, as this book will become your practical guide to getting things done and a starting point to all things CentOS.

What this book covers

Chapter 1, Installing CentOS, is a series of recipes that introduces you to the task of installing your server, updating, and enhancing the minimal install with additional tools and adding a desktop environment. It is designed to get you started and to provide a reference that shows you a number of ways to achieve the desired installation.

Chapter 2, Configuring CentOS, is designed to follow on from a successful installation to offer a helping hand and provide you with a number of recipes that will enable you to achieve the desired server configuration. From changing the time zone and updating the hardware clock to binding multiple IP addresses, you will not only learn how to resolve a fully qualified domain name but you will be shown how to work with multiple Ethernet devices and manage SELinux.

Chapter 3, Working with CentOS, provides the building blocks that will enable you to champion your server and take control of your environment. It is here to kick start your role as a server administrator, by disseminating a wealth of information that will walk you through a variety of steps that are required to develop a fully considered and professional server solution.

Chapter 4, Managing Packages with Yum, serves to introduce you to the definitive package manager for CentOS 6 server. From upgrading the system to finding, installing, removing, and enhancing your system with additional repositories, it is the purpose of this chapter to explain the open source command-line package management utility known as the Yellowdog Updater, Modified.

Chapter 5, Securing CentOS, discusses the need to implement a series of solutions that will deliver the level of protection you need to run a successful server solution. From escalating user privileges to preventing dictionary-based attacks, you will see how easy it is to build a server that not only considers the need to reduce risk from external attack but one that will provide additional protection for your users.

Chapter 6, Working with Samba, focuses on the power and simplicity of file sharing with Samba in order to provide CentOS 6 server with the ability to provide a sense of community within the workplace.

Chapter 7, Working with Domains, considers the steps required to implement domain names, domain resolution, and DNS queries on a CentOS 6 server. The domain name system is an essential role of any server and whether you are intending to support a home network or a full corporate environment, it is the purpose of this chapter to provide a series of solutions that will deliver the beginning of a future-proof solution.

Chapter 8, Working with Databases, provides a series of recipes that delivers instant access to MySQL and PostgreSQL with the intention of explaining the necessary steps required to deploy them on a CentOS 6 server.

Chapter 9, Providing Mail Services, introduces you to the process of enabling a domain-wide Mail Transport Agent to your CentOS 6 server. From building a local POP3/SMTP server to configuring SASL and dealing with SPAM, the purpose of this chapter is to provide the groundwork for all your future e-mail-based needs.

Chapter 10, Working with Apache, investigates the role of this well known server technology to full effect, and whether you are intending to run a development server or a live production server, this chapter provides you with the necessary steps to deliver the features you need to become the master of your web based publishing solution.

Chapter 11, Working with FTP, concentrates on the role of VSFTP with a series of recipes that will provide the guidance you need to install, configure and manage the File Transfer Protocol you want to provide on a CentOS 6 server.

What you need for this book

The requirements of this book are relatively simple and begin with the need to download the CentOS operating system. The software is free, but you will need a computer that is capable of fulfilling the role of a server, an Internet connection, some spare time, and a desire to have fun.

In saying that, many readers will be aware that you do not need a spare computer to take advantage of this book as the option of installing CentOS on virtualization software is always available. This approach is quite common and where the recipes contained within these pages remain applicable, you should be aware that the use of virtualization software is not considered by this book. For this reason any requests for support regarding this the use of this software should be directed towards the appropriate supplier.

Who this book is for

This is a practical guide for building a server solution, and rather than being about CentOS itself, this is a book that will show you how to get CentOS up and running. It is a book that has been written with the novice-to-intermediate Linux user in mind who is intending to use CentOS as the basis of their next server. However, if you are new to operating systems as a whole, then don't worry; this book will also serve to provide you with the step-by-step approach you need to build a complete server solution with plenty of tricks of the trade thrown in for good measure.

Conventions

In this book, you will find a number of styles of text that distinguish between different kinds of information. Here are some examples of these styles, and an explanation of their meaning.

Code words in text, database table names, folder names, filenames, file extensions, pathnames, dummy URLs, user input, and Twitter handles are shown as follows: "Again, if you experience any difficulties, simply check the logfile located at /var/log/maillog."

A block of code is set as follows:

```
include "/etc/named.rfc1912.zones";
zone "XXX.XXX.XXX.in-addr.arpa" IN {
type master;
file "/var/named/hostname.domainname.lan.db";
allow-update { none; };
};
```

Any command-line input or output is written as follows:

```
vi /etc/named.conf
```

New terms and **important words** are shown in bold. Words that you see on the screen, in menus or dialog boxes for example, appear in the text like this: "The second step is to choose the button labeled **Configure Network** (located in the lower-left portion of the screen) and use the resulting **Network Connections** dialog box to record any changes to your Ethernet settings."

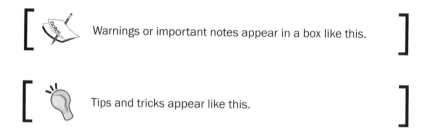

[Warnings or important notes appear in a box like this.   ]

[Tips and tricks appear like this.   ]

Reader feedback

Feedback from our readers is always welcome. Let us know what you think about this book—what you liked or may have disliked. Reader feedback is important for us to develop titles that you really get the most out of.

To send us general feedback, simply send an e-mail to feedback@packtpub.com, and mention the book title via the subject of your message.

If there is a topic that you have expertise in and you are interested in either writing or contributing to a book, see our author guide on www.packtpub.com/authors.

Customer support

Now that you are the proud owner of a Packt book, we have a number of things to help you to get the most from your purchase.

Errata

Although we have taken every care to ensure the accuracy of our content, mistakes do happen. If you find a mistake in one of our books—maybe a mistake in the text or the code—we would be grateful if you would report this to us. By doing so, you can save other readers from frustration and help us improve subsequent versions of this book. If you find any errata, please report them by visiting http://www.packtpub.com/submit-errata, selecting your book, clicking on the **errata submission form** link, and entering the details of your errata. Once your errata are verified, your submission will be accepted and the errata will be uploaded on our website, or added to any list of existing errata, under the Errata section of that title. Any existing errata can be viewed by selecting your title from http://www.packtpub.com/support.

Piracy

Piracy of copyright material on the Internet is an ongoing problem across all media. At Packt, we take the protection of our copyright and licenses very seriously. If you come across any illegal copies of our works, in any form, on the Internet, please provide us with the location address or website name immediately so that we can pursue a remedy.

Please contact us at copyright@packtpub.com with a link to the suspected pirated material.

We appreciate your help in protecting our authors, and our ability to bring you valuable content.

Questions

You can contact us at questions@packtpub.com if you are having a problem with any aspect of the book, and we will do our best to address it.

1
Installing CentOS

In this chapter, we will cover:

- ▶ Downloading CentOS and confirming the checksum on a Windows desktop
- ▶ Performing an installation of CentOS using the graphical installer
- ▶ Running a netinstall over HTTP
- ▶ Installing CentOS in Text Mode and building a minimal installation
- ▶ Re-installing the boot loader
- ▶ Updating the installation and enhancing the minimal install with additional administration and development tools
- ▶ Finishing the installation process with Firstboot
- ▶ Adding the GNOME desktop environment, changing the runlevel, and installing additional software

Introduction

This chapter is a collection of recipes that will guide you through the process of un-wrapping the box and exploring a wide range of installation techniques by downloading CentOS and confirming the checksum on a Windows desktop; performing an installation of CentOS using the graphical installer; running a netinstall over HTTP; installing CentOS in Text Mode and building a minimal installation; re-installing the boot loader; updating the installation and enhancing the minimal install with additional administration and development tools; finishing the installation process with Firstboot; adding the GNOME desktop environment, changing the runlevel and installing additional software.

Downloading CentOS and confirming the checksum on a Windows desktop

In this recipe we will learn how to download and confirm the checksum of one or more CentOS 6 disk image(s) using a typical Windows desktop computer.

CentOS is made available in various formats by HTTP, FTP, or via a Torrent-based client from a series of mirror sites located across the world. It supports both the 32-bit and 64-bit architectures, and having downloaded one or more image files, it is often a good idea to validate those files' checksum in order to ensure that any resulting media should function and perform as expected.

Getting ready

To complete this recipe it is assumed that you are using a typical Windows-based computer (Windows 7, Windows Vista, or similar) with full administration rights. You will need an Internet connection to download the required installation files and access to a standard DVD/CD disk burner with the appropriate software in order to create the relevant installation disks.

How to do it...

Regardless as to what type of installation files you download, the following techniques can be applied to all image files supplied by the CentOS project:

1. So let's begin by visiting `http://www.centos.org/mirrors-list` in your browser.

    This URL was correct at the time of writing this book, but if it's no longer functional or is not available, then simply visit `http://www.centos.org` and navigate to **Downloads | Mirrors | CentOS Public Mirror List** or review the links associated with the latest release announcements made on the home page.

2. The mirror sites are categorized, so from the resulting list of links, choose a mirror that best suits your current location. For example, if you are in London (UK), you can choose **European Mirrors (Countries N-Z)**.

3. From the resulting list and depending on your preferred method of downloading the CentOS images, scroll down and choose a mirror site by selecting either, the **HTTP** or the **FTP** link.

4. Having made your selection, you will now see a list of directories or folders that will allow you to choose the version of CentOS you want to install. To proceed, simply select the appropriate folder that reads **6.X**, where X is the required minor release of CentOS 6.

5. Having chosen the preferred minor release of CentOS you want to install, you will now see an additional list of directories that includes **centosplus**, **contrib**, **cr**, **extras**, **fasttrack**, **isos**, **os**, and **updates**. To proceed, choose the **isos** directory.

6. At this point you are now given the opportunity to choose the preferred architecture. The directory labeled i386 is a container for the 32-bit version while the directory labeled x86_64 is a container for the 64-bit version. Make the appropriate selection to proceed.

7. You will now be presented with a series of files available for download. Begin by downloading a copy of the valid checksum result labeled or identified as md5sum.txt.

> As this is a standard text file, place your mouse on the link, right-click and choose **Save As** to download a copy of md5sum.txt. When finished, store this file in a safe place for future reference. For the purpose of this recipe, it is assumed that all downloads will be stored in your C:\Users\<username>\Downloads folder.

8. Now, depending on which installation image best suits your needs, start downloading the relevant file(s) in the usual way.

If you are new to CentOS or are intending to follow the recipes found throughout this book, then the minimal installation is ideal. However, you should be aware that there are other options available to you.

For a full 64-bit DVD-based installation, you will need both:

```
CentOS-6.X-x86_64-bin-DVD1.iso
CentOS-6.X-x86_64-bin-DVD2.iso
```

For a full 32-bit DVD-based installation, you will need both:

```
CentOS-6.X-i386-bin-DVD1.iso
CentOS-6.X-i386-bin-DVD2.iso
```

For a minimal installation, you should choose either:

```
CentOS-6.X-i386-minimal.iso (32-bit version)
CentOS-6.X-x86_64-minimal.iso (64-bit version)
```

For a network installation, you should choose either:

```
CentOS-6.X-i386-netinstall.iso (32-bit version)
CentOS-6.X-x86_64-netinstall.iso (64-bit version)
```

If you choose to download a torrent file, then you will need to extract these files in the usual way in order to build the appropriate ISO image file(s).

9. When you have finished downloading the required files, visit http://mirror.centos.org/centos/dostools/ in your browser.

10. Now download the following DOS-based tool in order that we can use it to validate our installation files:

    md5sum.exe

The full URL is http://mirror.centos.org/dostools/md5sum.exe.

11. It is assumed that you have downloaded all the files to the typical downloads folder of the current user profile on your Windows desktop (C:\Users\<username>\Downloads), so when the download is complete, open **Command Prompt** (typically found at **Start | All Programs | Accessories | Command Prompt**) and type the following command to access this location:

    cd downloads

12. To see the list of files and the relevant extensions, type the following command:

    dir

13. The command prompt should now list all the files in your download folder (including all image files, md5sum.txt, and md5sum.exe). Based on the file names shown, modify the following command in order to check the checksum of your ISO image file and type:

```
md5sum.exe your_image_file_name_here.iso
```

> For example, you can type
> md5sum.exe CentOS-6.X-x86_64-minimal.iso

14. Press the *Return* key to proceed and then wait for the command prompt to respond. The response is known as the **sum** and the result could look like this:

```
087713752fa88c03a5e8471c661ad1a2   *CentOS-6.X-x86_64-minimal.iso
```

15. Now look at the value given, this is known as the sum, and compare against the relevant listing for your particular image file listed in md5sum.txt. If both numbers match, then you can be confident that you have indeed downloaded a valid CentOS image file.

16. Now repeat this process for any remaining image files and when you have finished, simply burn your image file(s) to a blank CD-Rom or DVD-Rom using your preferred desktop software.

How it works...

The act of downloading an installation image and validating the file's integrity is just the first step towards building the perfect server, and although the process of downloading CentOS is very simple, many do forget the need to confirm the checksum.

So what have we learned from this experience?

We began this recipe by showing you how to download CentOS by outlining the various options available to you. It is not expected that you will need to do this often, but during the course of this recipe you also learned how to navigate the CentOS Project website and select the best download location based on your current location.

Having done this, our next step was to obtain a copy of md5sum.txt before downloading the preferred image files.

> The choice as to whether you selected a 32-bit or 64-bit version is largely dependent on the specification of your intended server. However, given the abilities of most modern computers, for most people the obvious choice will be the 64-bit version in order that you can take advantage of the improved code base and support more than 4 GB of RAM.

The time required to complete the task of downloading the relevant files will depend largely on the speed of your Internet connection, but it was important that we obtained a copy of `md5sum.exe` in order to confirm file integrity and compare the value given against those listed in `md5sum.txt`.

The DOS-based tool was obtained from `http://mirror.centos.org/centos/dostools/md5sum.exe`.

Having completed these steps, we then proceed to open a command prompt session and navigate to the expected destination of all the files by typing:

```
cd downloads
```

We then proceeded to view the contents of `C:\Users\<username>\Downloads` by typing the following command:

```
dir
```

This action lists the filenames concerned, thereby enabling us to modify the following command in order to validate the appropriate ISO files:

```
md5sum.exe your_image_file_name_here.iso
```

The resulting response provides us with the checksum value of the file in question in order that we can compare it with the corresponding value found in `md5sum.txt`.

For example, the content of `md5sum.txt` may look like this:

```
087713752fa88c03a5e8471c661ad1a2  CentOS-6.X-x86_64-minimal.iso
```

Whereas the display in command prompt may show:

```
087713752fa88c03a5e8471c661ad1a2  *CentOS-6.X-x86_64-minimal.iso
```

You should repeat this process for all image files, and if these values match, then you can be confident that your download is verified. A fact that not only reduces the chance of wasting optical disks, but with security in mind, it also implies that what you downloaded is what you were expecting to download (and not something else).

So remember, with every new release the CentOS team will update the main website and enable you to download the required image files. Unless the CentOS project states otherwise, you will only need to do this once, as all minor updates can be managed like any other operating system (discussed later in this book). However, if you do intend to download them again, then it is always a good idea to check the integrity of your image files with the `md5sum` checksum tool.

See also

- ▸ CentOS project home page: `http://www.centos.org`
- ▸ CentOS project – mirror list: `http://www.centos.org/mirrors-list`
- ▸ CentOS project – approved vendors: `http://www.centos.org/vendors`
- ▸ CentOS project – download FAQ regarding md5 checksum:
  `http://www.centos.org/modules/smartfaq/faq.php?faqid=46`
- ▸ CentOS project – how to burn an ISO image:
  `http://www.centos.org/docs/5/html/CD_burning_howto.html`

Performing an installation of CentOS using the graphical installer

In this recipe we will learn how to perform a typical installation of CentOS using the graphical tools provided by the system installer.

In many respects this is considered to be the recommended approach to installing your system as it not only provides you with the chance to create the desired hard disk partitions, but also provides the ability to customize package selection. Your installation will then form the basis of a server on which you can build, develop, and run any type of service you may want to provide in the future.

Getting ready

Before we begin, it is assumed that you have followed a previous recipe in which you were shown how to download CentOS, confirm the checksum of the relevant image files, and create the relevant installation disks.

Depending on which installation image(s) were downloaded, in order to complete this recipe you will be expected to have completed the initial stages of a network install or that you are using one of the following DVD suites:

- ▸ To complete a full 64-bit installation you will need:

  ```
  CentOS-6.X-x86_64-bin-DVD1.iso
  CentOS-6.X-x86_64-bin-DVD2.iso
  ```

- ▸ To complete a full 32-bit installation you will need:

  ```
  CentOS-6.X-i386-bin-DVD1.iso
  CentOS-6.X-i386-bin-DVD2.iso
  ```

In addition to this, you should be confident that your server can meet the following minimum specifications:

▶ An Intel or AMD-based CPU (Pentium, AMD, Via, AMD64/EM64T)

▶ At least 768 MB RAM (1 GB or more recommended)

▶ At least 10 GB hard disk space

Of course, it should be said that the preceding specification acts as guidance only and further details concerning the minimum system requirements can be found at the end of this recipe.

For a typical server you should always consider the need to maximize your resources in terms of RAM and available hard disk space. You should also plan for the long term. Remember, the use of a 64-bit capable CPU will not only tend to run faster with a 64-bit operating system but the system as a whole will be able to take advantage of more than 4 GB of RAM and therefore provide a long-term, scalable solution that can grow with the needs of your network.

How to do it...

To begin this recipe, start by booting your computer from the first CentOS installation DVD and wait for the welcome screen:

1. On the welcome splash screen, use the *Up* and *Down* arrow keys to select and highlight **install or upgrade an existing system**. When you are ready, press the *Return* key to proceed.

2. Having loaded the necessary files, you will be presented with the **disc found** screen and asked if you would like to test the integrity of your DVD. Remember, file integrity in this context refers to the quality of the data on your DVD media only, so if you are confident that your installation media is error free and wish to continue with the installation, simply use the *Left* and *Right* arrow keys to choose **Skip** and press the *Return* key to proceed.

3. Alternatively, if you would prefer to test the integrity of your optical media, choose **OK** and follow the onscreen instructions. A single test should take between three to five minutes and you will have the opportunity to test one or more discs. When this process is complete, choose **Continue** to exit this phase and return to the main installation menu.

You should be aware that the verification process performed during this phase will not always guarantee a trouble-free installation as it will not monitor hardware or measure environmental conditions. This feature is not always used, but it can serve to increase the frequency of success by checking the file integrity of your installation media.

4. The CentOS installer will now prepare the onscreen environment and present the installation welcome screen. From this point onwards you can now use your keyboard and mouse, there is no time limit for completing any section, but remember to enable the number lock on your keyboard if you intend to use the keypad. When you are ready, choose the **Next** button to proceed.

5. On the language selection screen, select the preferred system language. All changes to your language settings will take immediate effect, so when you are ready, choose the **Next** button to proceed.

6. On the keyboard selection screen, select the appropriate keyboard for the system. When you are ready, choose the **Next** button to proceed.

7. On the next screen you are required to choose the type of devices your installation intends to support. You have two primary choices, and if you intend to install CentOS on a SAN device, then choose specialized storage devices. However, in most cases (and for a typical computer) that will be using a local hard disk; so simply choose the default option of basic storage devices. When you are ready, choose the **Next** button to proceed.

> If you are using a new hard disk or a virtual disk, you may see what could be described as a warning/error message. The message may read:
>
> **The storage device below may contain data**
>
> Don't worry, this is to be expected and the message is simply asking you to initialize your hard disk because it is considered to be blank, unpartitioned, or a virtual drive. In most cases, especially if you have more than one hard drive, simply enabling the checkbox and choosing yes, discarding any data will complete the task of disk initialization and enable you to proceed to the next step.

8. On the network settings screen you will be required to complete the following two steps:

   1. In the first step you will need to determine the hostname of your server. As you can see in the text field located at the top-left hand portion of the screen, this value will automatically default to **localhost.localdomain**. Setting the hostname is an important part of installing a server, so change this value to something more suitable, but don't worry, as this book will show you, this value can be changed after the installation process.

2. The second step is to choose the button labeled **Configure Network** (located in the lower-left portion of the screen) and use the resulting **Network Connections** dialog box to record any changes to your Ethernet settings. To do this, simply highlight the relevant Ethernet device listed under the **Wired** tab and choose **Edit**. Check the box labeled **connect automatically** and then make the necessary changes to the **IPv4/IPv6** values including the address, netmask, gateway, and DNS servers. You may even elect a DHCP connection at this stage if your network supports this feature. When finished, choose **Apply** and then close the **Network Connections** dialog box. Your computer will now try to initialize and activate the relevant Ethernet connection(s).

3. When you have finished both these steps, choose **Next** to proceed.

9. On the next screen, you are required to confirm a time zone for your server. You can do by using the interactive map or by simply scrolling through the list of locations to select your nearest city. When finished, ensure the checkbox labeled **System Clock Uses UTC** is checked before choosing **Next** to proceed.

10. On the next screen you will be required to create and confirm a root password for the root user. Typically, it is advised that you should avoid using simple phrases, dictionary-based words, or include any whitespaces. Passwords should consist of no less than six characters, so when you are ready, input your choice and choose **Next** to proceed.

11. On the next screen, you will be asked to determine a hard disk layout for the server as a whole. This will determine the installation type and you can choose from **Use All Space** (use the entire hard drive and utilize the default partition scheme), **Replace Existing Linux system (s)** (remove all current Linux partitions and replace with the default partition scheme), **Shrink Current System** (shrink the current file system to make room for the default partition scheme), **Use Free Space** (use the remaining free space to create the default partition scheme), or **Create Custom Layout**. You are given the option to review the partition scheme and the ability to customize your partitions is a useful option. However, if you are new to Linux or are not yet comfortable with the concept of building a custom layout, then for the purpose of this recipe you should select **Use All Space** and click **Next** to proceed.

12. You will now be asked to confirm your hard disk partitioning instruction. If you feel that you have made a mistake, now is the time to correct it by choosing **Go Back**. However, if you are confident that the correct choice has been made, then simply click the button labeled **Write changes to disk** in order to complete this phase of the installation process.

13. CentOS will now format your hard disk(s) before proceeding to the next screen where you will be invited to make any relevant changes to the boot loader. Otherwise known as the **GRand Unified Bootloader** (**GRUB**) unless you feel confident enough to change the location of boot loader, it is always best to accept the defaults. However, should you wish to set a boot loader password to improve security, then this can be achieved by selecting the checkbox labeled **Use a boot loader password** followed by the **Change password** button in order to make the relevant changes.

14. When you are ready, click **Next** to proceed.

15. On the package group selection screen, you will notice that CentOS provides for a number of **Package Selection Groups** that simplifies the process of selecting individual packages. Use the descriptions provided to make your primary choice, but for a typical server (and for someone who wishes to take full advantage of the recipes contained within this book) it is often better to begin with a minimal install and add packages as and when you need them.

    On the other hand, and should you feel inclined to do so, you can take this opportunity to explore the individual packages found on your installation media by choosing to customize the software selection. To do this, simply check the box labeled **Customize Now** before leaving this screen.

    When you are ready, click **Next** to proceed.

16. CentOS will now resolve any dependencies and the installer will begin writing to the hard disk. This may take some time, but a progress bar will indicate the status of your installation. When finished, the congratulations screen will inform you that the entire process is complete and that the installation was successful. So when you are ready, click **Reboot** to finalize this recipe and to recover the installation media.

17. Congratulations, you have now installed CentOS 6.

How it works...

In this recipe you have discovered how to install the CentOS 6 operating system, and having covered the typical approach to the graphical installation process you are now in a position to develop the server with additional configuration changes and packages that will suit the role you intend the server to fulfill.

So what have we learned from this experience?

We started by initializing the main installer and determining whether we would like to check the installation media for possible corruption and defects. Of course, validating the data on your disk is always a useful process and it can save time in the long run, but you should be aware that it will not necessarily guarantee a trouble-free installation. For this reason, most users who have already validated the checksum tend to skip this process.

The next steps then welcomed us to CentOS and invited us to confirm the appropriate language, keyboard, location, hostname, root password, network, and storage settings.

For example, any changes to the language setting were immediate, whereas the configuration of your network settings was simply a matter of ensuring the Ethernet device would connect automatically and modifying the appropriate IPv4/IPv6 settings. You were able to create a static or dynamic IP address, while the setting of a root password was simply a matter of choosing an appropriate series of alpha-numeric values that did not consist of known words, typical phrases, or contain any whitespace. Whatever password you decide on, it should consist of no less than six characters to avoid any warnings issued by the installer.

During the next stage, we then considered the need to partition the hard disks by selecting the default option known as **Use All Space**. By choosing this option, you were allowing the installer to determine the relative sizes of each partition and to build a logical volume that would assign GRUB to a default location. Of course, diving in to the depths of partition management was beyond the purpose of this recipe, but you did see that the various options that enable you to build your own custom layout should this be the preferred option.

You were then given the option to change the location of GRUB. This is not always deemed to be necessary, as moving GRUB can be an awkward process for even the most experienced users but ignoring this, you did discover an option that would enable you to password-protect the boot loader and provide additional system-wide protection.

Finally we came upon the package group selection screen where we discovered that CentOS not only enables us to choose a minimal install, but it also provides for a significant number of package selection groups that are designed for convenience.

The sole purpose of these groups is to simplify the process of selecting the correct packages for your installation. I think you would agree that most of the group titles are self-explanatory, but it is generally accepted that a minimal install is by far the most efficient method of installing any server because it is far easier to add and configure packages when we need them rather than simply installing everything at once. This rule of thumb not only reduces your initial workload, but it also ensures that your server remains safe and secure which is of a particular concern if it is located in the public domain.

So in conclusion, I think it would be appropriate to say that there is always more to discover about the installation process and that there are many different ways to install your server, but at this early stage you should now take the time to sit back and relax. Well done, you have now completed the recommend installation process and yes, you can now install CentOS.

See also

- ▸ CentOS project home page: http://www.centos.org
- ▸ CentOS project Wiki home page: http://wiki.centos.org
- ▸ CentOS product specifications: http://wiki.centos.org/About/Product

Running a netinstall over HTTP

In this recipe we will learn how to initiate the process of running a netinstall over HTTP (using the URL method) in order to install CentOS 6.

The CentOS network installation is a process by which a small image file is used to boot the computer and enable the download of all the necessary files that will be required to complete the installation of the full operating system.

Using this approach implies the advantage of not being required to download the DVD-based image files and for computers that do not have access to DVD drive; this can be of enormous benefit. Moreover, where you will only download the packages you need, unless you are intending to install more than one server then the entire netinstall-based approach (starting from downloading the initial installation image to finalizing the installation of your computer) not only provides greater flexibility, but it will also save time and offers the benefit of the full installer.

Getting ready

Before we begin, it is assumed that you have followed a previous recipe in which you downloaded the netinstall image of Centos 6, confirmed the checksum values of the image file, and that you have already created the relevant installation disk.

To complete this recipe you will need an active Internet connection, and because this recipe will serve as a starting point to the graphical installation process, you should be confident that your server can meet the following minimum requirements:

- An Intel-based or AMD-based CPU (Pentium, AMD, Via, AMD64/EM64T)
- At least 768 MB RAM (1GB or more recommended)
- At least 10 GB hard disk space

You should be aware that these specifications act as guidance only and further details concerning the minimum system requirements can be found at `http://wiki.centos.org/About/Product`.

How to do it...

To begin this recipe, insert the netinstall disc, boot your computer from the optical drive, and wait for the welcome screen to appear:

1. On the welcome splash screen, use the *Up* and *Down* arrow keys to select and highlight **install or upgrade and existing system**. When you are ready, press the *Return* key to proceed.

2. Having unpacked the necessary files, you will be presented with the **disc found** screen and asked if you would like to test the integrity of your installation disc. Remember, file integrity in this context refers to the quality of the data on the disc only, so if you are confident that your installation media is error-free and wish to continue with the installation, simply use the *Left* and *Right* arrow keys to choose **Skip** and press the *Return* key to proceed.

3. Alternatively, if you would prefer to test the integrity of your optical media, choose **OK** and follow the onscreen instructions. A single test should take a few minutes depending on your hardware. When this process is complete, choose **Continue** to exit this phase and return to the main installation menu.

 You should be aware that the verification process performed during this phase will not always guarantee a trouble-free installation as it cannot monitor hardware or measure environmental conditions. This feature is not always used but it can serve to increase the frequency of success by checking the file integrity of your installation media.

4. On the **Language Selection** screen, use the *Up* and *Down* arrow keys to select the preferred language. When ready, press the *Return* key to proceed.

5. On the **Keyboard Selection** screen, use the *Up* and *Down* arrow keys to select the preferred keyboard settings and press the *Return* key to proceed.

6. At this point you will now be asked to confirm the installation method. As we will be installing over HTTP (also referred to as the URL method), you should choose **URL** and press the *Return* key to proceed.

7. On the **Configure TCP/IP** screen, you will be asked to configure your network settings. By using the *Up* and *Down* arrow keys in conjunction with the *Space bar*, place a * in the preferred values. If your local area network supports dynamic IP assignment, then choose **DHCP** and when you are ready, highlight **OK** and press the *Return* key to proceed.

If you have elected to use a static IP address you will be presented with the **Manual TCP/IP Configuration** screen. This implies that you will be expected to confirm your IP address, Netmask, Gateway, and Nameserver (or DNS) settings by typing in the respective values as required. When you are finished, highlight **OK** and press the *Return* key to proceed.

8. At this stage, your server will now attempt to configure the Ethernet devices before inviting you to complete the **URL Setup** screen. So depending on whether you have chosen a 32-bit or 64-bit installation, in the first dialog box use one of the following values:

    ❏ For a 64-bit installation use
       `http://mirror.centos.org/centos/6/os/x86_64`

    ❏ For a 32-bit installation use
       `http://mirror.centos.org/centos/6/os/i386`

    ❏ Otherwise, you can obtain a list of local mirror sites from
       `http://www.centos.org/mirrors`

    Alternatively, you can also use a personal repository on your local network should you have access to such a facility.

Remember, if you need to enable an HTTP proxy, do this now by entering the relevant details. If you are in doubt, know that you do not use a Proxy or you are unaware of such a feature on your network then leave this section blank.

    When you are ready, by using the *Tab* key, highlight **OK** and press the *Return* key to proceed.

9. On success, the installer will begin to retrieve the appropriate `install.img` file. This may take several minutes to complete, but once resolved a progress bar will then indicate all the download activity. When this process has finished, the installer will prepare the onscreen environment and present you with the installation welcome screen.

From this point onwards you will be able to install CentOS using the graphical installer in the usual way but with one difference. Having resolved the necessary package dependencies all required packages will be downloaded from the Internet.

How it works...

The purpose of this recipe was to introduce you to the concept of the CentOS network installation process in order to show you just how simple this approach can be. By completing this recipe you have not only saved time by limiting your initial download to those files required by the installation process, but you have been able to take advantage of the full graphical installation method without the need for a complete DVD suite.

So what have we learned from this experience?

We have learned how to boot from the netinstall image, initialize the main installer, test the optical media for errors, provide the relevant network settings for the host computer, and provide a URL in order to download the relevant files.

The URL in this case was web-based and dependent on the preferred architecture, but as an alternative you could have modified this instruction to use a local mirror site or even implement an installation from a local repository from your local network.

So in conclusion, it must be said that if you are intending to install more than one server at a time (with a full array of packages), then this may not be the best approach, but for a single server or multiple servers using a minimal install, then the netinstall image represents a far more flexible approach. Rather than waiting to download a complete set of installation files you may never need, the installer will download the required files directly from the chosen location thereby ensuring that you will not only reduce the overall time it takes to get your server up and running, but you will be able to take advantage of the full installation without the need for a DVD drive.

See also

 ▸ CentOS project home page: `http://www.centos.org`
 ▸ CentOS project Wiki home page: `http://wiki.centos.org`
 ▸ CentOS product specifications: `http://wiki.centos.org/About/Product`

Installing CentOS in Text Mode and building a minimal installation

In this recipe we will learn how to install CentOS in Text Mode.

For new users, Text Mode may not be the first choice when deciding how to install your server but it does remain a popular and useful option for a variety of reasons.

Installing a system in Text Mode offers reduced functionality when compared to its graphical counterpart, but this approach excels in an environment where your computer may not meet the general minimum requirements or your graphical display options are limited. Text Mode is a streamlined method, and this approach not only makes it a very simple method to use, but it also ensures that it remains a fast and efficient way to install a CentOS server by reducing the risk of variation and guaranteeing that every installation will be the same.

Getting ready

Before we begin, it is assumed that you have followed a previous recipe in which you were shown how to download CentOS, confirm the checksum values of the image files, and that you have created and labeled the relevant installation disk(s).

For the purpose of this recipe, it will be assumed that you are using the twin DVD-based installation disks. In many respects, installing your system by Text Mode is similar to using the minimal installation image file and for this reason some configuration screens may not be available unless used in the graphical mode.

Text Mode is automatically activated if the system is running less than 652 MB of RAM and for this reason, you should be confident that your system meets the following minimum requirements:

- An Intel-based or AMD-based CPU (Pentium, AMD, Via, AMD64/EM64T)
- At least 392 MB RAM
- At least 8-10 GB hard disk space

 You should be aware that these requirements act as guidance only and further details concerning the minimum system requirements can be found at http://wiki.centos.org/About/Product.

How to do it...

To begin this recipe you should boot your computer from the CentOS installation media of your choice and wait for the welcome screen to appear:

1. When presented with the welcome splash screen, press the *Tab* key to reveal the boot instruction, add a single space using the *Space bar*, and then enter the following:

   ```
   text
   ```

2. Now press the *Return* key to access the Text Mode installer.

3. When the installer is ready, you will be presented with the **disc found** screen and asked if you would like to test the integrity of your DVD. Remember, file integrity in this context refers to the quality of the data on your DVD media only, so if you are confident that your installation media is error-free and wish to continue with the installation, simply use the *Left* and *Right* arrow keys to choose **Skip** and press the *Return* key to proceed.

4. Alternatively, if you prefer to test the integrity of your optical media, choose **OK** and follow the onscreen instructions. A single test will take between 3-5 minutes depending on your hardware and you will have the opportunity to test one or more discs. When this process is complete, choose **Continue** to exit this phase and return to the main installation menu.

You should be aware that the verification process performed during this phase will not always guarantee a trouble-free installation as it cannot monitor hardware or measure environmental conditions. This feature is not always used but it can serve to increase the frequency of success by checking the file integrity of your installation media.

5. If your computer meets the minimum specification, the CentOS installer will now prepare the onscreen environment and present the installation welcome screen. You will now see the **OK** button, so when you are ready, press the *Return* key to proceed.

6. On the **Language Selection** screen, use the *Up* and *Down* arrow keys to highlight the preferred language. When you are ready, press the *Return* key to proceed.

7. On the **Keyboard Selection** screen, use the *Up* and *Down* arrow keys to select the preferred keyboard settings and when you are ready, press the *Return* key to proceed.

If you are using a new hard disk or a virtual disk, you may see what could be described as an error/warning message. The message may read as follows:

Error processing drive

If you see this message, simply use the *Tab* key to highlight the relevant option in order to re-initialize your disk. In most cases, especially if you have more than one hard drive, choosing **re-initialize all** will complete the task and enable you to proceed to the next step.

8. On the **Time Zone Selection** screen, you will be asked to choose your current location. Make sure a star symbol remains in the **system clock uses UTC** option and use the *Up* and *Down* arrow keys to make your selection. When finished, press the *Tab* key to highlight the **OK** button and then press the *Return* key to proceed.

9. On the **Root Password** screen, enter a preferred password. This password will be used to invoke system-based administrative tasks, so it is always a good idea to refrain from using dictionary words, simple phrases, or words that contain white spaces. When ready, press the *Tab* key to highlight the **OK** button and press the *Return* key to proceed.

 If you have used what is considered to be a weak password, the installer will notify you of this fact and ask you to re-confirm your decision to continue.

10. The ability to partition your hard disk in Text Mode is limited, so on the **Partitioning Type** screen, use the arrow keys to choose **use entire drive**. When you are ready, press the *Tab* key to highlight the **OK** button and press the *Return* key to proceed.

11. On the **write storage configuration to disk** screen, you will be asked to confirm the disk partitioning instruction. Use the *Left* and *Right* arrow keys to highlight **write changes to disk** and press the *Return* key to proceed.

12. The CentOS installer will now build the partitions and begin the installation process. This may take a while to complete, but when finished, you will be presented with the complete screen stating: **Congratulations, your CentOS installation is complete**. When you are ready, press the *Return* key to proceed and reboot your computer.

How it works...

In this recipe, you have discovered how to install the CentOS 6 operating system using Text Mode. In many respects it is very similar to using the minimal installation file and if you have read the official documentation supplied by the CentOS project, they advise that it may not be the recommended approach. However, depending on the type of hardware you have at your disposal you may not have an alternative.

So what have we learned from this experience?

We started by initializing Text Mode at the welcome screen by pressing the *Tab* key to reveal the boot instruction, adding a single white space, and entering the following:

```
text
```

So in practice, your screen instruction will look like this:

```
>vmlinuz initrd=initrd.img text
```

When finished, pressing the *Return* key enables us to continue the installation process and check the installation media for possible corruption and defects.

Validating the data on your disk is a quick and painless process but remember, at this stage the installer will only validate the data contained on your installation disk(s). It will not reliably detect any hardware issues, so in effect merely completing this process does not necessarily guarantee a trouble-free installation. For this reason, most confident users who have already confirmed the checksum will generally skip this step.

The following stages then welcome us to CentOS and invite us to review and confirm the appropriate language settings, keyboard settings, and time zone location. Completing these configuration screens is again very simple and this is one of the benefits of streamlining. However, for veterans of other installation methods, you will quickly notice that the number of options have been limited.

If you were using a new hard disk, then it is quite possible that you were asked to initialize the disk by choosing **re-initialize all**. Initializing the hard disk is a process that is generally confined to new hard disks only; it is common to all operating systems and may have taken just a few seconds to complete. Once complete, you were then invited to create a root password before choosing the preferred partition scheme: **use entire drive**.

Passwords should not contain whitespaces, or consist of simple phrases, or dictionary-based words. They should be longer than six characters in length and they should not be easily identifiable, so avoid using dictionary-based words, simple phrases, or actual names. The use of whitespaces should be avoided at all cost.

Again, veterans of the graphical installation method would have noticed that there were no options regarding the configuration of advanced storage methods such as LVM, RAID and iSCSI, customizing the partition layout, customizing the boot loader layout, and the selection of packages during the final phase of the installation. In fact, streamlining the CentOS 6 text installer has removed all of this and instead simply provided you a fast-track route to installing the necessary files that would make a complete minimal install.

You could argue that this approach has made it simpler, whereas you could also argue that the lack of such options can be a hindrance. It is not what the official documentation would call the recommended approach by any means, but this method does have its advantages. Text Mode is used for convenience, and it represents just another tool in your kit-bag, so regardless of whether you benefit from this streamlined approach or not, you now know that CentOS is accessible to even more computers than you originally thought.

See also

- ▸ CentOS project home page: http://www.centos.org
- ▸ CentOS project Wiki home page: http://wiki.centos.org
- ▸ CentOS product specifications: http://wiki.centos.org/About/Product

Re-installing the boot loader

In this recipe we will learn how to re-install the CentOS boot loader.

During the installation process it is possible that you may accidentally damage or even remove the GRUB boot loader and thereby render your server inaccessible. Accidents can happen and it is the purpose of this recipe to show you how to get your server back up and running.

Getting ready

To complete this recipe, you will require a standard installation disk of the CentOS 6 operating system. You will also require the use of a computer display, a standard keyboard, and an optical disk drive.

How to do it...

To begin this recipe you should boot your computer from the CentOS installation DVD and wait for the welcome screen to appear.

1. From the main menu, choose **Rescue installed system**.

2. On the **Language Selection** screen, use the *Up* and *Down* arrow keys to highlight the preferred language. When you are ready, press the *Return* key to proceed.

3. On the **Keyboard Selection** screen, use the *Up* and *Down* arrow keys to select the preferred keyboard setting and press the *Return* key to proceed.

4. On the **Rescue Method** screen, use the *Up* and *Down* arrow keys to select **Local/DVD** as the source and press the *Return* key to proceed.

5. On the **Setup Networking** screen, use the *Left* and *Right* arrow keys to choose **NO** and press the *Return* key to proceed.

6. We have now entered the **Rescue** screens which includes various confirmation sub-screens. To begin this section, use the *Left* and *Right* arrow keys to choose **Continue** and press the *Return* key to proceed.

7. On the first sub-screen, choose **OK** and press the *Return* key to proceed.

8. Again, in the following sub-screen choose **OK** and press the *Return* key to proceed.

9. On the next screen, choose **Start shell** and by using the *Tab* key, highlight **OK** and press the *Return* key to proceed.

10. By completing the preceding steps, you will launch a `Shell` session. You will notice this at the bottom of your display. The current status of the `Shell` session will read as follows:

```
Starting Shell
bash-4.1#_
```

11. At the prompt, type the following instruction before pressing the *Return* key to complete your request:

```
chroot /mnt/sysimage
```

12. Now type the following instruction before pressing the *Return* key to complete your request:

```
cd /boot/grub
```

13. We will now use the `fdisk` command to find the name of all the current partitions. To do this, type the following instruction and then press the *Return* key to complete your request:

```
fdisk -l
```

14. Look for the * symbol in the `fdisk` listing under boot, and assuming that your boot disk is on /dev/sda1 (change this as required) type:

```
grub-install /dev/sda1
```

15. If no error is reported the console should respond as follows:

```
# this device map was generated by anaconda (hd0) /dev/sda
```

16. This message has confirmed that GRUB has now been successfully restored. To proceed we must now leave the session by typing:

```
exit
```

17. To complete this recipe, type:

```
reboot
```

How it works...

GRUB, otherwise known as the **GRand Unified Bootloader**, is a boot loader package that provides access to the CentOS system. It is a very important file, but accidents can happen and on occasion it has been known to suffer damage or even be removed.

If this happens it is very possible that your server will not boot and for this reason this recipe serves to invoke a process that is known as **Rescue Mode** in order to re-install this file.

So what have we learned from this experience?

We started by learning how to access Rescue Mode and configuring the necessary language and keyboard preferences in order that we can interact with the session.

In the following stages, Rescue Mode then enabled us to mount the relevant disk partition with full read/write capability in order that we could target the correct location and re-install GRUB.

Depending on the original configuration and purpose of your server, you may need to review the contents of `/boot/grub/grub.conf` and make additional entries. This is particularly needed for any multi-boot environment in order that GRUB can be configured to manage additional operating systems.

So in conclusion, we could say that this was a very simple recipe, but it is also a very important recipe; and as damage to GRUB is typically associated with an installation procedure it was felt that such a recipe should remain close at hand. In many respects, it is always a good idea to keep a backup of your current `device.map`, `grub.conf`, and `menu.lst` files but without the benefit of hindsight, and with the assistance of this recipe, a typical disaster may have been averted as the result of following a very straightforward process.

Of course, it may not save you on every occasion and experience may prove that deciding to back up the contents of all the major files in `/boot/grub` will provide additional insurance, but at this moment, just rest easy, the boot loader has been restored and both you and your server are ready to get back to work.

Updating the installation and enhancing the minimal install with additional administration and development tools

In this recipe we will learn how to enhance the minimal install with additional tools that will give you a variety of administrative and development options that will prove vital during the lifetime of your server.

The minimal install is probably the most efficient way you can install a server, but having said that, a minimal install does require some additional features in order to make it a more compelling model. We are all aware that a server will require a variety of administration and development tools and with this in mind, this recipe will show you how to install the extra packages that will not only prove useful throughout the reading of this book, but they will endeavor to improve your workflow and your overall enjoyment of CentOS.

Getting ready

To complete this recipe, you will require a minimal installation of the CentOS 6 operating system with root privileges with a connection to the Internet in order to facilitate the download of additional packages.

How to do it...

We will begin this recipe by updating the system.

1. To do this, log in as root and type:

   ```
   yum -y update
   ```

2. CentOS will now search for the relevant updates and, if available, they will be installed. On completion and depending on what was updated (that is, kernel and new security features to name but a few), you can decide to reboot your computer. To do this type:

   ```
   reboot
   ```

3. Your server will now reboot and having returned to the login screen, we will now complete the main recipe and enhance our current installation with a series of package groups that will prove to be very useful in the future. To do this, log in as root and type:

   ```
   yum -y groupinstall "Base" "Development Libraries" "Development
   Tools"
   ```

4. When the installation process is complete, simply reboot your server by typing the following command:

   ```
   reboot
   ```

How it works...

The purpose of this recipe is to enhance a minimal installation of the CentOS 6 operating system and by doing this you have not only introduced yourself to the **Yum Package Manager** (something to which we will return to later on in this book), but you now have a system that is capable of running a vast amount of applications right out of the box.

So what have we learned from this experience?

We started the recipe by updating the system in order to ensure that our system was up to date:

```
yum -y update
```

At this stage it is often a good idea to reboot the system. The reason behind this is typically based on the desire to take advantage of a new kernel or revised security updates (that is, SELinux or IPTables). It is not expected that we will do this very often, but rebooting the server was simply a matter of using the following command:

```
reboot
```

In the next phase the recipe showed you how to add a series of package groups that may prove to be more than useful in the future. To save time we wrapped the instruction to install three main package groups in a single command like so:

```
yum -y groupinstall "Base" "Development Libraries" "Development Tools"
```

The preceding action alone installs over 200 individual packages thereby giving your server the ability to compile code and run a vast array of applications out of the box. This list includes Perl, Python, GCC, Make, nslookup, ping, and a vast array of other necessary and important packages you may need over the life time of your server.

For example, you can run `nslookup` as follows:

```
nslookup www.packtpub.com
```

Moreover, instead of using the **Vi** text editor, you now have the opportunity to use the Nano text editor and many more. Which, given its lack of complexity, usually makes the process of managing your server that much simpler.

For example, if you are ever asked to edit or create a new a file. Instead of typing the following:

```
vi /path/to/some_file_name
```

You could type:

```
nano /path/to/some_file_name
```

You will be happy to know that this form of text editor replacement will work for all the examples shown throughout this book.

On top of this, you will also have the chance to use **vim-enhanced**, another fantastic text editor that supports scripts and color coding, but as a tutorial on this subject is beyond the purpose of this recipe I have included some links at the end of this section that will get you started.

The final part of this recipe was to action another reboot by typing:

```
reboot
```

Again this is not always required, but given the number of new packages you have just installed, it is often advisable in order for you to enjoy the benefits of your new server.

See also

- ▶ GNU Nano project's home page: `http://www.nano-editor.org`
- ▶ GNU Nano Guide: `http://mintaka.sdsu.edu/reu/nano.html`
- ▶ The Vi Lovers home page: `http://thomer.com/vi/vi.html`
- ▶ Vim project home page: `http://www.vim.org/`
- ▶ Vim documentation and help: `http://vimdoc.sourceforge.net/htmldoc/help.html`

Finishing the installation process with Firstboot

In this recipe we will learn how to finalize the installation process by enabling **Firstboot**, a simple application that enables you to manage the first-time installation of your server in a slightly less complicated way.

Firstboot can function in both the console and desktop environments and its intention is to activate the Setup agent. It has a single purpose that is often considered to be an optional extra, it isn't always going to be necessary, but for beginners and experienced users alike, it does provide instant access to a tried and tested process that will enable you to finalize the installation of any CentOS server in a fast and efficient manner.

Getting ready

To complete this recipe, you will require a minimal installation of the CentOS 6 operating system with root privileges and a connection to the Internet in order to facilitate the download of additional packages.

How to do it...

On a minimal installation Firstboot is not installed by default and for this reason we will begin this recipe by installing the necessary package and its related dependencies.

1. To do this, log in as root and type the following command:

   ```
   yum -y install firstboot
   ```

2. When the installation is finished, simply enable the package to run at boot by typing the following command:

   ```
   chkconfig firstboot on
   ```

3. At a convenient time, simply reboot the system to access Firstboot by typing:

   `reboot`

4. On a successful reboot, you will be presented with the Firstboot application. To begin, simply use the *Up* and *Down* arrow keys in conjunction with the *Tab* key to jump between the elements on the screen. Make the appropriate changes to your system and use the *Return* key to confirm your choices. On certain screens you are given the opportunity to use the *Space bar* in order to nominate or activate a particular setting. Choose **Quit** to exit Firstboot at any time.

5. Having quit Firstboot, you will be invited to access your server in the usual way but remember, any permanent changes to your security settings may not take effect until you reboot your server. So if this is the case, return to your console and type:

   `reboot`

How it works...

Firstboot is a simple package with the sole purpose of activating the Setup agent. It is not intended to be complicated and for this reason you probably found that it was both easy to install and even easier to activate.

So what did we learn from this experience?

We start the recipe by installing the necessary packages. In this case, the target package was called Firstboot and so we issued the following command to the server:

`yum -y install firstboot`

The system then proceeded to install a number of different dependencies that includes many setup utilities, but as Firstboot runs as a service, to access these utilities you should ensure that the service is running. So our next step was to return to the console and type:

`chkconfig firstboot on`

 If you prefer to ensure that Firstboot will only launch with the desktop environment, simply modify the preceding command to read as follows:

`chkconfig --level 5 firstboot on`

Having done this, we then proceeded to reboot the system like so:

`reboot`

On a successful reboot, you are then invited to run the various tools associated with this service. Of course, a discussion regarding the actual settings you should employ is a subject we will return to later on in this book, but having successfully completed this recipe you now understand that this small addition does have specific uses that serve to simplify the process of finalizing the installation of any CentOS server.

On a console-based server, the act of running Firstboot will enable you to run a screen by screen setup process that covers the main aspects of a first-time installation. For experienced users, this can prove to be a welcome reminder, but for new users Firstboot can prove to be a useful introduction to CentOS by offering a one-stop, tried and tested starting point. It may not be a necessary feature, but this small tool does go some way to make CentOS a very easy experience.

There's more...

As the name implies, Firstboot will only run once. However, should you ever wish to return to this screen in the future, simply log in to your server as the root user and ensure the service is set to run at boot by typing:

```
chkconfig firstboot on
```

Now remove the following file by typing:

```
rm /etc/sysconfig/firstboot
```

You will be asked if removing this file is intended, so type y (yes) and press the *Return* key to confirm your decision like so:

```
rm: remove regular file 'etc/sysconfig/firstboot' ? y
```

Having done this Firstboot is now active and will be ready to run on your next reboot.

Adding the GNOME desktop environment, changing the runlevel, and installing additional software

In this recipe we will learn how to simplify access to your server by providing you with the option to add the GNOME desktop, change the runlevel in order that the desktop can be seen on boot, and enhance your system with an array of additional software packages typically associated with such an environment.

Adding a desktop environment is not a requirement of running a server and in many respects you can consider this action to be entirely optional. Members of the server community at large may frown with regard to the relevance of this feature, and if you are intending to run a standalone web server or mail server, then there is no reason for needing one, but the reality is, many people do find the practice of running a graphical user interface a welcome addition and in certain circumstances it really can save a huge amount of time depending on the nature and purpose of your server.

Getting ready

To complete this recipe, you will require a minimal installation of the CentOS 6 operating system with root privileges, a console-based text editor of your choice, and a connection to the Internet in order to facilitate the download of additional packages. The system should also have a computer display, a keyboard, and a mouse.

How to do it...

Before we begin, 64-bit users should be aware that the desktop environment will result in your system using a mixture of 32-bit and 64-bit software. This may change over time, but at the time of writing this book, most desktop applications are still 32-bit.

1. To install the GNOME desktop environment, log in as root and type the following command to install the necessary packages and dependencies:

   ```
   yum groupinstall "Desktop" "X Window System" "Fonts" "Desktop
   Platform"
   ```

2. The preceding action will install around 530 MB of packages, but for you to begin using the desktop environment at boot, you will need to change the runlevel. A **runlevel** is a preset operating state that determines which programs are executed at system startup. In this case, we are intending to execute the desktop environment and to do this, simply open the following configuration file by typing:

   ```
   vi /etc/inittab
   ```

3. Now scroll down towards the bottom of this file and locate the following line:

   ```
   id:3:initdefault:
   ```

4. Change this line to read:

   ```
   id:5:initdefault:
   ```

5. Now save your work. But before we finish, it is important to consider the need to add some software in order to enhance your enjoyment of the desktop environment. To do this, return to your console and type:

    ```
    yum groupinstall "General Purpose Desktop" "Graphical
    Administration Tools"
    ```

6. Finally, you will need to reboot your computer in order to allow the changes to take immediate effect. To do this, type:

    ```
    reboot
    ```

How it works...

During the course of this recipe, you have not only learned how to install the GNOME desktop environment, but have also successfully reconfigured the runlevel of your server and installed some additional software packages that will enhance your overall enjoyment of CentOS.

So what have we learned from this experience?

We began by installing the GNOME desktop environment by introducing ourselves to the Yum Package Manager's ability to install package groups. Yum is something we will return to later in this book, but in this instance we were required to install all the necessary components needed by a typical desktop, and we achieved this by typing:

```
yum groupinstall "Desktop" "X Window System" "Fonts" "Desktop Platform"
```

Having completed this initial step, we were then asked to reconfigure the runlevel of the server in order that the desktop environment would be initiated during the boot process. Without completing this step, the server will continue to boot in console mode.

 If you would prefer not to see the desktop at startup, simply leave the current runlevel as is (at level 3), and having accessed your system, you can always type the StartX command to initiate the desktop environment.

As described in this recipe, a runlevel is a preset operating state that determines which programs are executed at system startup. In this case, we are only considering the needs of X Window System and where a console-based server will typically start at runlevel 3, we need to modify this in order to activate the desktop environment that functions at runlevel 5.

To do this, we opened the main configuration file by typing:

```
vi /etc/inittab
```

You were then asked to scroll down towards the bottom of this file and find the following line:

```
id:3:initdefault:
```

Having found it, you were then asked to replace it with the following:

```
id:5:initdefault:
```

Finally, and last but not least, with a desktop environment everyone wants software, and by typing the following command, you were given the opportunity to enhance your system with a variety of tools that would make you feel at home:

```
yum groupinstall "General Purpose Desktop" "Graphical Administration
Tools"
```

> Remember, if you have not created an administrative user (see the appropriate recipe in this book) at this stage, then you should consider running Firstboot (see the appropriate recipe in this chapter) in order to run the desktop `setup agent`. Without completing either of these steps, you will be required to log in as the root user, which is not advisable for a desktop environment.

To complete this recipe, you were then required to reboot the server and having accessed your desktop environment, you can now navigate to **System | Administration | Add/Remove Software** to manage new and existing packages.

2
Configuring CentOS

In this chapter, we will cover:

- ▶ Changing the time zone and updating the hardware clock
- ▶ Synchronizing the system clock with NTP
- ▶ Setting a static IP address
- ▶ Binding multiple IP addresses to a single Ethernet device
- ▶ Bonding two Ethernet devices to increase bandwidth and improve performance
- ▶ Changing the hostname and resolving a fully qualified domain name
- ▶ Switching SELinux off
- ▶ Disabling the IPv6 module

Introduction

This chapter is a collection of recipes that covers the practice of priming your server by changing the time zone and updating the hardware clock; synchronizing the system clock with NTP; setting a static IP address; binding multiple IP addresses to a single Ethernet device; bonding two Ethernet devices to increase bandwidth and improve performance; changing the hostname and resolving a fully qualified domain name; switching SELinux off; and disabling the IPv6 module.

Changing the time zone and updating the hardware clock

In this recipe we will introduce the concept of **TZDATA** in order that we can learn how to change a server's time zone and update the hardware clock.

Over the lifetime of your server, the need to change the time and date for one or more users may not happen very often but when it does the process of managing this modification can seem to be quite complicated. You may want to make this change for any number of reasons, you can even use this approach to implement an independent time zone solution for different users, but regardless as to the reason why, it is the purpose of this recipe to illustrate a series of best practices that can be applied to your server and provide you with the solution you need.

Getting ready

To complete this recipe, you will require a working installation of the CentOS 6 operating system with root privileges, a console-based text editor of your choice, and a connection to the Internet to facilitate the download of additional packages.

How to do it...

TZDATA is a compilation of the world's time zone information and we will start this recipe by showing you how to use the `tzselect` utility and applying the new time zone setting to a user of your choice.

1. To begin, log in as root and type the following command in order to install the necessary `tzdata` package:

   ```
   yum install tzdata
   ```

2. Now start the `tzselect` utility by typing:

   ```
   tzselect
   ```

    Remember, you can press *Ctrl + C* to interrupt the `tzselect` utility at any time.

3. Having initiated the `tzselect` utility, you will be asked a series of questions that begins as follows:

   Please identify a location so that time zone rules can be set correctly.

4. From the values shown on screen, choose a numeric value to confirm your selection and press the *Return* key to proceed.

5. You will now be asked the following:

   Please select a country.

6. This question refers to the preferred time zone, so in a similar manner, choose a numeric value to make your selection and press the *Return* key to proceed. Based on the information provided, the utility will then respond by asking you to confirm the final details. As an example, for a user located in London (UK), the response will be as follows:

   The following information has been given:

   Britain (UK)

   Therefore TZ='Europe/London' will be used.

   Local time is now:Wed May 30 22:21:20 BST 2012.

   Universal Time is now:Wed May 30 21:21:20 UTC 2012.

   Is the above information OK?

   1) Yes

   2) No

7. Again, choose a numeric value to confirm your settings and press the *Return* key to proceed. By completing this action, you will now finalize the purpose of the `tzselect` utility, and it will respond in the following way:

   You can make this change permanent for yourself by appending the line

   TZ='Europe/London'; export TZ

   to the file '.profile' in your home directory; then log out and log in again.

   Here is that TZ value again, this time on standard output so that you

   can use the /usr/bin/tzselect command in shell scripts:

   Europe/London

8. With reference to the preceding example shown, return to your console and make a note of the following value:

   ```
   TZ='XXXXXX/XXXXXXX'; export TZ
   ```

    For example, if the TZ value given was `Los Angeles (USA)`, then you would record: `TZ='America/Los_Angeles'; export TZ`. However, if the TZ value given was `London (UK)`, then you would record: `TZ='Europe/London'; export TZ`.

9. Now open the appropriate user profile with your favorite text editor as follows:

```
vi /home/username/.profile
```

 If you cannot find this file, or this file does not exist, as an alternative you can use `/home/username/.bash_profile`.

10. Scroll to the bottom of the file and substitute the TZ values shown with those values you obtained from the `tzselect` utility like this:

```
TZ0
```

```
'Europe/Moscow'; export TZ
```

 On the whole, most people will use the location-based method to confirm any preferred time zone settings, but there may be an occasion when you would prefer to use the Posix Time Format. If this is the case, then simply modify the previous command by substituting the following value, `POSIX-format-here with a relative value`, as follows:

`TZ='POSIX-fomat-here'; export TZ`

The value chosen should be a number based on the difference in time between you current location and GMT such as `GMT-5`.

11. When finished, save and close your file. The relevant user can now re-login and use the `date` command to confirm their new time zone settings at any time:

```
date
```

12. Repeat these given steps for any remaining users on the server.

How it works...

As we have seen, the `tzselect` utility can be used to tell you the time (anywhere in the world) by simply looking at your system clock and comparing it with **Coordinated Universal Time** (**UTC**). Its purpose is not to complete the task of updating your server's time zone, but it does provide the necessary information that will facilitate such changes for one or more users.

So what have we learned from this experience?

Having started by installing the relevant package, you were then guided to start the `tzselect` utility and use the supplied TZ value to update a user's profile.

Updating a user's profile was simply a matter of amending the appropriate file for each user. In most cases you would update the file found at /home/username/.profile. However, if this file was not available, then an alternative option located at /home/username/.bash_profile can be used.

For example, a revised bash profile will look like this:

```
# .bash_profile
# Get the aliases and functions
if [ -f ~/.bashrc ]; then
   . ~/.bashrc
fi
# User specific environment and startup programs
PATH=$PATH:$HOME/bin
export PATH
TZ='Europe/Moscow'; export TZ
```

You were also shown how to use the Posix Time Format, and if you did indeed decide to use this variation, then your revised bash profile will look like this:

```
# .bash_profile
# Get the aliases and functions
if [ -f ~/.bashrc ]; then
   . ~/.bashrc
fi
# User specific environment and startup programs
PATH=$PATH:$HOME/bin
export PATH
TZ='GMT-5'; export TZ
```

Remember, in the context of this recipe, the measurement of time is session based, so having made the preceding modifications, a user would then be required to re-login before they will notice any changes. They can do this by typing the following command:

`date`

Moreover, it is important to note that a change to a specific profile will not affect another user and none of these changes will affect the server as a whole. So with this in mind, this recipe can be used to enable multiple users to maintain different clocks.

So having completed this recipe, we can say that we now know how to obtain the required TZ value and provide a unique time zone setting for each user. As previously stated, it may not be a feature that you use on a regular basis, but it does provide a flexible solution in as much that you are now able you to configure a user account independently of the system as a whole and deliver a fully localized server environment regardless of how many users you serve or where they are located.

There's more...

Setting the time for your users is only one aspect of managing time on a server and it should not be forgotten that your server will run two clocks—a hardware-based clock that is supported by the battery on the motherboard and a secondary clock that is maintained by the operating system. Where the former is used to set the system clock during the boot process, the latter will be the clock that is used to keep a track of time.

Both of these time values can be run independently of each other (local time versus UTC) and on occasion this may even prove to be useful when considering a dual-boot situation. However, and in the case of most servers, it is common practice to ensure that both the hardware clock and system clock use the same reference in order to account for daylight.

As the root user you can use the following syntax to set a new date and time for your server's operating system by simply replacing MMDDhhmmYYYY.ss (Month, Day, Hour, Minute, Year, and seconds) with the correct values:

```
date MMDDhhmmYYYY.ss
```

For example, to change the time and date value to May 17, 13:21:22, 2012, you can use the following syntax:

```
date 051713212012.22
```

> As an alternative approach you can simplify this procedure by changing these values independently. You can change the date by typing:
>
> ```
> date --set="YYYYMMDD"
> ```
> You can change the time by typing:
> ```
> date +%T -s "HH:MM:SS"
> ```

When ready, you should now synchronize the system with your hardware clock by typing:

```
hwclock-systohc
```

Finally, reboot your server to finalize the changes made:

```
reboot
```

> You should be aware that changing time values on a regular basis can affect other aspects of your server and as a result, you may need to ensure that any date and time-based service or application is not affected inadvertently.

On a successful reboot, you can confirm the status of your hardware clock with the following command:

```
hwclock-show
```

Similarly you can view the current operating system date and time by typing the following command:

```
date
```

Linking time and location

As many of the applications and features running on your server will use the current clock to determine the correct time, having completed the preceding steps it is often a good idea to ensure if the correct time zone information is linked to your server's local time settings.

To do this simply, log in as root, and remove the old location values by typing:

```
rm /etc/localtime
```

Confirm the request and then by referring to the list of files located in /usr/share/zoneinfo, create the following symbolic link by replacing XXX with a value more representative of your location:

```
ln -sf /usr/share/zoneinfo/XXX /etc/localtime
```

For example, if you were to type, ln -sf /usr/share/zoneinfo/Europe/London /etc/localtime, this would be correct for servers located in or near London, while the command ln -sf/usr/share/zoneinfo/Europe/Moscow /etc/localtime would be correct for servers located in or around Moscow.

Finally, you should reboot your server to allow any changes to take immediate effect:

```
reboot
```

Synchronizing the system clock with NTP

In this recipe, we will learn how to synchronize the system clock with an external time server using NTP.

Time remains an essential tool for your server because every aspect of managing, securing, running, and debugging a network involves determining when events happen or are about to take place. From the need to time stamp documents, e-mails, logfiles, or by simply interacting with shared devices and services, everything on your server is dependent on maintaining an accurate system clock and it is the purpose of this recipe to show you how to achieve this with the **Network Time Protocol** (**NTP**).

Getting ready

To complete this recipe you will require a working installation of the CentOS 6 operating system with root privileges, a console-based text editor of your choice, and a connection to the Internet to facilitate the download of additional packages.

How to do it...

If you are using the minimal installation recommended by this book, then the **Network Time Protocol** (**NTP**) is not installed by default and for this reason we will need to install the relevant package:

1. To begin, log in as root and type:

    ```
    yum -y install ntpd
    ```

2. The default installation of NTP will use a public server that has access to the atomic clock, but in order to optimize the service we will need to make a few simple changes in order to streamline and optimize what time servers are used. To do this, we shall open the main configuration file with your favorite text editor like so:

    ```
    vi /etc/ntp.conf
    ```

3. Scroll down and look for the following lines:

    ```
    # Use public servers from the pool.ntp.org project.
    # Please consider joining the pool (http://www.pool.ntp.org/join.
    html).
    server 0.centos.pool.ntp.org
    server 1.centos.pool.ntp.org
    server 2.centos.pool.ntp.org
    ```

4. Replace the values shown with a list of preferred time servers like so:

    ```
    # Use public servers from the pool.ntp.org project.
    # Please consider joining the pool (http://www.pool.ntp.org/join.
    html).
    server 0.uk.pool.ntp.org
    server 1.uk.pool.ntp.org
    server 2.uk.pool.ntp.org
    server 3.uk.pool.ntp.org
    ```

 Visit `http://www.pool.ntp.org/` to obtain a list of local servers. Remember, the use of three or more servers will have a tendency to increase the accuracy of the NTP service.

5. Now find the following lines:

```
# Hosts on local network are less restricted.
#restrict 192.168.1.0 mask 255.255.255.0 nomodifynotrap
```

6. Before starting our time service, we should add and confirm a network range in order that we can determine who can and who cannot receive time service-based requests. To do this, uncomment the preceding line and replace the values to reflect your network environment like so:

```
# Hosts on local network are less restricted.
Restrict XXX.XXX.XXX.XXX mask YYY.YYY.YYY.YYY nomodifynotrap
```

7. When complete, save and close the file before synchronizing your server by using the following command:

```
ntpdate NTP_SERVER_ADDRESS_HERE
```

 For example, you can use `ntpdate pool.ntp.org`.

8. The initial synchronization request requires priming, so you may want to run and repeat this command several times before ensuring that the service will start during the boot process, by using the following command:

```
chkconfig ntpd on
```

9. When finished, you can start the NTP service like so:

```
service ntpd start
```

10. You should reboot to ensure that the relevant changes take effect:

```
reboot
```

11. Well done, you have now installed and configured the NTP service. The overall process of time synchronization will take some time to complete, but you will be able to use the standard **NTP query program** (**ntpq**) in order to review a list of known peers as and a summary of their current state. To do this, return to your console and type:

```
ntpq-p
```

How it works...

The Network Time Protocol (NTP) is a daemon that sets and maintains system time through a process of synchronization with a remote server. It is a very important service, and quite easy to implement, but if you have followed the minimal install procedure recommended by this book, you will be aware that NTP is not installed by default.

So what have we learned from this experience?

By beginning with the installation of the NTP service we have discovered that certain aspects of the initial configuration had to be defined in order to optimize the time servers used and to avoid exposing the server's time keeping service to unwanted requests. This was achieved by customizing and un-commenting the following lines:

```
# Use public servers from the pool.ntp.org project.
# Please consider joining the pool (http://www.pool.ntp.org/join.
html).
server 0.centos.pool.ntp.org
server 1.centos.pool.ntp.org
server 2.centos.pool.ntp.org

# Hosts on local network are less restricted.
Restrict XXX.XXX.XXX.XXX mask YYY.YYY.YYY.YYY nomodifynotrap
```

During the course of this recipe we have also learned how to prime the service by initiating contact with a third-party time server before configuring the service to be made available at boot process by typing:

```
chkconfig ntpd on
```

Having started the service and rebooted the server, we then learned that the standard NTP query program (ntpq) could be used to monitor our new configuration. You can do this any time by typing:

```
ntpq-p
```

It is important to realize that the process of synchronizing your server may not be instantaneous and it can take a while for the process to complete. However, you can now relax in the full knowledge that you now know how to install, manage, and configure the NTP service.

There's more...

All daemons are prone to the environmental conditions found on your network, and the NTP service is not an exception. Periodic packet breaks can be disruptive, but even if you have not experienced this yet, it may be advantageous to explore a solution that will make your NTP service far more persistent when probing the third-party servers.

Known as the `iburst` option, this feature is designed to tell the NTP service to issue a burst of eight packets to the remote server instead of one in order to offer an improved approach to the time synchronization process. Implementing this method is very simple and to begin, simply return to your console and open the main configuration file in your favorite text editor like so:

```
vi /etc/ntp.conf
```

Scroll down the file and locate your time servers. Now simply append your time servers with a whitespace followed by the term `iburst`. For example, your new configuration file will look like this:

```
# Use public servers from the pool.ntp.org project.
# Please consider joining the pool (http://www.pool.ntp.org/join.
html).
server 0.uk.pool.ntp.org iburst
server 1.uk.pool.ntp.org iburst
server 2.uk.pool.ntp.org iburst
server 3.uk.pool.ntp.org iburst
```

When finished, simply save and close your file before rebooting your server or restarting the NTP service with the following command:

```
service ntpd restart
```

Synchronizing multiple machines

Based on this recipe, we can now use the NTP service to synchronize multiple machines.

Having configured the master time server, all subsequent machines in your local environment can now use the local master instead of a third-party (external) source, and by doing this you will not only speed-up the process of allocating the measurement of time among local machines, but you will also improve the security of your local network.

To begin, simply open the main configuration file on each of the slave computers. You can do this on all operating systems, but the instructions may vary.

On CentOS, this is achieved by opening the main configuration file in your favorite text editor like so:

```
vi /etc/ntp.conf
```

Now scroll down and locate the listing for your time servers. Based on the examples used in the main recipe, your new configuration file may look like this:

```
# Use public servers from the pool.ntp.org project.
# Please consider joining the pool (http://www.pool.ntp.org/join.
html).
server 0.uk.pool.ntp.org iburst
server 1.uk.pool.ntp.org iburst
server 2.uk.pool.ntp.org iburst
server 3.uk.pool.ntp.org iburst
```

If the network address for the new local time server is `time.masterserver.lan`, then simply modify your configuration file to reflect this value:

```
# Use public servers from the pool.ntp.org project.
# Please consider joining the pool (http://www.pool.ntp.org/join.
html).time.masterserver.lan
```

You can also use the `iburst` option like so:

```
# Use public servers from the pool.ntp.org project.
# Please consider joining the pool (http://www.pool.ntp.org/join.
html).time.masterserver.lan iburst
```

When finished, simply save and close your file before restarting the local time service in order to allow the changes to take immediate effect:

```
service ntpd restart
```

Now repeat this action on all computers across your network. Remember, the approach may be different for each operating system, but by using a local time server this recipe can be used to benefit all the computers on your network.

Modifying the logfile's location

By using the default settings, all NTP activity will be recorded at `/var/log/messages`. Of course, NTP activity can be filtered using the `grep` command, but if you would prefer to use to a separate logfile, then simply make the following adjustment.

To begin, open the main configuration in your favorite text editor:

```
vi /etc/ntp.conf
```

Scroll to the bottom of this file and add the following new line:

```
logfile /var/log/ntpd.log
```

When finished, simply save and close the file before restarting the NTP service like so:

```
service ntpd restart
```

By doing this we are merely asking the NTP service to make a separate logfile at `/var/log/ntpd.log`. Of course, you can always modify the name of this logfile to something more appropriate to your own needs, and having made this configuration change, it would be appropriate to point out that a select number of NTP-based events will persist in `/var/log/messages`. However, having implemented this simple solution, you should now find that the NTP log is far more concise and a lot easier to read.

Fudging time

If your network does not have Internet connection or the Internet connection is intermittent, then a fallback solution is often required. In such cases you can implement a process known as **reflective synchronization**. This may sound complicated, but in reality we are simply telling the NTP service that the monitoring system's internal clock is correct and it should be used as our definitive time keeper if a fallback is required.

To do this, open the main configuration file in your favorite text editor like so:

```
vi /etc/ntp.conf
```

Now scroll down and locate the following lines:

```
# Undisciplined Local Clock. This is a fake driver intended for backup
# and when no outside source of synchronized time is available.
#server  127.127.1.0  # local clock
#fudge  127.127.1.0 stratum 10
```

This is where we will literally `fudge` time by simply un-commenting the relevant lines like so:

```
# Undisciplined Local Clock. This is a fake driver intended for backup
# and when no outside source of synchronized time is available.
server  127.127.1.0  # local clock
fudge  127.127.1.0 stratum 10
```

When complete, save and close your file before restarting the NTP service:

```
service ntpd restart
```

See also

- ▸ The NTP home page: `http://www.ntp.org/`
- ▸ The NTP Pool project's home page – list of time servers: `http://www.pool.ntp.org/`

Setting a static IP address

In this recipe we will learn how to configure a static IP address for a new or existing CentOS server.

While a dynamically assigned IP address or DHCP reservation may be fine for most desktop and laptop users, if you are setting up a server it is often the case that you will require a static IP address. From web pages to e-mail, databases to file sharing, a static IP address will become a permanent location from which your server will deliver a range of applications and services, and it is the intention of this recipe to show you how easily it can be achieved.

Getting ready

To complete this recipe, you will require a working installation of the CentOS 6 operating system with root privileges and a console-based text editor of your choice.

How to do it...

For the purpose of this recipe, you will be able to find all the relevant files in `/etc/sysconfig/network-scripts/`. But before making any changes to your original configuration, it is always a good idea to create a simple backup of the existing configuration files for future reference.

1. To do this, log in as root and type the following command:

   ```
   cp /etc/sysconfig/network-scripts/ifcfg-eth0 /etc/sysconfig/
   network-scripts/ifcfg-eth0.bak
   ```

2. The preceding command will make a copy of `ifcfg-eth0` and name it `ifcfg-eth0.bak`. Now repeat the previous step for any remaining Ethernet devices.

3. When you are ready to proceed, open the following file in your favorite text editor by typing:

   ```
   vi /etc/sysconfig/network-scripts/ifcfg-eth0
   ```

4. Now work down the file and apply the following changes:

   ```
   NM_CONTROLLED="no"
   BOOTPROTO=none
   DEFROUTE=yes
   PEERDNS=no
   PEERROUTES=yes
   IPV4_FAILURE_FATAL=yes
   ```

    For the purpose of this recipe, all IPv6 values have been ignored. You will also notice that the PEERDNS value has been set to no, this is a temporary measure and we will return to this subject later in this recipe.

5. Now add your IPv4 information by customizing the values of XXX.XXX.XXX.XXX as required:

   ```
   IPADDR=XXX.XXX.XXX.XXX
   NETMASK= XXX.XXX.XXX.XXX
   BROADCAST= XXX.XXX.XXX.XXX
   ```

If you are experiencing difficulty in determining your broadcast address, it is simply defined as `XXX.XXX.XXX.255`. For example, if your IP address was `192.168.1.100` and your Netmask was `255.255.255.0`. Then your broadcast address will be `192.168.1.255`.

6. When ready, save and close the file before repeating this step for any remaining Ethernet devices. When doing this, remember to assign a different IP address to each device.

7. Having completed the configuration of your Ethernet card(s), we now need to make some additional changes starting with the following configuration file:

    ```
    vi /etc/sysconfig/network
    ```

8. We must now add a default gateway. Typically, this could be the address of your router and to do this, simply add a new line at the bottom of the file like so and customize the value as required:

    ```
    GATEWAY=XXX.XXX.XXX.XXX
    ```

9. When finished, save and close this file before restarting your network service:

    ```
    service network restart
    ```

How it works...

In this recipe, you have seen the process associated with changing the state of your server's IP address from a dynamic value obtained from an external DHCP provider to that of a static value assigned by you. This IP address will now form a unique network location from which you will be able to deliver a whole host of services and applications. It is a permanent modification and yes, you could say that the process itself was relatively straightforward.

So what have we learned from this experience?

Having started the recipe by creating a backup of the original Ethernet configuration files, we then opened the primary Ethernet configuration located at `/etc/sysconfig/network-scripts/ifcfg-eth0` in order to make the following adjustments:

```
NM_CONTROLLED="no"
ONBOOT=yes
```

Having ensured that the Ethernet device will be available at boot, we no longer require the services of the **Network Manager**, and for this reason we disabled `NM_CONTROLLED` by setting the value to `no`.

We then applied the following change:

```
BOOTPROTO=none
```

As we are in the process of moving to a static IP address, `BOOTPROTO` has been set to `none` as we are no longer using DHCP.

To complete our configuration changes, we then moved on to add our specific network values:

```
IPADDR=XXX.XXX.XXX.XXX
NETMASK= XXX.XXX.XXX.XXX
BROADCAST= XXX.XXX.XXX.XXX
```

When finished, we were asked to save and close the file before repeating this step for any remaining Ethernet devices.

In the next phase we were then required to make some changes to the following configuration file:

```
vi /etc/sysconfig/network
```

The default file will look similar to the following:

```
NETWORKING=yes
HOSTNAME= your_computername_here
```

However, in order to assist the creation of a static IP address we were required to add a new setting known as the **default gateway**. This configuration change is important (in as much that it allows the server to contact the wider world), and it was achieved by simply adding a new line at the bottom of the file like so:

```
NETWORKING=yes
HOSTNAME=your_computername_here
GATEWAY=XXX.XXX.XXX.XXX
```

Having done this we were then asked to restart the network service in order to complete this recipe and to enable our changes to take immediate effect.

So you could say that having modified the configuration details for your Ethernet devices and by adding a default gateway, it was simply a process of telling your server not to use DHCP, to remain independent of the Network Manager and to access the world through a specific gateway address. So well done, you work is done and you can now enjoy the benefits of a static IP address.

There's more...

Having previously mentioned `PEERDNS`, we shall now come back to this in order to provide you with some additional background reading that will serve to enhance your understanding of the DNS system and improve the performance of your server.

You may or may not be familiar with the `/etc/resolv.conf` file. On a freshly installed system or a desktop this file is typically maintained by the Network Manager. To see the evidence of this, if you ever take the opportunity to open this file and read the default content, you will almost certainly see the words `Generated by NetworkManager` close to or at the top of this file.

Also known as the resolver, `resolv.conf` is used for DNS management and it is used to configure your server's access to the Internet **Domain Name System** (**DNS**). It does this by determining which name servers are to be used and in what order they are chosen and by optimizing this file we can intentionally manage how your server will experience the world at large.

Instead of editing this file directly we are going to use a trick of the trade that will modify `resolv.conf` automatically and do all the hard work for us.

To begin, open the primary Ethernet configuration file in your favorite text editor by typing:

```
vi /etc/sysconfig/network-scripts/ifcfg-eth0
```

Now scroll down and modify the `PEERDNS` value to look like this:

```
PEERDNS=yes
```

Now scroll down to the end of this file and add the following new lines:

```
DNS1=XXX.XXX.XXX.XXX
DNS2=XXX.XXX.XXX.XXX
DOMAIN=your_domain.com
```

The final addition refers to your preferred DNS name servers and you local domain name. Currently, a maximum of three DNS values are supported, but two will suffice for any typical system; so customize these values as necessary with something more appropriate to your own needs.

For example, you could use Google's Public DNS like so:

```
DNS1=8.8.8.8
DNS2=8.8.4.4
DOMAIN=your_domain.com
```

When finished, save and close the file and then type:

```
service network restart
```

Having completed these steps, you will be activating the `PEERDNS` control and as a result, the server will now read the new DNS information supplied by your Ethernet configuration file and append `/etc/resolv.conf`. So remember, if you ever need to change your DNS servers, simply manage them via the primary Ethernet device configuration file mentioned in the preceding steps.

Substituting the Netmask value with a prefix

It is commonly understood that you should always supply a Netmask value when determining your network configuration, but as an alternative, there is something called a **prefix**, and it does save time in typing out a long series of numbers.

The prefix is a shorthand way of specifying the Netmask value by implementing the **Classless Inter-Domain Routing** (**CIDR**) system. For both you and me this means:

Instead of typing this:

```
NETMASK= 255.255.255.0
```

We can replace it with this:

```
PREFIX=24
```

For the example shown here, the prefix shown is translated by the CIDR to imply the value `255.255.255.0`. Consequently, when writing your Netmask value, instead of writing this:

```
IPADDR=XXX.XXX.XXX.XXX
NETMASK= XXX.XXX.XXX.XXX
BROADCAST= XXX.XXX.XXX.XXX
```

You could use this:

```
IPADDR=XXX.XXX.XXX.XXX
PREFIX= XX
BROADCAST= XXX.XXX.XXX.XXX
```

Finding your HWADDR/MAC address

If you ever make a mistake and lose your Ethernet card's HWADDR/MAC address, simply return to your console and type the following command:

```
/sbin/ifconfig | grep -ihwaddr
```

Your server will then provide the HWADDR for each Ethernet device.

Binding multiple IP addresses to a single Ethernet device

In this recipe we will learn how to bind multiple IP addresses to a single Ethernet device in order to provide greater networking functionality to a new or existing CentOS server.

There are many advantages to using a static IP address, but combining this with the ability to use more than one will present you with a new range of configuration options. Clearly, the benefit of circumventing the need to purchase and install multiple Ethernet devices is obvious, but this approach will not only enable you to run multiple servers and websites, it can also enable you to create a private LAN using a local IP and have the alias hold your Internet IP. So with that in mind, it is the purpose of this recipe to show you how easily an IP-rich server can be achieved.

Getting ready

To complete this recipe, you will require a working installation of the CentOS 6 operating system with root privileges and a console-based text editor of your choice. It is assumed that the primary Ethernet device is configured to use a static IP address.

How to do it...

In order to reduce the amount of typing required to complete this recipe, we are going to make a working copy of the original Ethernet configuration files.

1. To begin, log in as root and type the following command:

    ```
    cp /etc/sysconfig/network-scripts/ifcfg-eth0 /etc/sysconfig/
    network-scripts/ifcfg-eth0:1
    ```

2. By doing this, we create a copy of `ifcfg-eth0` and name it `ifcfg-eth0:1`. You should be aware that the name of this new file is important as it will form the basis of our first virtual device. To proceed, open the virtual configuration file in your favorite text editor by typing:

    ```
    vi /etc/sysconfig/network-scripts/ifcfg-eth0:1
    ```

3. Scroll down and change the following values:

    ```
    DEVICE="eth0:1"
    NAME="System eth0:1"
    ```

4. Now delete the following line(s):

    ```
    HWADDR=XX:XX:XX:XX:XX:XX
    UUID=XXXXXXXX-XXXX-XXXX-XXXX-XXXXXXXXXXXX
    ```

5. Finally, you will want to add your new static IP address. To do this, simply scroll down and locate the following line in order to make the relevant changes:

    ```
    IPADDR=XXX.XXX.XXX.XXX
    ```

6. When finished, save and close the file and either reboot your server or restart the network settings by typing:

    ```
    service network restart
    ```

7. When this process is complete your new network settings will take immediate effect. You can test this by running the following command, which will respond by providing you with an instant report on the current IP address for both eth0 and eth0:1.

    ```
    ifconfig
    ```

How it works...

In this recipe you have seen how easy it is to create virtual adaptors in order to provide your server with an additional IP address. The ability to increase your IP pool is always welcomed by any server administrator and yes, by using this method you really can enjoy the benefit of an IP-rich environment without the additional expense of new hardware.

So what have we learned from this experience?

Working on the assumption that your Ethernet device was already running a static IP address, we discovered that by making a copy of the original file saves time, and by simply renaming certain values (DEVICE, NAME) and removing selected attributes (HWADDR and UUID), we can build a virtual adaptor with a separate and wholly distinct IP address with little to no effort.

We completed the recipe by restarting the network in order that CentOS could detect the new settings and automatically include them when the networking service resumes.

You can confirm this by invoking ifconfig, a console-based command-line utility that will provide you with current feedback on the current state of your Ethernet devices.

So in the end it is hoped that you would agree in saying that this process was very simple, and by taking note of the values given for both eth0 and eth0:1, you will now be able to reap the benefits of a gain in productivity that will be left for you to explore and enjoy.

There's more...

To add additional adaptors, simply repeat the steps in this recipe and create a new identity for your original Ethernet card using a different label.

Of course, the labels used by each Virtual Adaptor must be unique and they should follow a logical sequence (that is, eth0:1, eth0:2, eth0:3, and so on), but as this recipe has shown, the possibilities are endless and you can use the increased IP range to provide additional services.

Bonding two Ethernet devices to increase bandwidth and provide redundancy

In this recipe we will learn how to combine the features of multiple network interfaces as a single device in an arrangement known as **channel bonding** with the intention of improving the overall performance of your server.

If your server has more than one Ethernet device, the process of channel bonding allows you to bind these interfaces together into a single channel in order to increase bandwidth and provide redundancy. It may sound complicated and finding the best settings will require some experimentation on your behalf or the support of specific network-based hardware, but it is the purpose of this recipe to provide a suitable starting point that enables you to take control and discover a network configuration that suits you best.

Getting ready

To complete this recipe, you will require a working installation of the CentOS 6 operating system with root privileges, a console-based text editor of your choice, and a connection to the Internet in order to facilitate the download of additional packages. In addition to this, it is assumed that one or more Ethernet devices are currently configured to use a static IP address, and that you have created a backup of your existing configuration files.

How to do it...

Before we begin this recipe, we will be required to download a series of packages that will enable us to complete the process of making a bond and testing our configuration.

1. To do this, log in as root and download the following packages:

   ```
   yum -y install bind-utils ethtool
   ```

2. Having installed the necessary packages, we shall begin by creating a new file called bond0 that will become the bonding master. To do this, return to your console and type:

   ```
   vi /etc/sysconfig/network-scripts/ifcfg-bond0
   ```

3. Now add the following lines by substituting the relevant values marked as XXX.XXX.XXX.XXX with something more appropriate to the needs of your server:

   ```
   DEVICE="bond0"
   NAME="System bond0"
   NM_CONTROLLED="no"
   USERCTL=no
   ONBOOT=yes
   TYPE=Ethernet
   ```

```
BOOTPROTO=none
DEFROUTE=yes
PEERDNS=no
PEERROUTES=yes
IPV4_FAILURE_FATAL=yes
IPV6INIT=no
IPADDR=XXX.XXX.XXX.XXX
NETMASK=XXX.XXX.XXX.XXX
BROADCAST=XXX.XXX.XXX.XXX
```

4. When ready, save and close the file before proceeding to modify your existing Ethernet configuration files:

   vi /etc/sysconfig/network-scripts/ifcfg-eth0

5. Again, make the relevant changes but as a point of reference, here is an example of a single NIC:

```
DEVICE="eth0"
NM_CONTROLLED="no"
ONBOOT=yes
HWADDR=XX:XX:XX:XX:XX:XX
UUID=XXXXXXXX-XXXX-XXXX-XXXX-XXXXXXXXXXXX
TYPE=Ethernet
BOOTPROTO=none
NAME="System eth0"
USERCTL=no
MASTER=bond0
SLAVE=yes
```

6. Now repeat this step for each Ethernet device by substituting the appropriate values before continuing to the next step.

7. When the process of Ethernet device configuration is complete, the next step is to create the bonding module configuration file by typing the following command:

   vi /etc/modprobe.d/bonding.conf

8. Now add the following lines:

```
alias bond0 bonding
options bond0 mode=5 miimon=100
```

9. Save and close the file before proceeding to register the bonding module with CentOS as a device. To do this, type:

   modprobe bonding

10. And finally, to complete our configuration you should reboot or type:

```
service network restart
```

11. Well done. The process of channel bonding is now complete and you can test your new network settings by running the following command:

```
ifconfig
```

How it works...

In this recipe you have been provided with a walkthrough of the necessary steps involved in implementing channel bonding. Channel bonding (also known as **Ethernet bonding**) is a computer networking arrangement in which two or more network interfaces on a host computer are combined in order to provide redundancy or increased throughput. Of course, to get the best out of this arrangement some additional experimentation with the bonding values will be required but overall, this introduction has served to show you that creating a channel bond may not be as complicated as it was originally thought.

So what have we learned from this experience?

Having started this recipe by installing the appropriate packages, we then proceeded to create the bonding master at /etc/sysconfig/network-scripts/ifcfg-bond0, which would maintain the following range of settings:

```
DEVICE="bond0"
NAME="System bond0"
NM_CONTROLLED="no"
USERCTL=no
ONBOOT=yes
TYPE=Ethernet
BOOTPROTO=none
DEFROUTE=yes
PEERDNS=no
PEERROUTES=yes
IPV4_FAILURE_FATAL=yes
IPV6INIT=no
IPADDR=XXX.XXX.XXX.XXX
NETMASK=XXX.XXX.XXX.XXX
BROADCAST=XXX.XXX.XXX.XXX
```

By doing this, we have created a new device. This device is known as the bonding master that will use our real Ethernet cards as slaves. If a slave device fails, this type of configuration will ensure that the other slave will take over thereby reducing the margin of error.

In the next step, we then made some changes to our existing Ethernet devices:

```
DEVICE="eth0"
NM_CONTROLLED="no"
ONBOOT=yes
HWADDR=XX:XX:XX:XX:XX:XX
UUID=XXXXXXXX-XXXX-XXXX-XXXX-XXXXXXXXXXXX
TYPE=Ethernet
BOOTPROTO=none
NAME="System eth0"
USERCTL=no
MASTER=bond0
SLAVE=yes
```

From your initial experience of building a static IP address, you will notice that the first eight lines of both configuration files show that nothing of significance has changed. We have removed what is now considered to be redundant information, but this is because much of the information we have removed is now contained in `/etc/sysconfig/network-scripts/ifcfg-bond0`.

On the other hand, you will notice that the final three lines have not only declared that non-root users are not allowed to control the device, but they have agreed to confirm that the master is known as `bond0`, while the Ethernet device is considered to be a slave.

For example, the configuration file for a second Ethernet device may look like this:

```
DEVICE="eth1"
NM_CONTROLLED="no"
ONBOOT=yes
HWADDR=XX:XX:XX:XX:XX:XX
UUID=XXXXXXXX-XXXX-XXXX-XXXX-XXXXXXXXXXXX
TYPE=Ethernet
BOOTPROTO=none
NAME="System eth1"
USERCTL=no
MASTER=bond0
SLAVE=yes
```

So having made some basic changes to the current Ethernet configuration files (now known as slaves), the recipe then required us to register the bonding module as a device. This was achieved by creating a new file called `bonding.conf in/etc/modprobe.d` with the following preferences:

```
alias bond0 bonding
options bond0 mode=5 miimon=100
```

The previous settings indicate the type of bond we are trying to build and this is something you may wish to experiment with at a later date.

In all, there are six modes thereby giving you plenty of scope to reconfigure this recipe for your own needs. However, for the purposes of simplicity, we have used `mode=5`, a function that conforms to a process of adaptive transmit load balancing, a basic configuration path that does not require any specific type of network switch support.

The consequence of this modification is to allow the outgoing traffic to be distributed according to the current load on each slave (Ethernet) device and if one device fails the other device assumes responsibility for continuing with the task in hand.

 In this configuration, the `miimon` value is used to confirm just how often (in milliseconds) the links will be checked for failure.

To finalize this process we then proceeded to register the module and restart the network service.

Of course, there is always much more detail that could be provided but don't forget, any changes to the mode type or `miimon` value found in `/etc/modprobe.d/bonding.conf` is something that you can alter at your leisure if you want to improve the overall performance of your server.

There's more...

As a fallback it may be worth considering adding an additional setting to `/etc/sysconfig/network-scripts/ifcfg-bond0` that will serve to provide balance to the system. Channel bonding can be used in such a way that multiple devices can carry different configurations, but before you begin experimenting it is suggested that we finalize the main recipe by enabling both Ethernet cards to carry the same options until you have the time to test your configuration and improve it.

 Remember, there are six modes in total and although some of these modes will require specific hardware support, the aim of this recipe is to provide a starting point from which you can begin testing your server's performance by changing both the mode type or `miimon` settings to suit your environment.

To begin, open `ifcfg-bond0` in your favorite text editor like so:

vi/etc/sysconfig/network-scripts/ifcfg-bond0

Now add the following line at the bottom of the file:

```
BONDING_OPTS="miimon=100 mode=balance-tlb"
```

Alternatively, if you are currently using `mode=6`, you can use the following settings:

```
BONDING_OPTS="miimon=100 mode=balance-alb"
```

When you have finished, run the following command to restart the network:

```
service network restart
```

Changing the hostname and resolving a fully qualified domain name

In this recipe we will learn how to change the hostname and resolve the **Fully Qualified Domain Name** (**FQDN**) of your server.

The process of setting the hostname is typically associated with the installation process but on many occasions there comes a time when the name used is either incorrect for a technical reason or you just don't like it any more. For some people the name of the server lacks importance, but for many others, a good server demands a good name and so it is the purpose of this recipe is to show you how quickly the hostname can be changed with the intention to revise and resolve the resulting fully qualified domain name.

Getting ready

To complete this recipe you will require a working installation of the CentOS 6 operating system with root privileges and a console-based text editor of your choice.

How to do it...

To begin this recipe we shall start by accessing the system as root and opening the following file in order to name or rename your current server.

1. To do this, log in as root and using your favorite text editor type:

   ```
   vi /etc/sysconfig/network
   ```

2. Now change the hostname value to your preferred name and when finished save and close the file. For example, if you wanted to call your server `henry`, your configuration file will look like this:

   ```
   NETWORKING=yes
   HOSTNAME=henry
   ```

CentOS is case sensitive, so it is best to avoid using capitals and irregular characters when giving your computer a hostname. Restrict yourself to using an Internet-friendly alpha-numeric. The overall length should be no longer than 63 characters but try to keep it much shorter.

3. We will now confirm the settings for the server in order to complete the Fully Qualified Domain Name or FQDN. An FQDN consists of a hostname and the more familiar DNS-based domain name, and in order to do this we will need to open and edit the `hosts` file:

   ```
   vi /etc/hosts
   ```

4. A typical file may look like this:

   ```
   127.0.0.1        localhostlocalhost.localdomain localhost4
   localhost4.localdomain4
   ::1                     localhostlocalhost.localdomain localhost6
   localhost6.localdomain6
   ```

5. So let's concentrate on confirming the correct order and setting the correct values with the intention of making our file look similar to the following:

   ```
   127.0.0.1                localhost.localdomain localhost
   XXX.XXX.XXX.XXX       hostname.domainname.suffix hostname
   ::1                 localhost6.localdomain6 localhost6
   ```

6. You should now replace the values of the second line with something more appropriate to your needs. For example, if your server was called `henry`, (with an IP address of `192.168.1.100` and domain name of `henry.com`) your final file will look like this:

   ```
   127.0.0.1                localhost.localdomain localhost
   192.168.1.100          henry.henry.com henry
   ::1                 localhost6.localdomain6 localhost6
   ```

 For a server found on a local network, it advisable to use a non-Internet based address. For example, you could use `.local` or `.lan` or even `.home`; and by using these references you will avoid any confusion with the typical `.com`, `.co.uk`, or `.net` domain names.

7. When complete, save and close your file before rebooting your server to allow the changes to take immediate effect. To do this, return to your console and type:

   ```
   reboot
   ```

8. On a successful reboot you can now check your new hostname by typing the following command and waiting for the response:

```
hostname
```

9. To confirm the domain name, you should type the following command and wait for the response:

```
hostname -f
```

10. Finally, and as an alternative to the preceding method, to confirm the Fully Qualified Domain Name (FQDN), you can type the following command and wait for the response:

```
hostname -fqdn
```

How it works...

A hostname is a unique label created to identify a machine on a network. They are restricted to alpha-numeric based characters, and making a change to your server's hostname can be achieved by simply changing the values found in two system configuration files and rebooting your server.

So what have we learned from this experience?

In the first stage of the recipe, our intention was to change the current hostname used by our server that is maintained by a configuration file located at `/etc/sysconfig/network`.

A typical example of this file would look like this:

```
NETWORKING=yes
HOSTNAME=your_computername_here
```

Based on the example shown, if you did change the name of your server to `henry`, then your resulting configuration file would look like this:

```
NETWORKING=yes
HOSTNAME=henry
```

However, if you wanted to use a slightly different name, then you can use this:

```
NETWORKING=yes
HOSTNAME=webserver
```

Following this, and having saved our work, we were then required to confirm the Fully Qualified Domain Name or FQDN of our server. This is achieved by updating the hosts file found at `/etc/hosts`.

A typical example of the hosts file can look like this:

```
127.0.0.1         localhostlocalhost.localdomain localhost4 localhost4.
localdomain4
::1               localhostlocalhost.localdomain localhost6 localhost6.
localdomain6
```

The `hosts` file is used by CentOS to map hostnames to IP addresses and it is often found to be incorrect on a new, un-configured, or recently installed server. For this reason our first task was to reorganize the references shown in order to support both, the relevant IPv4 and IPv6 values as well as a hostname and domain name reference.

As a consequence of this, we found that the entire file would need rewriting in order to look like this:

```
127.0.0.1           localhost.localdomain localhost
XXX.XXX.XXX.XXX      hostname.domainname.suffix hostname
::1                 localhost6.localdomain6 localhost6
```

You were then informed that an FQDN should consist of both, a short hostname and the domain name. Based on the example shown in the main recipe, for a server named `henry` whose IP address is `192.168.1.100` and whose domain name is `henry.com`, the revised hosts file would now look like this:

```
127.0.0.1           localhost.localdomainlocalhost
192.168.1.100       henry.henry.com henry
::1                 localhost6.localdomain6 localhost6
```

Whereas the alternative name suggested previously will look like this:

```
127.0.0.1           localhost.localdomainlocalhost
192.168.1.100       webserver.webserver.com webserver
::1                 localhost6.localdomain6 localhost6
```

Saving this file would arguably complete this process. However, because the kernel makes a record of the hostname during the boot process, there is no choice but to reboot your server with the following command:

```
reboot
```

On a successful reboot, you were then shown three basic commands that would enable you to confirm your new settings, starting with a command to call your current hostname. You did this by typing:

```
hostname
```

To confirm the domain name, you were invited to use the following command:

```
hostname -f
```

Finally, the following command is used to confirm the Fully Qualified Domain Name or FQDN like so:

```
hostname -fqdn
```

So in conclusion you can say that this recipe has not only served to show you how to rename your server, but it has also served to dispel the many myths associated with your hostnames as opposed to domain names.

As we all know, a server is not only known by the use of a shorter, easier-to-remember, and quicker-to-type single-word based name, but it also consists of three values separated with a period. The relationship between these values may seem strange at first, especially where many people will see them as a single value, but by completing this recipe you have discovered that the domain name remains distinct from the hostname by the virtue that it is determined by the resolver subsystem and it is only by putting them together that your server will yield the Fully Qualified Domain Name or FQDN of the system as a whole.

There's more...

The `hosts` file consists of a list of IP addresses and corresponding hostnames and if your network contains computers whose IP addresses are not listed in an existing DNS record, then in order to speed up your network it is often recommended that you add them to the `hosts` file.

This can be achieved on any operating system, but to do this on CentOS, simply open the `hosts` file in your favorite text editor like so:

```
vi /etc/hosts
```

Now scroll down to the bottom of this file and add the following values by substituting the domain names and IP addresses shown here with something more appropriate to your own needs:

```
192.168.1.100     www.example1.lan
192.168.1.101     www.example2.lan
192.168.1.102     www.example3.lan
192.168.1.103     www.example4.lan
```

You can even use external address such as:

```
83.166.169.228   www.packtpub.com
```

This method provides you with the chance to create mappings between domain names and IP addresses without the need to use a DNS, and it can be applied to any workstation or server. The list is not restricted by size and you can even employ this method to block access to certain websites by simply repointing all requests to visit a known website to a different IP address. For example, if the real address of `www.website.com` is `192.168.1.200` and you want to restrict access to it, then simply make the following changes to the `hosts` file of the viewing computer:

```
192.168.1.201      www.website.com
```

It isn't failsafe, but in this instance, anyone trying to access `www.website.com` will automatically be sent to `192.168.1.201` instead of `192.168.1.200`.

When you have finished, remember to save and close your file in the usual way before proceeding to enjoy the benefits of faster and safer domain name resolution across any available network.

Switching SELinux off

In this recipe we will consider the need to switch **Security-Enhanced Linux** (**SELinux**) off in order to ease the process of installing packages and managing your server.

Security-Enhanced Linux is a very robust security mechanism that is enabled by default. It is designed to improve the security of your server but on occasion it has been the case that you have been required to disable it in order to install a new package or to speed up the process of server management. This is not a decision you will make in haste, but it is the purpose of this recipe to show you how this can be achieved and this solution can be seen as both, temporary or permanent, depending on your needs.

Getting ready

To complete this recipe, you will require a working installation of the CentOS 6 operating system with root privileges and a console-based text editor of your choice.

How to do it...

SELinux has three enforcement levels and in this recipe we will show you how to make a permanent change to the current status of Security-Enhanced Linux by switching it off. As this recipe can be seen as both, a temporary or permanent solution, by using the alternative options shown, you may also use this method to re-enable SELinux with an enforcement level of your choice at any time.

1. To begin this recipe, log in as root and type the following command:

   ```
   vi /etc/sysconfig/selinux
   ```

2. Scroll down and look for the line that reads:

   `SELINUX=`

3. To switch SELinux off, change the line to read as follows:

   `SELINUX=disabled`

SELinux has three possible states:

`enforcing`: Choose this value to determine that SELinux security policy is enforced. To set this condition, type `SELINUX=enforcing`.

`permissive`: Choose this value to determine that SELinux prints warnings instead of enforcing. To set this condition, type `SELINUX=permissive`.

`disabled`: Choose this value to determine that no SELinux policy is loaded. To set this condition, type `SELINUX=disabled`.

---

4. When complete, save and close before proceeding to reboot your server in order for the new changes to take effect. To do this, type:

   `reboot`

How it works...

SELinux is a major security component found within the CentOS operating system and in this recipe we have just discovered how easy it is to disable.

So what have we learned from this experience?

Security-Enhanced Linux is managed by a simple configuration file located at `/etc/sysconfig/selinux`. It is enabled during the boot process and it can run in one of three states. The term state refers to what is otherwise known as an **enforcement mode** and they can be summarized as follows:

▶ **Enforcing**: This level enforces security and access policies around both files and processes.

▶ **Permissive**: This level allows operations that would otherwise be blocked by SELinux security policies. In this state SELinux will report messages to `/var/log/audit/audit.log` indicating which operations would have been blocked. You should also be aware that in this state the mechanism that labels files and processes according to SELinux policies is still active in this enforcement mode.

▶ **Disabled**: This level completely disables SELinux, thereby permitting all operations and disabling logging and file/process labeling.

To determine the current state of **SELinux,** you can simply run the following command at any time:

`getenforce`

Of course, a discussion based on the benefits of SELinux is beyond the scope of this recipe but having made the decision to switch it off, the next step was to open the file located at `/etc/sysconfig/selinux`, to make the necessary configuration change and complete a full system reboot, like so:

`reboot`

> When SELinux is running, you can use the `setenforce` command. However, this will only affect the server if you are switching between enforcing or permissive mode. For the purpose of this recipe, the role of this command is negligible.

SELinux has an excellent pedigree and it does provide an outstanding level of protection if used correctly. However, not every server will need to use it or has need for it, and in these circumstances a need to change the default enforcement level may be required; and this is often the case when using particular types of software, providing particular services, installing and running control panels (such as **cPanel**, **DirectAdmin**, or **Plesk**) or during a process of making system-wide configuration changes.

For example, a default or typical SELinux configuration will typically look like this:

```
# This file controls the state of SELinux on the system.
# SELINUX= can take one of these three values:
#      enforcing - SELinux security policy is enforced.
#      permissive - SELinux prints warnings instead of enforcing.
#      disabled - No SELinux policy is loaded.
SELINUX=enforcing
# SELINUXTYPE= can take one of these two values:
#      targeted - Targeted processes are protected,
#      mls - Multi Level Security protection.
SELINUXTYPE=targeted
```

As you can see, it will show that the current enforcement level is set at `enforcing`. However, if you have deemed it necessary to enable a permissive approach to enforcement, then your configuration file will look like this:

```
# This file controls the state of SELinux on the system.
# SELINUX= can take one of these three values:
#      enforcing - SELinux security policy is enforced.
#      permissive - SELinux prints warnings instead of enforcing.
#      disabled - No SELinux policy is loaded.
```

```
SELINUX=permissive
# SELINUXTYPE= can take one of these two values:
#       targeted - Targeted processes are protected,
#       mls - Multi Level Security protection.
SELINUXTYPE=targeted
```

On the other hand, if you have made the decision to disable SELinux, then the same file will now look like this:

```
# This file controls the state of SELinux on the system.
# SELINUX= can take one of these three values:
#       enforcing - SELinux security policy is enforced.
#       permissive - SELinux prints warnings instead of enforcing.
#       disabled - No SELinux policy is loaded.
SELINUX=disabled
# SELINUXTYPE= can take one of these two values:
#       targeted - Targeted processes are protected,
#       mls - Multi Level Security protection.
SELINUXTYPE=targeted
```

In conclusion, this recipe has not only shown you how to configure the enforcement level of SELinux, but it has served to introduce you to the vast subject and debate Security-Enhanced Linux tends to inspire.

See also

> ▸ The U.S. National Security Agency:
> `http://www.nsa.gov/research/selinux/index.shtml`

> ▸ The UnOfficial SELinux FAQ: `http://www.crypt.gen.nz/selinux/faq.html`

Disabling the IPv6 module

In this recipe we will consider the need to disable the IPv6 module on a CentOS server.

IPv6 was designed to solve the problems of IPv4, but it is an accepted fact that not everyone uses it and not all hardware supports it. The deployment of IPv6 is accelerating but for this reason it is also a possibility that some environments will expect that IPv6 has been disabled on the server. This is certainly not unusual, and in these circumstances, you may find that disabling IPv6 will not only speed up networking, but it will also serve to reduce an administrative overhead and improve your current level of security.

Getting ready

To complete this recipe you will require a working installation of the CentOS 6 operating system with root privileges and a console-based text editor of your choice.

How to do it...

Before we start, you should be aware that this recipe is not advised if you are using or you are intending to use any IPv6-dependant features such as Bonding, Postfix, SELinux, and similar packages. For this reason it is advised that you research your current packages to make sure that any changes made here will not impact the server's performance.

1. To begin, log in as root and disable IPv6 by typing:

   ```
   echo "install ipv6 /bin/true" > /etc/modprobe.d/disable-ipv6.conf
   ```

2. Now run the following command to disable `ip6tables`:

   ```
   chkconfig ip6tables off
   ```

3. We must now disable any calls to IPv6 in its various locations. To do this we will start by opening the following configuration file:

   ```
   vi   /etc/sysconfig/network
   ```

4. Scroll down and add or amend the following line to read:

   ```
   NETWORKING_IPV6=no
   ```

5. To complete this process, you must now modify the configuration for each Ethernet device to show the following values:

   ```
   IPV6INIT=no
   ```

   ```
   IPV6_AUTOCONF=no
   ```

    You can do this by running `vi   /etc/sysconfig/network-scripts/ifcfg-ethX`, where X is the value for the relevant Ethernet device in question.

6. When you have finished, simply reboot the system to ensure that these changes take immediate effect:

   ```
   reboot
   ```

How it works...

IPv6 is a major component found within the CentOS operating system and by following this recipe you have seen how to completely disable IPv6 on your system. For those networks and applications that do not support this feature, disabling IPv6 can be a very good option in order to tighten system security and increase the overall performance of your system. However, given the pervasive nature of the IPv6 module, this recipe was required to draw on a similarly aggressive tone.

So what have we learned from this experience?

We began the process of disabling the IPv6 module by invoking the following command-line instruction that asks the system to write install `ipv6 /bin/true` in a new file found at `/etc/modprobe.d/disable-ipv6.conf`:

```
echo "install ipv6 /bin/true" > /etc/modprobe.d/disable-ipv6.conf
```

By doing this, you have now implied that whenever the system needs to load the IPv6 module, it is forced to execute the `true` command instead of actually loading the module; and as `/bin/true` does and means nothing, the module will not load.

 At the time of writing this book, this was the only effective way to disable IPv6 in CentOS. However, it is possible that this situation will be updated over time.

Following this, the next stage directed us to switch off IPv6 Tables (as they won't be needed any more) and disable all IPv6 network-based calls so they would not be triggered on boot.

Having completed this process, we were then required to reconfigure the Ethernet devices to run in IPv4 mode only. This was achieved by opening the main configuration file for each device with the intention of setting the following conditions:

```
IPV6INIT=no
IPV6_AUTOCONF=no
```

The final step then required a full system reboot in order for the changes to take immediate effect; and having followed this recipe you should now find that IPv6 has been disabled.

Remember, this method is very effective but as it was stated at the outset, disabling IPv6 is not advisable if you intend to use other IPv6-dependant features and packages at some point in the future.

There's more...

You can verify as to whether the IPv6 module is currently running by using the following command:

`ifconfig`

The sample output of a typical system using both IPv4 and IPv6 could look like this:

```
eth0      Link encap:EthernetHWaddr 00:1F:C6:89:50:75
inet addr:192.168.1.100  Bcast:192.168.1.255  Mask:255.255.255.0
inet6addr: fe80::21f:c6ff:fe89:5075/64 Scope:Link
          UP BROADCAST RUNNING MULTICAST  MTU:1500  Metric:1
          RX packets:1840 errors:0 dropped:0 overruns:0 frame:0
          TX packets:424 errors:0 dropped:0 overruns:0 carrier:0
collisions:0 txqueuelen:1000
          RX bytes:127636 (124.6 KiB)  TX bytes:44580 (43.5 KiB)
          Interrupt:26 Base address:0x2000
```

As an alternative you can also use grep, like so:

`lsmod | grep ipv6`

If the result of grep returns any output, then the response is telling you that the IPv6 module is enabled.

3
Working with CentOS

In this chapter, we will cover:

▶ Creating an administrative user and becoming root with the switch user command

▶ Introducing `mailx` and forwarding the root's e-mail to an external address

▶ Automating tasks with cron

▶ Synchronizing files and directories with rsync and working towards a full system backup with cron

▶ Issuing customized e-mail reports with Mutt

▶ Using logrotate to manage logfiles

▶ Extending log rotation by adding NTP to logrotate

▶ Enabling a custom service at boot

▶ Evaluating current memory usage with the `free` and `top` commands and clearing the memory cache

Introduction

This chapter is a collection of recipes that introduces you to the process of running and maintaining an enterprise class server by introducing you to a series of starting points that considers how to approach creating an administrative user and becoming root with the switch user command; introducing mailx and forwarding root's e-mail to an external address; automating tasks with cron; synchronizing files and directories with rsync and working towards a full system backup with cron; issuing customized e-mail reports with Mutt; using logrotate to manage logfiles; extending log rotation by adding NTP to logrotate; enabling a custom service at boot; evaluating current memory usage with the free and top commands and clearing the memory cache.

Creating an administrative user and becoming root with the switch user command

In this recipe we will learn how to create an administrative user and provide them with access to the su or switch user command that enables them to change the ownership of a login session in order to become root or any other user.

An experienced user will always tell you that routinely managing a server as the root user is not the best way to work. It might be convenient, but by doing this you are leaving yourself open to a whole host of issues that can give rise to a multitude of errors and unwanted side effects. Best practices will always tell you that the use of the root user account should be left until it is required, and with this in mind it is the purpose of this recipe to show you how to configure a day-to-day administrative user whose ability to assume the power of root and any other user is just a few strokes of the keyboard away.

Getting ready

To complete this recipe you will need a working installation of the CentOS 6 operating system with root privileges and a console-based text editor of your choice.

How to do it...

This recipe considers the act of creating an administrative user who has the option to become another user by invoking the su command. Otherwise known as the **switch user** command, you should not confuse this with sudo, which is discussed elsewhere in this book.

1. To begin, log in as root and create your new user account by typing:

   ```
   useradd your_new_username
   ```

2. This command will serve not only to create a new user, but it will also establish an associated user ID, make the relevant home directory, set the default shell to bash, and create a new primary group. However, in order to complete this process, you will be expected to provide a suitable password. To do this, type the following command:

   ```
   passwd your_password_here
   ```

Passwords should be no less than six characters in length, but no longer than sixteen characters in length. They should consist of alphanumeric values, and for obvious reasons you must avoid the use of including whitespaces. Do not use a dictionary-based word and refrain from using a known or obvious phrase.

3. Wait for the prompt and complete the password confirmation by retyping your password when asked. The process of creating the user account is now complete and you should stop here if you do not intend to provide them with any administrative powers. However, if you want to provide them with access to the switch user command, then the next task is to modify the user's attributes and to add them to the wheel group like so:

```
usermod -a -G wheel your_new_username
```

4. When ready, you should now ensure that the wheel module is activated in PAM. **PAM** or the **Pluggable Authentication Module** provides us a global method of authenticating users across the system as a whole without any individual program being required to know which authentication system will be used. PAM is a big subject, and an undertaking of what it does is beyond the scope of this recipe. However, PAM is common to all modern Linux-based systems and we now need to modify its preset conditions in order that members of the wheel group will have access to su. To do this, open the following file in your favorite text editor:

```
vi /etc/pam.d/su
```

5. Scroll down and uncomment the following line:

```
auth      required  pam_wheel.so use_uid
```

6. When complete, save and close the file in the usual way. You have now successfully activated the su command for the user concerned, but unlike sudo that enables a user to execute a single command as root, su is a very powerful command that will enable the user to become any other user (including root).

How it works...

The purpose of this recipe is to create a new user and provide them with the power to routinely change the ownership of a login session to become root or any other user. For the purpose of this recipe, the term "administrative powers" relates to the user being given access to the su or switch user command, and this should not be confused with sudo; which is discussed elsewhere in this book.

So what did we learn from this experience?

We began by invoking the following command in order to create a new user:

```
useradd your_new_username
```

The useradd command required us to supply a suitable name for the new user, which, in turn will then enable the server to establish the new identity with a default set of values and criteria that includes a user ID, home directory, primary group, and set the default shell to bash.

As an alternative, you can create new users by invoking the `adduser` command. However, as the `adduser` command is present as a symbolic link to the actual `useradd` command, regardless of what command you use, the work will be done by the `useradd` command.

Completing this process was simply a matter of confirming a suitable password by typing the following command:

```
passwd your_password_here
```

When finished, the next phase of the recipe introduced the act of providing your user with administrative powers.

To do this, we began by making the user in question a member of the wheel group by typing:

```
usermod -a -G wheel your_new_username
```

On all modern Linux systems, authentication is processed by PAM, and where all root powers are provided as a result of being a member of the wheel group our next task was to activate the wheel group within PAM. We did this by editing the configuration file found at `/etc/pam.d/su` and uncommenting the following line:

```
auth       required  pam_wheel.so use_uid
```

Having completed this task, it was simply a matter of saving the file in order to complete the process and from this point onwards, the new user would be able to become root or any other user by simply issuing the `su` or switch user command at any time.

There's more...

As an administrative user you can invoke the `su` command at any time by typing the following command:

```
su -
```

As no additional parameters were given, this command will automatically attempt to access the root user account. You will be expected to enter root's password, but having done this, the user will have absolute administrative access to the system because they are now the root user in every sense of the word.

It is important to remember that `su` does not keep a record of what actions are completed when an administrative user has become root. For these reasons you should reference your enquiries to `/var/log/messages`.

For example, you can create a new directory by typing:

```
mkdir some_new_directory
```

Or use this opportunity to review your hard disks by typing:

```
fdisk -l
```

Did you notice in the previous examples that because you are the root user you do not need to invoke `sudo`. Moreover, because you are the root user you will have full access to every command and every part of the server without any restrictions. This is the nature and purpose of the switch user command and for this reason it makes an ideal way of providing the server administrator with an everyday account that has the opportunity to assume the role of any other user at any time.

> The `sudo` command represents a flexible way of providing administrative powers without making a specific user or user group an administrator. Of course, we know that `sudo` will allow you to disseminate elevated privileges without revealing any details regarding the root user and a `sudo` command-based user can do most things, but not everything. They can assume some administrative powers, but they are not an administrator in the fullest sense of the word.

So with this in mind, and if you want to become a system user called `henry`, then you would enter the following command-line argument:

```
su - henry
```

Again, you will need to know the password for `henry`, but having provided this information, all future activity will be committed as `henry` until you exit the session.

To exit a current login session and return to your original user account you would need to type:

```
exit
```

However, as changing personality can be quite confusing, another useful command to remember is known as `whoami`. This simple command is used to confirm the identity of the current login session, and you can run this command at any time by simply typing:

```
whoami
```

Introducing mailx and forwarding the root's e-mail to an external e-mail address

In this recipe we will investigate the use of mailx and forward the root's e-mail to an external e-mail address of your choice in order to provide your server with a simple messaging system that can be used at any time.

E-mail capability for the root user is not activated by default and you may find it useful to ensure that this service is not only enabled, but that it is also able to issue any messages to a third-party address. At any given moment CentOS may be required to generate e-mail reports that should be issued to, or generated on the behalf of the root user, while those of you who enjoy the benefit of e-mail in order to issue simple reminders and notices will want a convenient solution that may not require a comprehensive mail server solution. We all know that e-mail capability is essential to every aspect of your role as the administrator and it is the purpose of this recipe to not only show you how to activate the root's e-mail, but to enable all messages to be sent to a destination of your choice.

Getting ready

To complete this recipe you will require a working installation of the CentOS 6 operating system with root privileges, a console-based text editor of your choice, and a connection to the Internet in order to facilitate the download of additional packages and the sending of e-mail messages to a third-party account.

How to do it...

In this recipe you are invited to install a package called **mailx**. The purpose of the `mailx` utility is to provide a send and receiving facility for messages, and for this reason you can easily adapt this feature to serve many other needs.

1. To begin, log in as root and install `mailx` like so:

    ```
    yum install mailx
    ```

2. In order to confirm that your environment is not blocking any potential e-mail activity and to confirm that `mailx` is installed correctly, simply replace the value `externalemail@domain.com` with something more appropriate and type the following command to send an e-mail to a third-party account:

    ```
    echo "Test Email" | mail -s "This is a test email." externalemail@
    domain.com
    ```

3. However, in order to forward the root's e-mail, we will now need to modify the aliases for your server. To do this, open the following file in your favorite text editor like so:

    ```
    vi /etc/aliases
    ```

4. Now scroll down and look for the following lines:

```
# Person who should get root's mail

#root:        marc
```

5. Uncomment the line and change the value `marc` to an e-mail address of your choosing:

```
# Person who should get root's mail

root:        youremail_address@youdomain.com
```

 As an alternative solution, instead of sending the root's e-mail to an external e-mail address, you could just as easily send it to one or more existing server users by replacing the preceding instruction with the following:

```
root:     username1, username2
```

6. Now save and close the file in the usual way before proceeding to run the following command in order to implement the changes:

```
newaliases
```

7. On completion of a successful test, simply invoke `mailx` to test the new configuration by sending an e-mail to the root user's account like so:

```
echo "Test Email" | mail -s "This is a test email" root
```

How it works...

Having completed this recipe, you are now able to forward the root's e-mail to a third-party account. You have been introduced to a command-line facility called `mailx` and you now have a simple tool that will enable you to send e-mail from the console.

So what have we learned from this experience?

In the first part of this recipe, we began by installing `mailx`. It may not have a graphical user interface, but for the purpose of sending simple messages from the command line in order to test our final configuration, it proved to be a perfect addition.

We installed the package with the following command:

```
yum install mailx
```

While sending a message from the command line proved to be as simple as typing the following instruction:

```
echo "Test Email" | mail -s "This is a test email." externalemail@domain.
com
```

In the second part of this recipe, we then returned to the main task of forwarding the root's e-mail by modifying the values found in /etc/aliases.

To open this file it was simply a matter of using your favorite text editor in the following way:

```
vi /etc/aliases
```

Then, we located the appropriate lines in order to activate the role of who should get the root's mail and to instruct CentOS where to send that e-mail:

```
# Person who should get root's mail
root:         youremail_address@youdomain.com
```

Having done this, and saved the file in the usual way, you were then required to run the following command in order to rebuild the database:

```
newaliases
```

At this stage it should be important to remember that any change to the aliases file will always imply the need to run the newaliases command before the changes take effect, but as a result of completing this recipe, we have discovered that the process was simple, very quick, and rather elegant, and you can easily test your new settings by electing to send an e-mail directly from the command line like so:

```
echo "Test Email" | mail -s "This is a test email" root
```

The ability to receive e-mail reports is a vital tool for any server administrator and during the course of this recipe we have discovered how to ensure that any message sent to the root user can be redirected to a third-party e-mail account. For this reason you will now have the confidence to know that you will never miss an important e-mail and with the assistance of mailx, the advantage of sending e-mail from the console will provide an added convenience.

There's more...

On occasion, e-mails may tend to get stuck in a queue. There are several ways of dealing with this that includes the ability to flush all mail, to send e-mails forcefully, or to delete e-mails. To begin managing this process you can type the following command:

```
mailq
```

If a queue is found, then the mailq command will display a summary of the mail messages queued for future delivery. Of course, there are occasions when many servers will often report to not have a queue and this is quite normal. So with this in mind it is expected that the server will typically respond like so:

```
Mail queue is empty
```

A comprehensive description of all the features regarding `mailx` is beyond the scope of this recipe, but it is hoped that this brief introduction to this feature-rich, console-based e-mail send-and-receive facility will inspire you to learn more by reviewing the supplied manual.

To do this, return to your console and type the following command:

```
man mailx
```

Automating tasks with cron

In this recipe we will investigate the role of server automation and the convenience of running specific tasks at predefined periods by introducing you to the time-based job scheduler known as **cron**.

Cron allows for the automation of tasks by enabling the administrator to determine a predefined schedule based on any hour, any day, or any month. It is a standard component of the CentOS operating system, and it is the purpose of this recipe to introduce you to the concept of managing recurring tasks in order to take advantage of this invaluable tool and to make CentOS work for you.

Getting ready

To complete this recipe you will require a minimal installation of the CentOS 6 operating system with root privileges and a console-based text editor of your choice.

How to do it...

The purpose of this recipe is to create a script that will write the time and date with a few words of your choice to a text file every fifteen minutes. This may seem to be a relatively simple exercise, but the intention is to show you that from such simplicity, cron can be used to do so much more that will make working with CentOS an absolute pleasure.

1. To begin this recipe, log in as root and create your first cron job by typing:

   ```
   crontab -e
   ```

2. We will now create a simple cron job that will write the date and time with the words `hello world` to a file located at `/root/cron-helloworld.txt` every fifteen minutes. To do this, add the following line:

   ```
   */15 * * * * echo `date` "Hello world" >>$HOME/cron-helloworld.txt
   ```

3. When complete, simply save the file using the name provided and exit the editor. The system will now respond with the following message:

   ```
   crontab: installing new crontab
   ```

4. The preceding message informs you that the server is now creating the new cron job. When finished, restart the cron service like so:

```
service crond restart
```

5. Having restarted the service, the new cron job will be activated and you can view the output of the script by reviewing the file found at `/root/cron-helloworld.txt` or by monitoring the logfile found at `/var/log/cron`.

How it works...

Cron is the name of a program that enables CentOS users to execute commands or scripts automatically at a specified time and date. Cron's settings are kept in a user-specific file called a **crontab**, and as we have seen in this recipe, this file can be edited to create automated tasks as often as they are required.

So what did we learn from this experience?

The example used was very simple, but in many ways this was the purpose of the original recipe. Crontab uses a daemon, `crond`, which runs constantly in the background and checks once a minute to see if any of the scheduled jobs need to be executed. If a task is found, then cron will execute it.

To edit an existing crontab file or to create a new crontab, you would type:

```
crontab -e
```

To view a list of current cron jobs, you can type:

```
crontab -l
```

Alternatively, to view a list of the current jobs for another user, you can type:

```
crontab -u username -l
```

Along with the commands just discussed, other common commands associated with cron include:

- `crontab -r`: Use this option to remove a crontab file
- `crontab -v`: Use this option to display the last time you edited a crontab file

Tasks or jobs are generally referred to as cron jobs and by avoiding complication in our first script it was the intention to show you that the nature of command construction was very simple. The formation of a cron job looks like this:

```
<minute> <hour> <day of the month> <month of the year> <day of the
week> <command>
```

Entries are separated by a single or tabbed space and the allowed values are primarily numeric (that is, 0-59 for minute, 0-23 for hour, 1-31 for day of the month, 1-12 for month of the year, and 0-7 for day of the week). However, in saying this, it is also true to say that there are more specific operators (that is, /, ,, -) and cron-specific shortcuts (that is, @yearly, @daily, @hourly, @weekly) that do allow for additional controls.

For example, where the / operator is used to step through specified units, our recipe shows that the use of */15 will run the task every fifteen minutes, while the use of */1 will run the task every minute. As an addition to this, you should be aware that the use of this syntax will align all commands on the hour.

So with this in mind, the most suitable template or starting point for anyone wanting to write their first cron job is to start with a series of five asterisks followed by the command, like this:

```
* * * * * command
```

Or more commonly, you could write it like this:

```
* * * * * /absolute/path/to/script.sh
```

Then proceed to configure the minute, hour, day, month, and day-of-the-week values as desired.

For example, if you want a particular PHP script to run at 8 P.M. (20:00 hrs) on every weekday (Monday-Friday), it may look like this:

```
0 20 * * 1-5 /full/path/to/your/php/script.php
```

So with this in mind, and by completing this simple recipe you can now see how cron can be used to manage a database backup, run a scheduled system backup, provide support to websites by activating scripts at predefined intervals, or run various bash scripts and a whole lot more.

There's more...

To delete or disable a cron job, it is simply a matter of either removing the instruction from an individual user's cron file or by placing a hash (#) at the beginning of the line. Individual cron files can be found at /var/spool/cron/<username> and the use of the hash will either disable the cron job or allow you to write comments.

For example, if you want to remove the cron job created in the main recipe, you can log in as root and begin by typing the following command:

```
crontab -e
```

At this point you may either remove the entire line or comment it out, like so:

```
# */15 * * * * echo `date` "Hello world" >>$HOME/cron-helloworld.txt
```

Save the file, and when finished, remember to restart the cron service by typing:

```
service crond restart
```

See also

- ▸ Cron Wikipedia home page: `http://en.wikipedia.org/wiki/Cron`
- ▸ *The Open Group Base Specifications Issue 7* – commands and utilities reference: `http://pubs.opengroup.org/onlinepubs/9699919799/utilities/crontab.html`

Synchronizing files and directories with rsync and working towards a full system backup with cron

In this recipe, we will investigate the need to synchronize files and directories with rysnc on the command line. We will then use this introduction to build on a previous recipe discussing cron and illustrate how a simple bash script can be used to implement a fully automated backup process.

Rsync can be used to synchronize files and directories across a variety of local and remote locations. It can interact with multiple operating systems, work over SSH, provide incremental backups, execute commands on a remote machine, and replace the need for the copy command. Rsync is an invaluable asset for any system administrator who intends to run a server or manage a network of computers as it not only simplifies the process of making backups in general, but it can be used to action a complete backup solution, and for this reason it is the purpose of this recipe to offer a suitable starting point for a small utility that will quickly become your trusted friend.

Getting ready

To complete this recipe, you will require a working installation of the CentOS 6 operating system with root privileges, a console-based text editor of your choice, and a connection to the Internet in order to facilitate the download of additional packages.

How to do it...

During the course of this recipe, it will be assumed that you know the location of the (target or source) files and directories you wish to synchronize and that a suitable destination is available.

1. To begin this recipe, log in as root and install rsync by typing:

   ```
   yum install rsync
   ```

2. Now create a backup directory by implementing the `mkdir` command, like so:

   ```
   mkdir /home/backup
   ```

   Typical usage of the mkdir command is as follows:

   ```
   mkdir directory_name
   ```

   For example, to create a new directory called `backup` within an existing folder called `home`, we use `mkdir /home/backup`. However you can also build a complete tree of directories by invoking the `-p` flag like so: `mkdir -p /home/backup/{docs,images,videos}`. In this way you can quickly create a new folder called `backup` that contains three additional folders called `docs`, `images`, and `videos`.

3. To begin the backup process, simply repeat the following command by modifying the value used for `/path/to/source/files/` with something more applicable to your needs:

   ```
   rsync --delete -avz /path/to/source/files/ /home/backup/
   ```

   In simple terms we have just provided rsync with an instruction to make a copy of the files found at `/path/to/source/files/` and copy them to `/home/backup/` using the following flags:

   `--delete`: Delete files that don't exist (on the sending system)

   `-a`: Archive mode (copy directories, files, and symlinks while preserving permissions, include modification times, ownership and group information)

   `-v`: Use verbosity and print all operations to the terminal. Not including this command will merely serve to reduce the amount of information shown

   `-z`: Compress file data

4. Having used the *Return* key to confirm the preceding instruction, your system will now respond with a live report of what is being copied. When this process has finished, you can then compare both directories to see that the contents are exactly the same. To do this, use the `diff` command:

```
diff /path/to/source/files/ /home/backup/
```

How it works...

In this recipe we considered the use of rsync through the command line. Of course, this is only one of the many ways that this tool can be used, but by using this approach it did allow us to explore a handful of the features provided by this very valuable utility.

So what did we learn from this experience?

Rsync is not intended to be complicated. It is a fast and efficient backup tool that is designed to be versatile by giving you complete access to an array of features on the command line. It can be used to maintain an exact copy (or mirror) of the target directory on the same machine or on a completely different system, and it does this by copying all the files once and then only updating the files that have changed the next time you run it. Rsync is intended to be flexible, and the evidence of this could be seen in the formulation of the command we used:

```
rsync --delete -avz /path/to/source/files/ /home/backup/
```

The use of the phrase `delete` is important, as it instructs rsync to delete files on the backup (which do not exist in the source), while the chosen flags imply that rsync should use (`-a`) archive mode in order to recursively copy files and directories while keeping all permissions and time-based information; (`-v`) verbosity mode so you can see what is happening; and to (`-z`) compress the data during the file transfer in order to save bandwidth and reduce the amount of time required to complete the entire process.

Rsync has many options that go beyond the purpose of this recipe, but if you want to exclude certain files you could always extend the original instruction by invoking the `--exclude` flag. By doing this, you can inform rsync to back up an entire directory but ensure that it does not include a predefined pattern of files and folders. Implementing the `--exclude` flag is relatively simple and it would imply a matter of modifying the original command like so:

```
rsync --delete -avz -exclude="files or folders to exclude" /path/to/
source/files/ /home/backup/
```

For example, if you are copying files from your server to a USB stick drive and you did not want to include large files (such as an `.iso` image), then your command may look similar to this:

```
rsync --delete -avz --exclude="*.iso" /path/to/source/ /path/to/external/
disk/
```

To extend this approach, with the intention of excluding a number of different file types, you can use the following command:

```
rsync --delete -avz --exclude="*.zip" --exclude="*.iso"  /path/to/source/
/path/to/external/disk/
```

On the other hand, if you want to take a full backup of the home directory and put it on an external disk while excluding the tmp folder and its contents, then your revised rsync instruction would look like this:

```
rsync -avz --exclude="tmp" /home/ /path/to/external/disk/
```

Alternatively, to exclude a specific file you can use:

```
rsync -avz --exclude="/home/path/to/file.txt" /home/ /path/to/external/
disk/
```

> When dealing with rsync, it is important to realize that the exclude path remains relative to the source. For this reason you do not need to include the first trailing slash /, so you could rewrite the instruction as `rsync -avz --exclude="home/path/to/file.txt" /source/ /destination/`.

On a final note, there is the subject of verbosity. Verbosity is very useful, but a tendency to use bytes as its primary unit for measurement can be a source of confusion. So in order to change this you can invoke rsync with the -h (or "human") option like so:

```
rsync -avzh --exclude="tmp" /home/ /path/to/external/disk/
```

Verbosity cannot be switched off or disabled, but you do have the option to use the -q or --quiet flag which enables us to decrease the amount of information displayed during a backup operation:

```
rsync -avzhq --exclude="tmp" /home/ /path/to/external/disk/
```

In conclusion, it will go without saying that a backup should be located on an external drive or on a separate partition, but having completed this introduction I think you will agree that rsync is ideally positioned in such a way that it will enable any server administrator to develop their own policy with regard to maintaining an effective backup of important data.

There's more...

You can run rsync at regular intervals using a cron job and thereby use it to implement a fully automated backup solution.

To do this, we will take the original command used in the main recipe, include an incidental logging feature, and ask cron to e-mail us when the process is complete. It will be expected that you have already installed `mailx` (as discussed in the *Introducing mailx and forwarding the root's e-mail to an external e-mail address* recipe), and that you are able to use a text editor of your choice.

As we need to run this process as root, we shall begin by creating a shell script in root's home directory. To begin, log in as root and create a backup directory by typing:

```
mkdir /root/bin/
```

We will now create a simple shell script by typing:

```
vi /root/bin/mybackup.sh
```

Now, by customizing the values shown, add the following three lines to `mybackup.sh`:

```
#!/bin/bash
rsync --delete --log-file=/path/to/$(date +%Y%m%d)_logfile.log -avzq /
path/to/source/directory/ /path/to/backup/directory/

cat /path/to/$(date +%Y%m%d)_logfile.log | mail -s "subject line here"
youremail@domain.com
```

> The preceding script uses `mailx` for e-mail capability. `mailx` has been discussed in a previous recipe which also detailed cron, but as an option you can always use Mutt (which is discussed in a following recipe found in this chapter). To use Mutt instead of `mailx`, simply replace the reference for mail with `mutt` like so:
>
> ```
> cat /path/to/$(date +%Y%m%d)_logfile.log | mutt
> -s "subject line here" youremail@domain.com
> ```

Remember, you should customize the values as required (that is, change the e-mail address used, select a source directory, and choose a destination directory) but whatever you do, you must keep the trailing slash.

In addition to this, you will notice that a small logging feature has been added on line three with the following code:

```
--log-file=/path/to/$(date +%Y%m%d)_logfile.log
```

This code will not only create a logfile, but it will serve to append the date to the beginning of the filename. This has been included for convenience and log rotation, so feel free to customize it as required.

When you have finished, simply save and close the file before making it executable, like so:

```
chmod a+x /root/bin/mybackup.sh
```

We will now add this script as a cron job to run on a daily schedule at 20:30 hours.
To do this, type:

```
crontab -e
```

Now add the following line:

```
30 20 * * * /root/bin/mybackup.sh
```

When finished, simply save the file using the assigned name and close the session.
On success, the system will now create a cron job and provide the following feedback:

```
crontab: installing new crontab
```

To finish this process you should restart the cron service by typing:

```
service crond restart
```

At the appropriate time you will receive an e-mail informing you that a backup has been made with a brief review of the actions taken. However, as this may be some hours away, if you would like to test your script right now, simply type the following commands one line at a time:

```
cd /root/bin/
```

```
./mybackup.sh
```

See also

▸ Rsync home page – official Rsync documentation:
`http://rsync.samba.org/documentation.html`

Issuing customized e-mail reports with Mutt

In this recipe we will investigate the need to issue customized e-mail reports with Mutt from the command line. We will then use this introduction to build on a previous recipe discussing cron and illustrate how a simple bash script can be used to automate a scheduled e-mail.

Mutt is a full-featured text-based Mail User Agent that supports the typical mail formats and protocols while providing comprehensive support for MIME, GPG, and PGP. By its very nature Mutt is a very useful package, and because it is a tool that all server administrators should become familiar with, it is the purpose of this recipe to show you how Mutt can be used to deliver customized reports and messages to a destination of your choice.

Getting ready

To complete this recipe you will require a working installation of the CentOS 6 operating system with root privileges, a console-based text editor of your choice, and a connection to the Internet in order to facilitate the download of additional packages.

How to do it...

Mutt is a powerful text-based mail client for CentOS. It is not installed by default, and having completed this recipe you will be able to send e-mail to a variety of sources. Mutt can be configured to use a variety of SMTP servers, but for the purpose of this recipe we will only consider the need to send outgoing e-mail as the root user and not concern ourselves with the need to accept incoming e-mail messages.

1. To begin, log in as root and install Mutt by typing:

   ```
   yum install mutt
   ```

2. Now test your installation by using Mutt to send a very basic e-mail on through the terminal, like so:

   ```
   echo " message body here" | mutt -s " subject line here"
   youremail@domain.com
   ```

3. Having checked that you have received the test message, we will now proceed to create an example report by sending a selection of logfiles from /var/log as an attachment to an e-mail address of your choice. To do this, simply type the following line by substituting the values shown with a preferred value for your message body, subject line and e-mail address:

   ```
   echo "Here is a log summary report sent by Mutt." | mutt -s "Log
   summary report" youremail@domain.com -a /var/log/messages -a /var/
   log/maillog -a /var/log/secure
   ```

4. When finished, press the *Return* key to finalize your instructions and then view your external e-mail client to read the e-mail.

How it works...

Mutt is a text-based mail client that is known for being a fast and highly configurable environment. It is available across most Linux-based distributions and as it is text-based, it remains ideal for any server administrator who wants the ability to send e-mails from the console or via a secure shell environment.

So what did we learn from this experience?

The purpose of the recipe was to show you how to send e-mails through the command line. So having begun this recipe by installing the relevant packages and sending a test e-mail, we then saw how easily you could create a real-time message at the console and issue attachments to a third-party e-mail address:

```
echo "Here is a log summary report sent by Mutt." | mutt -s "Log summary
report" youremail@domain.com -a /var/log/messages -a /var/log/maillog -a
/var/log/secure
```

The preceding command may look long and involved, but if we step back a little, we can see that the process of creating an e-mail on the command line is based on the following elements:

```
echo " Here is a log summary report sent by Mutt." | mutt -s "Log summary
report " youremail@domain.com
```

Of course, this was only a very simplistic message and it was enhanced by sending copies of the various logfiles found on your server by applying the attachment operator, like so:

```
echo " Here is a log summary report sent by Mutt." | mutt -s "Log summary
report " youremail@domain.com -a /path/to/filename
```

This was the approach taken in this recipe, but what if you want to send the file not as an attachment but as the actual body content instead? Don't worry, Mutt has this covered, by modifying our original command, like so:

```
cat /path/to/filename | mutt -s "Log summary report" youremail@domain.com
```

Or combine these techniques like this:

```
cat /path/to/filename | mutt -s "subject line" youremail@domain.com -a /
path/to/filename
```

Of course, the latter example does imply some redundancy, but if you happened to be sending a report to a mobile platform, it is often a good idea to use both approaches in order to cover any issues regarding the device's ability to handle file formats.

So as we have discovered, Mutt is not just an e-mail client. It is a tool that can be used beyond its shell and it shines when you consider its potential to send e-mails from the console environment. For those of you who want to dig deeper, then you can access the main software interface by typing:

```
mutt
```

Otherwise, you can learn more about Mutt by reviewing the onboard manual:

```
man mutt
```

There's more...

You can schedule e-mail-based messages by simply creating a cron job. To do this we will build on what we have already learned and convert our command-line approach to a scheduled shell script.

As we want to run this process as root, we will begin by creating a shell script in root's home directory. To begin, log in as root and create a backup directory by typing:

```
mkdir /root/bin/
```

We will now create a simple shell script by typing:

```
vi /root/bin/mymuttscript.sh
```

Now add the following to mymuttscript.sh:

```
#!/bin/sh
echo " Here is a log summary report sent by Mutt." | mutt -s "Log
summary report" youremail@domain.com -a /var/log/messages -a /var/log/
maillog -a /var/log/cron
```

Remember to customize the values shown, but when finished, save and close the file before making it executable, like so:

```
chmod a+x /root/bin/mymuttscript.sh
```

We will now add this script as a cron job to run on a daily schedule at 22:00 hours. To do this, type:

```
crontab -e
```

Then add the following line:

```
00 22 * * * /root/bin/mymuttscript.sh
```

Again, remember to customize the values shown but note that we have used the full path when adding the script location.

When finished, simply save the file using the assigned name and close the session. On success, the system will now create a cron job and provide the following feedback:

```
crontab: installing new crontab
```

To finish this process you will want to restart the cron service by typing:

```
service crond restart
```

▶ Mutt's official website: `http://www.mutt.org/`

Using logrotate to manage logfiles

In this recipe we will consider the practice of log rotation in order to learn how to improve the functionality and overall performance of the entire system.

Logfiles provide information on the health of your system and assist you in troubleshooting specific difficulties with a service or software application. They can be stored on a separate partition, but during the lifetime of your server, large logfiles can often become too difficult to search, inflate backups, or minimize the known disk space on your system. Logfiles are vital to your role as a server administrator, and as an out-of-control logfile can only serve to hinder, it is the purpose of this recipe to show you how to use a feature known as **logrotate** in order to keep your system in check.

Getting ready

To complete this recipe you will require a minimal installation of the CentOS 6 operating system with root privileges and a console-based text editor of your choice.

How to do it...

Logrotate is installed by default, but in order to complete this recipe we will need to activate the relevant features by making several changes to the logrotate configuration file.

1. Log in as the root user and with your favorite text editor, open the following file:

   `vi /etc/logrotate.conf`

2. Working down the file, start your configuration changes by specifying a value that will determine the frequency of log rotation by changing the default value to either `daily`, `weekly`, `monthly`, or `yearly`. For example, you can specify a `monthly` value like so:

   `monthly`

3. Now specify a numeric value that will determine how many archived logs will be kept before the process of log rotation will delete them. The default `rotate` command value is set at 4 but in order to maintain seven at a time you would use:

   `rotate7`

4. The `create` parameter will serve to tell the server to create a new logfile after each rotation, and as this is a desired feature we will leave this value alone. However, if you would like to compress the rotated (archived) logfiles in GZIP format, then you should uncomment the following line like so:

   compress

5. When complete, save and close the file before testing your new configuration by typing the following command:

   `logrotate -vf /etc/logrotate.conf`

How it works...

Log rotation is a process that solves many problems associated with logfile expansion. It is an essential task for any system administrator and the key to your success remains with the ability to master a small utility known as **logrotate**. Installed by default, logrotate is an invaluable tool that should be used by all servers and by following this recipe you now know how easy it is to activate and configure.

So what have we learned from this experience?

Logrotate provides us with a simple utility for maintaining logfiles. It runs on a predetermined schedule and enables the server to maintain order by archiving current logfiles, keeping them for period of time and then deleting the oldest logfiles based on the rotate value set within `logrotate.conf`. For example, to rotate seven logfiles you would use:

rotate7

Logrotate is managed as a cron job (a feature discussed in this chapter), where a typical installation will rotate up to four logs on a weekly basis, by following this recipe you can now appreciate that by changing a few simple parameters, you can not only modify this process to suit a schedule of your choice, but can also compress your logfiles with the intention of conserving disk space and making backups that much easier.

There's more...

Having already seen how, by using the `size` command, you can control the log rotation process, you can take this one step further and specify a file size that logrotate will use to determine whether or not to perform a rotation. By doing this, the `size` command will take priority over any rotation interval or rule and it will reset the time period if activated.

 Remember, unless you use an interval other than `daily`, then log rotation cannot be guaranteed to happen on the same day every week.

The `size` command is not found in `logrotate.conf` by default, so you will need to apply it manually by using it in conjunction with a value for the maximum file size you intend to specify for your logs.

To do this, log in as the root user. Open the main configuration file for `logrotate.conf` in your favorite text editor:

```
vi /etc/logrotate.conf
```

Now scroll down to the bottom of this file and add the following line by replacing X with a value more appropriate to your own needs:

```
size X
```

For example, if you wanted to rotate a log based on a file size of 500 KB, you can add the following line to `logrotate.conf`, like so:

```
size 500k
```

To rotate a log based on a file size of 5 MB, you can use:

```
size 500M
```

To rotate a log based on a file size of 1GB, you can use:

```
size 1G
```

Finally, you can test your new configuration by typing:

```
logrotate -vf /etc/logrotate.conf
```

Extending log rotation by adding NTP to logrotate

In a previous recipe you were shown how to configure logrotate. Logrotate is typically associated with system logfiles, but given that we have already shown you how to create a custom logfile for NTP, it is the purpose of this recipe to build on that knowledge and to show you how you can use logrotate for any custom application.

Getting ready

To complete this recipe, you will require a minimal installation of the CentOS 6 operating system with root privileges and a console-based text editor of your choice. It is assumed that you have followed a previous recipe that detailed the necessary steps to configure customized NTP logging.

How to do it...

In this recipe you are required to log in as root and create a new file that will maintain all the necessary instructions for logrotate. Remember, this is a custom solution based on a popular package, and with this in mind there is always plenty of room for you to develop it and adapt it to your own needs at some point in the future.

1. To begin, log in as root and type the following to create a new file called `ntp`:

   ```
   vi /etc/logrotate.d/ntp
   ```

2. Now add the following lines by changing the values to something more appropriate to your own needs:

   ```
   /var/log/ntpd.log {
   missingok
   notifempty
   size 50M
   rotate 5
   weekly
   create 0600 root root
               postrotate
   /sbin/service ntpd restart
   endscript
   }
   ```

3. When complete, save and close the file before proceeding to test the new settings by typing:

   ```
   logrotate -vfd /etc/logrotate.conf
   ```

How it works...

Having just discovered how to implement a custom solution that can be used to support NTP, this brief recipe has not only shown you how this will serve to enhance the value of logrotate to the server as a whole, but it has also illustrated a basic technique that can be tailored to suit almost any service and application that you may decide to implement in the future.

So what have we learned from this experience?

Having created a new file in `/etc/logrotate.d`, we added the following instructions that would determine how logrotate will treat the logfile in question:

```
/var/log/ntpd.log {
missingok
notifempty
size50M
```

```
rotate 5
weekly
create 0600 root root
postrotate
/sbin/service ntpd restart
endscript
}
```

So let's break this down:

In the first line we told logrotate the location of the relevant logfile and followed this with a regular code block like so:

```
/var/log/ntpd.log {
}
```

Inside the code block, we then added the appropriate instructions:

```
# This option specifies if there is no log file do not issue an error
or warning
missingok
# This option specifies not to rotate an empty log.
notifempty
# This option rotates the logs over 50M.
size50M
# This option specifies the need to keep 5 log files at a time.
rotate 5
# This option rotates the logs weekly.
weekly
# This option sets the permissions for the newly created log files.
create 0600 root root
# This option specifies the need to restart the NTP service.
# You have two options - prerotate or postrotate.
postrotate
        /sbin/service ntpd restart
endscript
```

For the full list of available options, return to your console and read the `logrotate.conf` manual by typing `man logrotate.conf`.

And finally we tested our configuration by using the following command:

```
logrotate -vfd /etc/logrotate.conf
```

By using the previous command to test our settings we have implied the use of several flags:

▶ −v: Logrotate reports on what is happening and when it happens

▶ −f: Logrotate is asked to process the request regardless of the current cron status

▶ −d: Logrotate is asked to process the request without actually rotating them

So as you can see, adding NTP to logrotate wasn't that difficult, but by completing this recipe we have also discovered how useful logrotate can be when we consider extending this utility to manage other services and applications. Of course, there is plenty of scope to tailor this recipe to your exact needs, but until then you should now have an excellent and very capable solution for managing the logfiles generated by NTP.

Using chkconfig to enable a custom service at boot

In this recipe we will consider the practice of using the chkconfig management tool in order to enable a custom service at boot.

CentOS provides us with a simple command-line tool for managing services that are started during the various runlevels of your system (discussed in *Chapter 1, Installing CentOS*). Most applications and services will include their own initialization script and these will be installed to /etc/init.d, but over the life time of your server you may wish to use or write your own custom service (from a script or for a bespoke application) that will require manual installation. You may even want to troubleshoot an existing service, but whatever your reasons, it is the purpose of this recipe to show you how it can be achieved.

Getting ready

To complete this recipe you will require a minimal installation of the CentOS 6 operating system with root privileges and a console-based text editor of your choice. It is assumed that you have already installed a custom service and that you know the name of this custom service.

How to do it...

Before we begin, it is often a good idea to make sure that your new service is not already enabled.

1. To do this, log in as root and page through the list of current services by typing:

    ```
    chkconfig -list | less
    ```

     Depending on the number of services running on your server, this command may display a long list of services. For this reason you may want to use the `grep` tool like so:

    ```
    chkconfig --list | grep [servicename]
    ```

    Alternatively, you may know the name of the service in question, so use `chkconfig --list [servicename]`.

2. If the application or service you are looking for is not shown, then simply add the new service to the `chkconfig` management tool by using the following command and replacing `servicename` with the name of the service in question:

    ```
    chkconfig --add [servicename]
    ```

     Remember, when an application or service is installed an initialization script is generated and automatically added to the `/etc/init.d`. So if you have difficulty in identifying the name of your service, visit `/etc/init.d`, locate the appropriate script and obtain the service name from its contents.

3. The appropriate links are then created automatically, but in order to enable the service or application at startup, you will need to type the following command by replacing `servicename` with the service name in question and customizing the runlevels as required:

    ```
    chkconfig --levels 235 [servicename] on
    ```

     As an alternative, you can simply use `chkcongfig [servicename] on`. However, as this is a custom script, the preceding example was used in order that you could specify the exact runlevels needed.

4. When complete, you can confirm if this process was successful by typing:

```
chkconfig --list [servicename]
```

5. Having seen the appropriate output, you now know that you have successfully added your custom script to the chkconfig management tool and the service will start at the next reboot.

How it works...

When an application or service is installed, an initialization script is generated and automatically added to /etc/init.d. However, chkconfig needs to be made aware that it exists. This is done automatically when the new initialization script (or init script) is part of a typical rpm (that is, installed via YUM) but it needs to be done manually if you add your own initialization script.

So what have we learned from this experience?

During the operation of your system, CentOS can experience a number of states or modes of operation in which applications and services may or may not be running. Otherwise known as runlevels, by using the chkconfig command you can specify at what state your application or service should be initialized.

The example output may look similar to the following:

auditd	0:off	1:off	2:on	3:on	4:on	5:on	6:off
crond	0:off	1:off	2:on	3:on	4:on	5:on	6:off
ip6tables	0:off	1:off	2:on	3:on	4:on	5:on	6:off
iptables	0:off	1:off	2:on	3:on	4:on	5:on	6:off
netconsole	0:off	1:off	2:off	3:off	4:off	5:off	6:off
netfs	0:off	1:off	2:off	3:on	4:on	5:on	6:off
network	0:off	1:off	2:on	3:on	4:on	5:on	6:off
ntpd	0:off	1:off	2:on	3:on	4:on	5:on	6:off
ntpdate	0:off	1:off	2:off	3:off	4:off	5:off	6:off
postfix	0:off	1:off	2:on	3:on	4:on	5:on	6:off
rdisc	0:off	1:off	2:off	3:off	4:off	5:off	6:off
restorecond	0:off	1:off	2:off	3:off	4:off	5:off	6:off
rsyslog	0:off	1:off	2:on	3:on	4:on	5:on	6:off
saslauthd	0:off	1:off	2:off	3:off	4:off	5:off	6:off
sshd	0:off	1:off	2:on	3:on	4:on	5:on	6:off
udev-post	0:off	1:on	2:on	3:on	4:on	5:on	6:off

Using `chkconfig` is a relatively simple process and we have learned that runlevels 2, 3, and 5 are typical for most initialization scripts. This is because runlevel 3 will place the service in multiuser mode with full networking capabilities, whereas runlevel 5 is generally associated with desktop computing.

A full list of runlevels looks like this:

0 Halt: This is the runlevel at which the system shuts down and is unsuitable for any type of application or service.

1 Single-User mode: This runlevel does not start any networking or multiuser services, but it does boot the system into single-user mode under which only the root user can log in. This runlevel is ideal for system administrators who wish to perform system maintenance or repair activities.

2 Multi-user mode, console logins only (without networking): This runlevel does not start the network but it does boot the system into a multiuser environment with text-based console login capability.

3 Multi-User mode, console logins only: This runlevel gives all the features of runlevel 2, but it provides full networking services. This is the most common runlevel for server-based systems that do not require or use a graphical desktop environment.

4 Not used/User-definable: This runlevel is undefined and can be configured to provide a custom environment.

5 Multi-User mode, with display manager as well as console logins (X11): This runlevel is similar to runlevel 3, but is generally associated for systems with desktop environments.

6 Reboot: This runlevel reboots the system and is unsuitable for any type of application or service.

For example, to initialize the Apache web service during the boot process at runlevels 2, 3, and 5 you would use the `chkconfig` command like this:

```
chkconfig --levels 235 httpd on
```

Whereas MySQL will look like this:

```
chkconfig --levels 235 mysqld on
```

In conclusion it should be important to realize that the `chkconfig` management tool will only affect the service in question at the next reboot. So as an alternative to rebooting, you may want to consider running the following command in order to start you service now:

```
service [servicename] start
```

There's more...

Having discussed starting a service, we will now review the steps you need to take should you wish to disable and remove a service.

If you no longer require the use of a service, you can disable it at boot by using the `chkconfig off` switch, like so:

```
chkconfig [servicename] off
```

You should then proceed to stop the service from running with the following command:

```
service [servicename] stop
```

The preceding command will take immediate effect. However, in order to finalize this procedure you may want to remove it from the `chkconfig` management tool by typing:

```
chkconfig --del [servicename]
```

 Remember, if a service has been removed from the `chkconfig` management tool, you will need to re-register it using this recipe should you wish to initialize the same service with `chkconfig` in the future.

Evaluating current memory usage with the free and top commands and clearing the memory cache

In this recipe we will consider the merit of monitoring your current memory usage with a view to periodically clearing the cache.

The CentOS operating system has an efficient memory management process that will serve to restore cached memory as an ongoing process. However, there are occasions when the server may decide that the cached memory is being used for a particular reason which can inadvertently lead to memory retention and deny your server access to a vital and necessary resource. Memory is vital to a server, and it is the purpose of this recipe to show you how to force the server to release any cached memory.

Getting ready

To complete this recipe, you will require a minimal installation of the CentOS 6 operating system with root privileges and a console-based text editor of your choice.

How to do it...

As the administrator of your server it is often a good idea to make regular checks as to how the memory is being allocated, and we are about to discover that there are several ways of doing this, but rather than considering this to be a troubleshooting technique, you should always keep in mind that the process of reviewing memory allocation forms the basis of effective server management.

1. To begin, log in as root and review the status of your current memory usage by typing:

    `free -m`

    The `free` command shows the total amount of free and used physical and swap memory in the system as well as the buffers used by the kernel. It is very simple to use and the output may look similar to following:

	total	used	free	shared	buffers	cached
Mem:	4011	1052	2958	0	218	664
-/+ buffers/cache:		769	3242			
Swap:	2047	0	2047			

2. It is often a good idea to get a second opinion on the current status of your server memory, and for this reason you should type the following command:

    `top`

    The `top` command is used to provide a real-time view of your system. The list is dynamic and it will be refreshed every few seconds. The actual output for your system will be different, but it could look similar to this:

PID USER	PR	NI	VIRT	RES	SHR	S	%CPU	%MEM	TIME+	COMMAND
1 root	20	0	19204	1436	1176	S	0.3	0.1	0:00.46	init
2 root	20	0	0	0	0	S	0.1	0.0	0:00.00	kthreadd
3 root	RT	0	0	0	0	S	0.0	0.0	0:00.00	migration/0
4 root	20	0	0	0	0	S	0.0	0.0	0:02.23	ksoftirqd/0
5 root	RT	0	0	0	0	S	0.0	0.0	0:00.00	migration/0
6 root	RT	0	0	0	0	S	0.0	0.0	0:00.03	watchdog/0
7 root	RT	0	0	0	0	S	0.0	0.0	0:00.00	migration/1
8 root	RT	0	0	0	0	S	0.0	0.0	0:00.00	migration/1
9 root	20	0	0	0	0	S	0.0	0.0	0:01.08	ksoftirqd/1

    Use the M key to toggle the results by memory consumption

    Use the P key to toggle the results by CPU consumption.

    Press the Q key to quit.

3. From the results shown, if you have determined that too much memory is being cached, then you should proceed by typing the following lines one at a time:

```
sync
echo 3 > /proc/sys/vm/drop_caches
```

4. When complete, re-type the `free` command to review any changes made to your server:

```
free -m
```

Based on previous example shown, we have now been able to restore a healthy amount of RAM from the cache, as shown in the following output:

	total	used	free	shared	buffers	cached
Mem:	4011	144	3866	0	0	28
-/+ buffers/cache:		116	3895			
Swap:	2047	0	2047			

How it works...

As we all know, a server just like any other computer requires memory and by following this simple recipe you could say that you are now able to monitor and moderate memory usage. You have been introduced to two new commands, and without probing too deeply, this recipe has served to show you how both of these commands can be used in order to provide insight regarding your server's CPU utilization, memory allocation, and the status of any swap memory used.

So what have we learned from this experience?

We have discovered that the `free` command provides a simple way of showing you how much memory is being used on your system. It shows the total amount of RAM (`Mem`) and swap space (`Swap`) alongside the value of RAM currently in use. However, it can be misleading so you should always pay close attention to the second line of the output which shows the actual amount of RAM available for any applications and services:

```
total          used        free       shared     buffers        cached
Mem:           4011        1052        2958          0            218          664
-/+ buffers/cache:          769        3242
Swap:          2047           0        2047
```

By adding together the values for `used` and `free` RAM, you will obtain the total installed RAM. Whereas any memory listed as `shared` is an indication of how much memory is common to more than one process.

In addition to this, and as a second opinion, we have also learned how to review the server's need for memory by using the `top` command. Admittedly, we have probably not had time to dive deeper into its usage, but you did discover that it was not only able to show you a measurement for any current memory allocation, but you were also able to review the active processes and relate that information against current CPU utilization.

 CPU utilization is shown as a measurement of the load average and where this is generally regarded to be a complicated subject, it would be easier for us to remember that the load average is a measurement of CPU utilization over a period of time. Typically, a load average of a value no greater than 1 often implies that your processes are not waiting to use the CPU, whereas a load average above 1 indicates that your system is behaving in a manner that is less responsive than it should be. Values above 2 can be regarded as problematic and imply the need for additional troubleshooting.

So with all that information at hand, the best way to calculate the amount of free RAM is made by simply calculating the total amount of free RAM and adding this to the total amount of buffers and cached RAM, like so:

```
Free  RAM + (buffers + cached) = X
```

Whereas the total amount of RAM being used by any services and applications could be calculated like so:

```
Used RAM - (buffers + cached) = X
```

Obviously, there will be a time difference when running the two commands and both will utilize some RAM in order to function, but based on the results it is expected that you will notice how the two results correlate very well.

So having done the math you are now in a position to decide as to whether you would like to free up any RAM. A process that involved typing the following two lines:

```
sync
echo 3 > /proc/sys/vm/drop_caches
```

The `drop_caches` command is designed to be safe and it is coupled with the `sync` command in order to ensure that the entire cache is cleared. The act of clearing this cache will obviously imply that a greater load on the CPU (because the cache has gone) will be experienced, but you should also be aware that the amount of RAM available to the system will increase as well.

Arguably you could say that there will be a performance decrease because you are not taking advantage of the cache. This is very true and as a result it may have a negative effect over the short term. However, in a situation where you server was busy compiling data, handling large files, archiving, installing packages, scanning drives, or benchmarking (in fact, any role that can cause an excessive cache to build up), by completing this short recipe you server's memory will be refreshed and in a short period of time it will recover with a clean cache to the long term benefit of your users.

There's more...

Using the preceding method is very simple, but it can be a little inconvenient to do this during the typical working day, so to make your role a little simpler, why don't we take this method and apply it to a cron job that can run at set intervals every day?

Cron is the name of a program that enables users or administrators to execute one or more commands or scripts automatically at a specified time and date. An individual task is called a cron job and where a better introduction for the creation of cron jobs can be found elsewhere in this chapter, the convenience of allowing our server to refresh its cache after hours seems very sensible and an opportunity not to be missed.

To begin, log in as the root user and type:

```
crontab-e
```

This `crontab` interface will allow you to create a cron job. The format of creating a task is very simple and it looks like this:

```
minute hour day-of-month month day-of-week function-to-be-performed
```

This is generally represented as:

```
* * * * * function-to-be-performed
```

So scroll to the bottom of the cron file and add the following line:

```
30 23 * * * /root/memcache.sh
```

The preceding instruction will create a cron job that will require the script found at `/root/memcache.sh` to run at 23:30 hours or 23:30 P.M. every day. Alternatively, if you would prefer the same script to run at the same time every Friday (day 5), then simply make the following adjustment:

```
30 23 * * 5 /root/memcache.sh
```

`Crontab` will use your default editor and in most cases this will be VI, so when you are ready, save and close the file by accepting the default name provided.

Now having created our cron job we will need to create the script that will contain our instructions to clear the cache. To do this, create a file in `/root called memcache.sh`, like so:

```
vi /root/memcache.sh
```

Now add the following content to that file:

```
#!/bin/sh
sync; echo 3 > /proc/sys/vm/drop_caches
```

When finished, remember to save and close the file before restarting the cron service:

```
service crond restart
```

Well done, you have now created a cron job that will clear the memory of your server at 23:30 hours or 11:30 P.M. every day.

4
Managing Packages with Yum

In this chapter, we will cover:

- ▶ Updating the system with Yum
- ▶ Cleaning the Yum cache
- ▶ Automating Yum updates with Yum-cron
- ▶ Installing packages with Yum
- ▶ Removing packages with Yum
- ▶ Finding packages with Yum
- ▶ Installing Yum Priorities to support additional repositories
- ▶ Enhancing CentOS with the EPEL and Remi repositories

Introduction

This chapter is a collection of recipes that introduces you to the power of the Yum Package Manager by providing you with the opportunity to learn how to begin updating the system with Yum; cleaning the Yum cache; automating Yum updates with Yum-cron; installing packages with Yum; removing packages with Yum; finding packages with Yum; installing Yum Priorities to support additional repositories; and enhancing CentOS with the EPEL and Remi repositories.

Updating the system with YUM

In this recipe we will investigate the role of the Yum Package Manager with regard to running a system update.

Every once in a while you may become aware of an update or may simply wish to discover if an update exists. Applying patches and updates is a regular task for all server administrators and in this recipe you will learn how to achieve this with the help of Yum.

Getting ready

To complete this recipe you will require a working installation of the CentOS 6 operating system with root privileges, a console-based text editor of your choice, and a connection to the Internet in order to facilitate the download of additional packages.

How to do it...

Before we begin this recipe, you will be required to access the server with full root privileges in order that we can update the system. You can run this recipe as often as required but it should be done frequently, based on a schedule of your own choosing in the full knowledge that on occasion, some updates may require a full system reboot.

1. We will begin by checking to see whether there are any updates for your installed packages. To do this, log in as root and type:

    ```
    yum check-update
    ```

2. If no updates are available, then the update process will end and no further work will need to be done. However, if updates are available, Yum will now return a list of all package updates from the repositories known to your system. To complete the update process, type the following command:

    ```
    yum -y update
    ```

3. By using the -y flag the preceding command will now bypass the need to confirm the transaction summary and your system will now undergo an immediate update process. When complete, you will be provided with a final report that identifies what dependencies have been installed and what packages have been updated.

4. Generally speaking no further work is required and you may resume typical operations. However, if a new kernel has been installed or an important security update has taken place, it may be necessary to reboot the system in order for the new changes to take effect. To do this, type:

    ```
    reboot
    ```

While there is much debate as to whether an update will require a full system update, unless Yum explicitly states the need to do so, in practice a full system reboot is only to be considered after a `kernel` update, an update to `glibc`, and particular security-based features that are activated during the boot process.

How it works...

Yum is the default package management system for CentOS and part of its role is to automatically calculate what packages may require updating, what dependencies are required, and to manage the entire process of updating your system. So as you can see, Yum makes the process of updating your system very simple.

So what have we learned from this experience?

We started the recipe by checking to see if any updates were available to our system with the following command:

```
yum check-update
```

In this way, Yum will now check a central repository to confirm if an update is applicable to our system.

A repository is a remote directory or website that contains prepared software packages and utilities. Yum will use this facility to automatically locate and obtain the correct RPM packages (and dependencies) and if an update is available, then Yum will respond accordingly with a full summary of what packages and dependencies are available.

For this reason, Yum is a very useful tool and without doubt its mechanism does serve to simplify the processes associated with package management because it saves us from having to find and install new applications or updates manually.

If no updates are available, then Yum will respond as follows:

```
Loaded plugins: fastestmirror, refresh-packagekit
Loading mirror speeds from cached hostfile
 * base: anorien.csc.warwick.ac.uk
 * extras: anorien.csc.warwick.ac.uk
 * updates: mirror.rmg.io
Setting up Update Process
No Packages marked for Update
```

However, if updates are available, then we can proceed to update the system by typing the following command:

```
yum -y update
```

In this instance the preceding command includes the −y flag. This is done in order to circumvent the need to agree with the transaction summary given, and to confirm that we have already agreed to make these updates after running the previous check.

As an alternative approach, you could ignore the previous instruction by typing:

```
yum update
```

By doing this, you will be presented with a transaction summary, like so:

```
Transaction Summary
================================================================
Install        1 Package(s)
Upgrade       14 Package(s)


Total download size: 86 M
Is this ok [y/N]:
```

In this instance, to update your system you would simply confirm the request by using the Y key.

So having used Yum to update your system, you can be confident that this same recipe can be run as often as it is required. During this recipe we have learned that Yum will automate the entire process of resolving dependencies and it will obtain the relevant packages needed to complete the update request. Typically, there is no need to reboot the system, but when finished you may want to consider restarting certain services in order for the changes to take immediate effect.

There's more...

Yum will serve to ensure that all of the requirements for an application are met during installation and it will automatically install the packages for any dependencies that are not already present on your system. However, and I am sure you will be pleased to hear this, if a new application has requirements that conflict with existing software, Yum will abort the process without making any changes to your system.

Based on this knowledge, if you would like to determine which packages provide for a specific file or feature, simply run the following command at any time by substituting your_filenam_here with something more relevant to your own needs:

```
yum provides your_filename_here
```

See also

► Yum project wiki – Yum guides: `http://yum.baseurl.org/wiki/Guides`

Cleaning the YUM cache

In this recipe we will investigate the role of YUM with regard to ensuring that the working cache remains current.

As a part of its typical mode of operation, Yum will create a cache that consists of metadata and packages. These files are very useful, but over time they will accumulate in size to such an extent that you may find that Yum is acting erratically or not as intended. The frequency of this happening can vary from system to system but it generally implies that the Yum cache system requires your immediate attention. Such a situation can be quite frustrating but it is the purpose of this recipe to provide a quick solution that will serve to assist you in cleaning the cache and restoring Yum to its original working state.

Getting ready

To complete this recipe you will require a working installation of the CentOS 6 operating system with root privileges, a console-based text editor of your choice, and a connection to the Internet in order to facilitate the download of additional packages.

How to do it...

Before we begin, it is important to realize that while we are troubleshooting a current problem, this same recipe can be used in an everyday situation to ensure that best working practices are maintained.

1. We will begin this recipe by asking Yum to clean any cached package information. To do this, log in as root and type:

   ```
   yum clean packages
   ```

2. Allow time for your system to respond and when finished, type the following command to remove any cached XML-based metadata:

   ```
   yum clean metadata
   ```

3. Again, wait for Yum to respond and when ready, type the following command to remove any cached database files:

   ```
   yum clean dbcache
   ```

4. Following this you will want to clean all the files to confirm the preceding instructions and to ensure that unnecessary disk space is not used. To do this, type:

```
yum clean all
```

5. Finally, you will want to rebuild the Yum cache by typing:

```
yum makecache
```

How it works...

Yum is a very powerful tool that is known for its ability to resolve package dependencies and automate the process of package management, but as with all things, there are times when even the best utilities can get confused and may report errors or behave erratically. Fixing this issue is relatively simple and the approach outlined in this recipe will also serve to keep your package manager in a healthy running state for the life time of your operating system.

So what have we learned from this experience?

During its typical operation Yum will create a cache of metadata and packages found in /var/cache/yum. These files are essential, but as they grow in size this cache will ultimately serve to slow down the overall use of this utility and may even cause some issues.

To address this situation we started by using the following command to clean the current package-based cache:

```
yum clean packages
```

We then followed this by cleaning the metadata cache, which would remove any excess XML-based files:

```
yum clean metadata
```

Yum uses SQLite as a part of its normal operation, so the next step was to remove any remaining database files:

```
yum clean dbcache
```

The next step was to clean all files associated with enabled repositories in order to reclaim any unused disk space:

```
yum clean all
```

Finally, we restored Yum to its normal working state by rebuilding the cache:

```
yum makecache
```

So in conclusion, even though this recipe was aimed at troubleshooting a typical issue, you now know that the same recipe can be run as often as required in order to keep Yum in an optimal working state.

There's more...

On a typical server, Yum is a tool that will solve the most complex problems related to package dependencies and package management. However, in instances where you have knowingly mixed incompatible repositories or you have used incomplete sources, there is a risk that Yum will not be able to help.

 Remember, in this situation you should consider the following advice to be a temporary remedy only. A tendency to ignore any warnings provided by Yum will only lead to bigger problems later on.

If such instances occur and if the error is RPM-based, as a temporary fix you can skip broken packages by using the following command:

```
yum -y update --skip-broken
```

This command will allow Yum to continue working by bypassing any packages with errors, but as stated earlier, this should be regarded as a temporary fix only. You should always be aware that a system with broken dependencies is not considered to be a healthy system. This situation is to be avoided at all costs and under these circumstances fixing such errors should become your first priority.

See also

▶ Yum project wiki – Yum guides: http://yum.baseurl.org/wiki/Guides

Automating Yum updates with Yum-cron

In this recipe we will investigate the role of Yum in conjunction with Yum-cron in order to automate the task of updating your system.

For some users the prospect of managing daily or even weekly updates with Yum may prove to be a time-consuming and unwelcome task. It could be that you are managing more than one server, or that your time is taken elsewhere with other types of tasks, but whatever the reason it is the purpose of this recipe to show you how to automate this process in order to alleviate the task of administration and to remove the need for daily attendance.

Getting ready

To complete this recipe you will require a working installation of the CentOS 6 operating system with root privileges, a console-based text editor of your choice, and a connection to the Internet in order to facilitate the download of additional packages.

How to do it...

The purpose of this recipe is to show you how Yum-cron can be used to automate nightly Yum updates. To do this we will need to install the relevant package and disable the pre-installed updater before activating the schedule.

1. To begin this recipe, log in as root and type:

   ```
   yum install yum-cron
   ```

2. Ensure that the service will start at runtime like so:

   ```
   chkconfig yum-cron on
   ```

3. We will now disable the pre-installed update service like so:

   ```
   chkconfig yum-updatesd off
   ```

4. Now stop the pre-installed updater by typing the following command:

   ```
   service yum-updatesd stop
   ```

5. We will now turn our attention to making a few changes to the configuration file. So, by using your preferred text editor, open the yum-cron file as follows:

   ```
   vi /etc/sysconfig/yum-cron
   ```

6. Modify the following lines to reflect these changes:

   ```
   ERROR_LEVEL=1
   MAILTO=your_email_address_here
   ```

7. When complete, save and close the file before typing:

   ```
   service yum-cron start
   ```

8. The service will now be activated and your server should respond as follows:

   ```
   Enabling nightly yum update: [ OK ]
   ```

9. Finally, run the update process to prepare your system and resolve any outstanding conflicts:

   ```
   yum update
   ```

How it works...

Yum-cron is a simple but powerful utility that is optimized for servers and replaces the yum-updatesd daemon that is typically associated with desktop usage. Yum-cron is not installed by default, nor will it reboot your computer after an update, but for a typical server you will discover that this optimized package is far more subtle and works with a lot less overhead.

So what did we learn from this experience?

Running Yum is known to be a manual task, but by installing and activating this simple package you can automate this process. We started the recipe by installing the relevant packages and disabling the current `yum-updatesd` daemon with the following commands.

We installed `yum-cron`:

```
yum install yum-cron
```

We enabled `yum-cron` at boot:

```
chkconfig yum-cron on
```

We disabled `yum-updatesd` at boot:

```
chkconfig yum-updatesd off
```

We started the `yum-cron` service:

```
service yum-cron start
```

We stopped the `yum-updated` service:

```
service yum-updatesd stop
```

The next step was to open the following file in order to make a few brief but necessary configuration changes:

```
vi /etc/sysconfig/yum-cron
```

Yum-cron executes the `/etc/cron.daily/0yum.cron` file at specified times. It is configured by opening and changing the values found in `/etc/sysconfig/yum-cron`. The file is well commented and clearly indicates the level of control provided. For example, in the main recipe it was decided to activate reporting and indicate that we would want all error messages supplied by e-mails regardless of the actual importance:

```
ERROR_LEVEL=1
MAILTO=your_email_address_here
```

Of course, the comments found in this file show that this level of detail is not necessary and that you can equally set the level of reporting through a number range of 0 to10, but for most of us, we generally prefer to know what the server did and so `Error_Level=1` will prove to be the most suitable value to use.

To finalize this process we then started the service with the following command:

```
service yum-cron start
```

Before updating Yum to ensure that any current conflicts are resolved:

```
yum update
```

In conclusion, I think you would agree that the process of installing and configuring this package was very straightforward. Automating the update process may not suit every server environment, and you will need to check what has been installed as certain updates will always require a system reboot or a service restart in order for the changes to take effect, but having installed this package, you will find that the manual process of running a package update is just one less task you need to worry about.

See also

▸ Yum project wiki – Yum guides: `http://yum.baseurl.org/wiki/Guides`

Installing packages with YUM

In this recipe we will investigate the role of using YUM to install new packages on your server.

An important task for any server administrator is the installation of applications and services. There are several different ways to achieve this but the most effective method involves the Yum Package Manager. Yum is able to search any number of repositories, automatically resolve package dependencies, and specify the installation of one or more packages. Yum is the definitive way to install your packages on your server and it is the purpose of this recipe to show you how it is done.

Getting ready

To complete this recipe you will require a working installation of the CentOS 6 operating system with root privileges, a console-based text editor of your choice, and a connection to the Internet in order to facilitate the download of additional packages.

How to do it...

This recipe will show you how to install one or more packages by invoking the Yum install option. To do this, you will need to log in as the root user and complete the following process:

1. To install a single package, replace the `package_name` value with the appropriate value and type:

   ```
   yum install package_name
   ```

2. Your system will now provide a transaction report that will require your approval. So when prompted, simply respond by using the *Y* or *N* key to either accept or decline the transaction, as follows:

   ```
   Is this ok [y/N]: y
   ```

3. If you have declined the transaction, then no further work is required and you will exit the package management routine. However, if you have confirmed the transaction, then watch the progress of your installation, like so:

```
Downloading Packages:
XXXXXXXX-version_number.el6.x86_64.rpm      | XX kB      00:01
Running rpm_check_debug
Running Transaction Test
Transaction Test Succeeded
Running Transaction
Installing :XXXXXXXX                                         1/1
Verifying  : XXXXXXXX                                        1/1


Installed:
XXXXXXXX


Complete!
```

How it works...

All packages are stored in the RPM format, and it is the role of Yum to provide access to those files which are stored in various repositories on the Internet. Yum is the power behind package management for CentOS and it really does make the installation process very easy, but what have we learned from this experience?

Having invoked the `install` command, Yum will conduct a search of the various repositories in order to find the relevant headers and metadata associated with the package in question.

For example, if you wanted to install a package called `wget`, you would begin by issuing the `install` command like so:

`yum install wget`

Yum will now locate the package and generate a transaction summary that will not only indicate the required disk size and expected installation size, but it will also indicate any necessary dependencies required by the requested package:

```
Loaded plugins: downloadonly, fastestmirror, refresh-packagekit
Loading mirror speeds from cached hostfile
 * base: anorien.csc.warwick.ac.uk
 * extras: anorien.csc.warwick.ac.uk
 * updates: mirror.prolocation.net
```

```
Setting up Install Process
Resolving Dependencies
--> Running transaction check
---> Package wget.x86_64 0:1.12-1.4.el6 will be installed
--> Finished Dependency Resolution


Dependencies Resolved


=================================================================================
Package          Arch          Version          Repository      Size
=================================================================================
Installing:
wget          x86_64          1.12-1.4.el6          base          481 k

Transaction Summary
=================================================================================
Install          1 Package(s)


Total download size: 481 k
Installed size: 1.8 M
Is this ok [y/N]:
```

As you can see, in order to provide us with a simple transaction summary, Yum has checked several different repositories (base, `extras`, and `updates`) and having resolved the need for any necessary dependencies, Yum is asking us to confirm the request before continuing with the installation process:

```
Downloading Packages:
wget-1.12-1.4.el6.x86_64.rpm                           | 481 kB       00:01
Running rpm_check_debug
Running Transaction Test
Transaction Test Succeeded
Running Transaction
Installing : wget-1.12-1.4.el6.x86_64                                1/1
Verifying  : wget-1.12-1.4.el6.x86_64                                1/1
```

```
Installed:
  wget.x86_64 0:1.12-1.4.el6
```

```
Complete!
```

So as you can see, by using the *Y* key we will be providing Yum the permission to fulfill the request which, in turn, will result in the download, verification, and installation of the package(s) concerned.

There's more...

There are times when you may wish to install more than one package at a time. To do this, simply invoke the same `install` command, but instead of naming a single package, simply identify the full list of packages you may require in such a way that it forms a long shopping list:

```
yum install package_name1 package_name2 package_name3
```

The numbers of packages you can install in this way is unlimited, but always leave a single space between each package name and keep the command on a single line. For very long installation instructions, line-wrapping may occur.

For example, if you wanted to install `wget` and `yum-utils` in a single transaction, you would then type:

```
yum install wget yum-utils
```

You do not need to list the packages in any particular order and the request will be processed in exactly the same way as it was in the original recipe:

```
Loaded plugins: downloadonly, fastestmirror, refresh-packagekit
Loading mirror speeds from cached hostfile
 * base: anorien.csc.warwick.ac.uk
 * extras: anorien.csc.warwick.ac.uk
 * updates: mirror.prolocation.net
Setting up Install Process
Resolving Dependencies
--> Running transaction check
---> Package wget.x86_64 0:1.12-1.4.el6 will be installed
---> Package yum-utils.noarch 0:1.1.30-14.el6 will be installed
--> Finished Dependency Resolution

Dependencies Resolved
```

```
==============================================================
Package          Arch        Version          Repository       Size
==============================================================
Installing:
wget             x86_64      1.12-1.4.el6     base             481 k
yum-utils        noarch      1.1.30-14.el6    base             101 k

Transaction Summary
==============================================================
Install      2 Package(s)


Total download size: 582 k
Installed size: 2.1 M
Is this ok [y/N]:
```

At this point, the transaction will remain pending until it is confirmed or declined. Again, use the *Y* key to confirm your request in order that the process will complete like so:

```
Downloading Packages:
(1/2): wget-1.12-1.4.el6.x86_64.rpm                    | 481 kB      00:01
(2/2): yum-utils-1.1.30-14.el6.noarch.rpm              | 101 kB
00:00
-------------------------------------------------------------------------
---------
Total
                                    322 kB/s | 582 kB      00:01
Running rpm_check_debug
Running Transaction Test
Transaction Test Succeeded
Running Transaction
Installing : yum-utils-1.1.30-14.el6.noarch                          1/2
Installing : wget-1.12-1.4.el6.x86_64                                2/2
Verifying  : wget-1.12-1.4.el6.x86_64                                1/2
Verifying  : yum-utils-1.1.30-14.el6.noarch                          2/2

Installed:
  wget.x86_64 0:1.12-1.4.el6
yum-utils.noarch 0:1.1.30-14.el6


Complete!
```

See also

▶   Yum project wiki – Yum guides: `http://yum.baseurl.org/wiki/Guides`

Removing packages with YUM

In this recipe we will investigate the role of using YUM with the intention of removing packages from your server.

During the lifetime of your server, it is possible that the need for certain applications and services may no longer be required. In such situations it is typical that you will want to remove such packages in order to optimize your working environment, and it is the purpose of this recipe to show you how this is done.

Getting ready

To complete this recipe you will require a working installation of the CentOS 6 operating system with root privileges, a console-based text editor of your choice, and a connection to the Internet.

How to do it...

This recipe will show you how to remove one or more packages by invoking the `yum remove` option. To do this, you will need to log in as the root user and complete the following process:

1. To remove a single package, replace the `package_name` value with the appropriate value and type:

    ```
    yum remove package_name
    ```

2. Wait for the transaction summary and confirmation prompt to be displayed, and then press either, the *Y* key to confirm or *N* key to decline the transaction, like so:

    ```
    Is this ok [y/N]: y
    ```

3. If you have declined the transaction, then no further work is required and you will exit Yum. However, if you have confirmed the transaction, then simply watch the progress of package removal until it is confirmed, like so:

    ```
    Downloading Packages:
    Running rpm_check_debug
    Running Transaction Test
    Transaction Test Succeeded
    Running Transaction Installing: package_name        1/1
    Erasing: package_name                               1/1
    ```

```
        Verifying: package_name                                    1/1


        Removed:
        package_name


        Complete!
```

How it works...

Applications that are no longer required can be removed with Yum. The process is very intuitive and only requires you to confirm the name of the packages you want to remove.

So what have we learned from this experience?

Having invoked the `remove` command, Yum will search your system to discover the relevant package; and by reading the package headers and metadata it will also determine what dependencies this will affect.

For example, if you wanted to remove a package called `wget`, we would begin by issuing the `remove` command like so:

```
yum remove wget
```

Yum in turn, will now locate the package details from your system and obtain a transaction summary that may include any necessary dependencies that are no longer required:

```
Loaded plugins: downloadonly, fastestmirror, refresh-packagekit
Setting up Remove Process
Resolving Dependencies
--> Running transaction check
---> Package wget.x86_64 0:1.12-1.4.el6 will be erased
--> Finished Dependency Resolution
base                                               | 3.7 kB     00:00
extras                                             | 3.0 kB     00:00
updates                                            | 3.5 kB     00:00


Dependencies Resolved


================================================================
Package       Arch       Version          Repository       Size
================================================================
```

```
Removing:
wget          x86_64       1.12-1.4.el6       @base         1.8 M


Transaction Summary
================================================================
Remove        1 Package(s)


Installed size: 1.8 M
Is this ok [y/N]:
```

This transaction will remain pending until you instruct Yum to remove the package(s) concerned. When confirmed, Yum will complete the transaction which, in return, will result in the removal of the package or packages, like so:

```
Downloading Packages:
wget-1.12-1.4.el6.x86_64.rpm            | 481 kB        00:01
Running rpm_check_debug
Running Transaction Test
Transaction Test Succeeded
Running Transaction
Installing : wget-1.12-1.4.el6.x86_64                    1/1
Verifying  : wget-1.12-1.4.el6.x86_64                    1/1


Installed:
  wget.x86_64 0:1.12-1.4.el6


Complete!
```

There's more...

You may want to remove more than one package at a time and you can do this by invoking the `remove` command with the full list of packages like this:

```
yum remove package_name1 package_name2 package_name3
```

The number of packages you can remove in this way is unlimited, but always leave a single space between each package name and keep the command on a single line. However, a long list of packages will probably result in a substantial increase in the number of dependencies that will also be removed, so you should spend some moments reading the summary report before proceeding.

For example, if you wanted to install both `wget` and `yum-utils` in a single transaction you would type:

```
yum remove wget yum-utils
```

You do not need to list the packages in any particular order and the full transaction will look similar to the following:

```
Loaded plugins: downloadonly, fastestmirror, refresh-packagekit
Setting up Remove Process
Resolving Dependencies
--> Running transaction check
---> Package wget.x86_64 0:1.12-1.4.el6 will be erased
---> Package yum-utils.noarch 0:1.1.30-14.el6 will be erased
--> Finished Dependency Resolution


Dependencies Resolved


================================================================
Package        Arch       Version         Repository        Size
================================================================
Removing:
wget           x86_64     1.12-1.4.el6     @base        1.8 M
yum-utils      noarch        1.1.30-14.el6     @base        301 k


Transaction Summary
================================================================
Remove          2 Package(s)


Installed size: 2.1 M
Is this ok [y/N]:
```

At this point you should review the transaction and confirm or decline the request. You should take extra care if the summary makes reference to any dependencies as these may be required by other RPMS.

When satisfied, use the *Y* key to complete the process like so:

```
Downloading Packages:
Running rpm_check_debug
Running Transaction Test
```

```
Transaction Test Succeeded
Running Transaction
  Erasing    : yum-utils-1.1.30-14.el6.noarch        1/2
  Erasing    : wget-1.12-1.4.el6.x86_64              2/2
  Verifying  : wget-1.12-1.4.el6.x86_64              1/2
  Verifying  : yum-utils-1.1.30-14.el6.noarch        2/2


Removed:
wget.x86_64 0:1.12-1.4.el6yum-utils.noarch 0:1.1.30-14.el6


Complete!
```

On the other hand, if you want to remove a particular package and you are concerned that certain dependencies should remain on the system, it is often a good idea to end the current transaction and simply de-activate or disable the software concerned.

See also

> ► Yum project wiki – Yum guides: `http://yum.baseurl.org/wiki/Guides`

Finding packages with YUM

In this recipe we will investigate the role of using YUM to find a package.

Yum was developed to improve the installation of RPMs and it is used to access a growing list of packages that provide a full range of services offered by your server. Yum is simple to use, but if you are not sure what a package is called, then your duties as the server administrator can become that much harder.

To overcome this, Yum maintains an extensive range of discovery tools and it is the purpose of this recipe to show you how use this functionality in order to search the various repositories and find the package you need.

Getting ready

To complete this recipe you will require a working installation of the CentOS 6 operating system with root privileges, a console-based text editor of your choice, and a connection to the Internet.

How to do it...

This recipe will show you how to find one or more packages by invoking Yum's searching options. To do this, you will need to log in as the root user and complete the following process:

1. To search for a single package, replace the `keyword` value with the appropriate phase, string or parameter, and type:

    ```
    yum search keyword
    ```

2. Wait for a summary of the search results and when a list is generated, you can query any package shown by simply replacing `package_name` with the appropriate value:

    ```
    yum info package_name
    ```

3. If the preceding results prove satisfactory and you want to view a list of dependencies associated with the package in question, type:

    ```
    yum deplist package_name
    ```

 This command is particularly useful when debugging dependencies or when working with source-based installations.

How it works...

Searching for packages with Yum can be achieved in the same way as you would search for anything on the World Wide Web. The types of words you can search for can be as specific or as general as you like. They can even consist of full or partial words, and having found a package that you may be interested in, you would have noticed that this recipe has also served to show you how to discover additional information about the package in question.

So what have we learned from this experience?

Yum maintains extensive search features and it allows you to query packages by keyword, package name, and pathname. For example, if you want to locate the correct package for compiling C, Objective-C, and C++ code, you can use the following query:

```
yum search compiler
```

The result of this query would be as follows:

```
Loaded plugins: downloadonly, fastestmirror, refresh-packagekit
Loading mirror speeds from cached hostfile
 * base: centos.mirror1.spango.com
 * extras: anorien.csc.warwick.ac.uk
 * updates: centos.weepeetelecom.nl
```

base		3.7 kB	00:00
extras		3.0 kB	00:00
updates		3.5 kB	00:00
updates/primary_db		1.2 MB	00:03

```
========================= N/S Matched: compiler ==========================
========
Pyrex.noarch : A compiler/language for writing Python extension modules
checkpolicy.x86_64 :SELinux policy compiler
compat-gcc-34.x86_64 : Compatibility GNU Compiler Collection
compat-gcc-34-c++.x86_64 : C++ support for compatibility compiler
compat-gcc-34-g77.x86_64 : Fortran 77 support for compatibility compiler
ecj.x86_64 : Eclipse Compiler for Java
gcc.x86_64 : Various compilers (C, C++, Objective-C, Java, ...)
gprolog.x86_64 : GNU Prolog is a free Prolog compiler
iasl.x86_64 : Intel ASL compiler/decompiler
mingw32-gcc.x86_64 :MinGW Windows cross-compiler (GCC) for C
mingw32-gcc-c++.x86_64 : MinGW Windows cross-compiler for C++
mingw32-gcc-gfortran.x86_64 :MinGW Windows cross-compiler for FORTRAN
mingw32-gcc-objc.x86_64 :MinGW Windows cross-compiler support for
Objective C
mingw32-gcc-objc++.x86_64 : MinGW Windows cross-compiler support for
Objective C++
mingw32-runtime.noarch :MinGW Windows cross-compiler runtime
ocaml.x86_64 : Objective Caml compiler and programming environment
pl.i686 : SWI-Prolog - Edinburgh compatible Prolog compiler
pl.x86_64 : SWI-Prolog - Edinburgh compatible Prolog compiler
samba4-pidl.x86_64 : Perl IDL compiler
teckit.i686 : Conversion library and mapping compiler
teckit.x86_64 : Conversion library and mapping compiler
teckit-devel.i686 : Conversion library and mapping compiler
teckit-devel.x86_64 : Conversion library and mapping compiler
xalan-j2-xsltc.noarch : XSLT compiler
yap.i686 : High-performance Prolog Compiler
yap.x86_64 : High-performance Prolog Compiler
```

As the preceding example shows, in searching our chosen terms, there are a number of related results and each package carries a brief description that enables us to use a simple process of elimination in order to select the most obvious or the most relevant value.

With this in mind, you can then query Yum to find out more information about the package in the following way:

```
yum info gcc
```

The result of running this query would be as follows:

```
Loaded plugins: downloadonly, fastestmirror, refresh-packagekit
Loading mirror speeds from cached hostfile
 * base: centos.mirror1.spango.com
 * extras: anorien.csc.warwick.ac.uk
 * updates: centos.mirror.triple-it.nl
Available Packages
Name        : gcc
Arch        : x86_64
Version     : 4.4.6
Release     : 4.el6
Size        : 10 M
Repo        : base
Summary     : Various compilers (C, C++, Objective-C, Java, ...)
URL         : http://gcc.gnu.org
License     : GPLv3+ and GPLv3+ with exceptions and GPLv2+ with
exceptions
Description : The gcc package contains the GNU Compiler Collection
version 4.4.
            : You'll need this package in order to compile C code.
```

So as we can see, the output from the `yum info` option reveals the full package details together with a detailed description of what functionality the package is intended to provide.

Generally speaking, you may not need to know any further details. However, there may be circumstances in which you would want to know how this package interacts with the server as a whole (especially if you are working with source installations or troubleshooting broken packages), so before we finish, we shall now look at one more example to see how this works:

```
yum deplist gcc
```

The result of this query will then reveal the following dependency information:

```
Loaded plugins: downloadonly, fastestmirror, refresh-packagekit
Loading mirror speeds from cached hostfile
 * base: centos.mirror1.spango.com
 * extras: anorien.csc.warwick.ac.uk
 * updates: centos.weepeetelecom.nl
Finding dependencies:
package: gcc.x86_64 4.4.6-4.el6
dependency: libgcc>= 4.4.6-4.el6
provider: libgcc.x86_64 4.4.6-4.el6
provider: libgcc.i686 4.4.6-4.el6
dependency: rtld(GNU_HASH)
provider: glibc.x86_64 2.12-1.80.el6
provider: glibc.i686 2.12-1.80.el6
provider: glibc.i686 2.12-1.80.el6_3.3
provider: glibc.x86_64 2.12-1.80.el6_3.3
dependency: libgomp.so.1()(64bit)
provider: libgomp.x86_64 4.4.6-4.el6
dependency: libc.so.6(GLIBC_2.4)(64bit)
provider: glibc.x86_64 2.12-1.80.el6
provider: glibc.x86_64 2.12-1.80.el6_3.3
dependency: libc.so.6()(64bit)
provider: glibc.x86_64 2.12-1.80.el6
provider: glibc.x86_64 2.12-1.80.el6_3.3
dependency: /sbin/install-info
provider: info.x86_64 4.13a-8.el6
dependency: libgomp = 4.4.6-4.el6
provider: libgomp.i686 4.4.6-4.el6
provider: libgomp.x86_64 4.4.6-4.el6
dependency: cloog-ppl>= 0.15
provider: cloog-ppl.x86_64 0.15.7-1.2.el6
provider: cloog-ppl.i686 0.15.7-1.2.el6
dependency: glibc-devel>= 2.2.90-12
provider: glibc-devel.x86_64 2.12-1.80.el6
provider: glibc-devel.i686 2.12-1.80.el6
```

```
provider: glibc-devel.i686 2.12-1.80.el6_3.3
provider: glibc-devel.x86_64 2.12-1.80.el6_3.3
dependency: libc.so.6(GLIBC_2.11)(64bit)
provider: glibc.x86_64 2.12-1.80.el6
provider: glibc.x86_64 2.12-1.80.el6_3.3
dependency: binutils>= 2.19.51.0.14-33
provider: binutils.x86_64 2.20.51.0.2-5.34.el6
dependency: libc.so.6(GLIBC_2.3)(64bit)
provider: glibc.x86_64 2.12-1.80.el6
provider: glibc.x86_64 2.12-1.80.el6_3.3
dependency: libgcc_s.so.1()(64bit)
provider: libgcc.x86_64 4.4.6-4.el6
dependency: cpp = 4.4.6-4.el6
provider: cpp.x86_64 4.4.6-4.el6
dependency: /bin/sh
provider: bash.x86_64 4.1.2-9.el6_2
dependency: libc.so.6(GLIBC_2.2.5)(64bit)
provider: glibc.x86_64 2.12-1.80.el6
provider: glibc.x86_64 2.12-1.80.el6_3.3
dependency: libc.so.6(GLIBC_2.7)(64bit)
provider: glibc.x86_64 2.12-1.80.el6
provider: glibc.x86_64 2.12-1.80.el6_3.3
```

So as you can see, it is quite a detailed report and if you do happen to have any broken packages, you could simply use this output to detail what dependencies you may or may not need to install in order to fix an underlying issue.

There's more...

Sometimes you may not want to search for a specific package and instead you may prefer to display the contents of your repositories in a catalog style format. Again, this is easy to do and Yum provides for this functionality with the following commands.

If you would like to simply list all the packages available to you from the current repositories used by your system, type:

```
yum list all
```

However, because this list may be quite exhaustive, you may prefer to page through the results by using:

```
yum list all | less
```

In a similar fashion, if you would simply like to list all the software currently installed on your system, type:

```
yum list installed | less
```

And of course, if you ever need any additional help you could simply review the help pages by typing:

```
yum --help
```

See also

> ▸ Yum project wiki – Yum guides: `http://yum.baseurl.org/wiki/Guides`

Installing Yum Priorities to support additional repositories

In this recipe we will investigate the task of preparing YUM to manage additional repositories by installing a plugin known as **Yum Priorities**.

Yum has the ability to search, remove, install, retrieve, and update packages from various remote locations. Such features make Yum a powerful tool, but if you ever decide to add an additional third-party repository, there is the chance that conflicts will render the system unstable.

Stability is one of the many advantages of using the CentOS operating system and it is the purpose of this recipe to show you how this confidence can be maintained while simultaneously allowing for the addition of new repositories.

Getting ready

To complete this recipe, you will require a working installation of the CentOS 6 operating system with root privileges, a console-based text editor of your choice, and a connection to the Internet in order to facilitate the download of additional packages.

How to do it...

This recipe will show you how to prepare Yum in order to manage the process of using one or more third-party repositories. To do this, you will need to install and configure a new package called Yum Priorities by following the steps shown here:

1. To begin this recipe, log in as root and type:

    ```
    yum install yum-plugin-priorities
    ```

2. Confirm the installation and when complete, type:

    ```
    vi /etc/yum/pluginconf.d/priorities.conf
    ```

3. You should ensure this file indicates that the plugin is enabled. This file should show the instruction `enabled = 1`. It is not expected that you will need to change anything in this file, but if you have made any changes, simply save and close the file before proceeding.

4. We now need to establish a priority value for each repository. This is a numeric value in ascending order where the highest priority is given lowest number. To do this, open the following file like so:

    ```
    vi/etc/yum.repos.d/CentOS-Base.repo
    ```

5. Add the following line at the end of the `[base]` section:

    ```
    priority=1
    ```

6. Now add the following line at the end of the `[updates]` section:

    ```
    priority=1
    ```

7. And finally, add the following line at the end of the `[extras]` section:

    ```
    priority=1
    ```

8. When complete, save and close the file before running `yum update`, like so:

    ```
    yum update
    ```

How it works...

Yum Priorities is a simple plugin that enables Yum to decide what repositories will assume the highest priority when installing and updating new packages. Using this plugin will reduce the chance of package confusion by ensuring that any particular package will always be installed or updated from the same repository. In this way you can add an unlimited number of repositories and enable Yum to stay in control of package management.

So what did we learn from this experience?

Enhancing Yum with this plugin was simply a matter of installing the package and ensuring that the package was enabled:

yum install yum-plugin-priorities

We did this by opening /etc/yum/pluginconf.d/priorities.conf with our preferred text editor and ensured that it read as follows:

```
[main]
enabled = 1
```

And having closed this file, it was simply a matter of configuring the priority-based requirements for /etc/yum.repos.d/CentOS-Base.repo, like so:

```
[base]
name=CentOS-$releasever - Base
mirrorlist=http://mirrorlist.centos.org/?release=$releasever&arch=$ba
search&repo=os
#baseurl=http://mirror.centos.org/centos/$releasever/os/$basearch/
gpgcheck=1
gpgkey=file:///etc/pki/rpm-gpg/RPM-GPG-KEY-CentOS-6
priority=1

#released updates
[updates]
name=CentOS-$releasever - Updates
mirrorlist=http://mirrorlist.centos.org/?release=$releasever&arch=$bas
earch&repo=updates
#baseurl=http://mirror.centos.org/centos/$releasever/
updates/$basearch/
gpgcheck=1
gpgkey=file:///etc/pki/rpm-gpg/RPM-GPG-KEY-CentOS-6
priority=1

#additional packages that may be useful
[extras]
name=CentOS-$releasever - Extras
mirrorlist=http://mirrorlist.centos.org/?release=$releasever&arch=$bas
earch&repo=extras
#baseurl=http://mirror.centos.org/centos/$releasever/extras/$basearch/
gpgcheck=1
gpgkey=file:///etc/pki/rpm-gpg/RPM-GPG-KEY-CentOS-6
priority=1

#additional packages that extend functionality of existing packages
[centosplus]
```

```
name=CentOS-$releasever - Plus
mirrorlist=http://mirrorlist.centos.org/?release=$releasever&arch=$bas
earch&repo=centosplus
#baseurl=http://mirror.centos.org/centos/$releasever/
centosplus/$basearch/
gpgcheck=1
enabled=0
gpgkey=file:///etc/pki/rpm-gpg/RPM-GPG-KEY-CentOS-6

#contrib - packages by Centos Users
[contrib]
name=CentOS-$releasever - Contrib
mirrorlist=http://mirrorlist.centos.org/?release=$releasever&arch=$bas
earch&repo=contrib
#baseurl=http://mirror.centos.org/centos/$releasever/
contrib/$basearch/
gpgcheck=1
enabled=0
gpgkey=file:///etc/pki/rpm-gpg/RPM-GPG-KEY-CentOS-6
```

We then discovered that the priority is set in ascending order, where the lowest values are given precedence over all others. This, of course, serves to simplify the overall process and for this reason we ensured that the default repositories were given a value of:

```
priority=1
```

This would ensure that the default repositories would maintain the highest priority, so when you do decide to add additional repositories, you could assign them a priority value of 2, 3, 4... and 10, or more.

On the other hand, it was notable that we only set this value across three main sections—[base], [updates], and [extras]. In simple terms, this was only because the other sections are shown to be disabled. For example, you may have noticed that the [centosplus] and [contrib] sections in /etc/yum.repos.d/ CentOS-Base.repo include the following line:

```
enabled=0
```

Whereas the [updates] and [extras] sections show this value as enabled=1.

Of course, if you intend to activate these repositories, then you will need to set a priority value for them, but for the purpose of this recipe such an action was not required.

Finally, we ran a simple update in order to activate our revised settings, like so:

```
yum update
```

So as we can see, Yum Priorities is an extremely flexible package that enables you to determine what repositories take priority when you want to expand your installation options. However, you should always be aware that Yum Priorities may not be appropriate for your system, as you are giving it the power to decide what packages are to be ignored, what packages are installed, and what packages are updated; in what order and from which repository you will get them from.

For most users who tend not to stay away from the typical server functions, this may not be an immediate concern, you may even safely ignore this warning, but if stability and security plays an overriding concern and you do intend to use additional packages from external repositories, then you should give careful consideration to the use of this plugin or at least consider and research the integrity of the third-party repositories used.

See also

▶   The Yum project home page: `http://yum.baseurl.org`

Enhancing CentOS with the EPEL and Remi repositories

In this recipe we will investigate the desire to take full advantage of the packages that are available to CentOS by installing both the EPEL and Remi repositories.

CentOS is an enterprise-based operating system that prides itself on stability and during the lifetime of your server it is possible that not every piece of software you need can be found in the default repositories. It is also possible that you may require updated packages of current software and for these reasons many server administrators choose to install both the EPEL and Remi repositories.

These are not the only repositories available, but because they represent one of the most popular combinations, it is the purpose of this recipe to show you how both the EPEL and Remi repositories can be added to your system.

Getting ready

To complete this recipe, you will require a working installation of the CentOS 6 operating system with root privileges, a console-based text editor of your choice, and a connection to the Internet in order to facilitate the download of additional packages.

How to do it...

Before we start, it is assumed that you have followed a previous recipe that showed you how to install and activate Yum Priorities.

1. To begin, log in as root and install the following tool that will be used to download the necessary packages we will need later on:

   ```
   yum install wget
   ```

2. From your home directory, type the following commands one line at a time to download the necessary files:

   ```
   wget http://dl.fedoraproject.org/pub/epel/6/i386/epel-release-6-7.
   noarch.rpm
   ```

   ```
   wget http://rpms.famillecollet.com/enterprise/remi-release-6.rpm
   ```

    The preceding URLs were correct at the time of writing this book, but over time these may change at the discretion of the repository owners. So if you do encounter an error from the previous commands, it may be worth confirming that the source URLs have not changed.

3. The preceding files should now be located in your home folder. To proceed, type the following command:

   ```
   rpm -Uvh remi-release-6*.rpm epel-release-6*.rpm
   ```

4. Now open the Remi repository file with your favorite text editor:

   ```
   vi /etc/yum.repos.d/remi.repo
   ```

5. Change `enabled=0` to `enabled=1` and add the line `priority=10`.

6. Now open the EPEL repository file with your favorite text editor:

   ```
   vi /etc/yum.repos.d/epel.repo
   ```

7. Again, change `enabled=0` to `enabled=1` and add the line `priority=10`.

8. To finish, update Yum like so:

   ```
   yum update
   ```

9. If updates are available, choose *Y* to proceed. Having completed the update process, you will now be able to download and install packages from both the Remi and EPEL repositories as an addition to those that are used by default.

How it works...

As this recipe has shown, by taking one of the most popular repository combinations available, you have seen that in order to use and enjoy the benefits of a third-party repository you are required to download specific installation packages. These packages should be unpacked and installed, the configuration files require enabling and then you simply need to run an update.

So what did we learn from this experience?

Having started the recipe by installing the `wget` tool, the task of installing both the Remi and EPEL repositories is a remarkably smooth process. `wget` is a simple utility that supports a variety of protocols (including HTTP, HTTPS, and FTP) and it enables us to download items on the command line:

```
wget http://dl.fedoraproject.org/pub/epel/6/i386/epel-release-6-7.noarch.
rpm
```

```
wget http://rpms.famillecollet.com/enterprise/remi-release-6.rpm
```

Of course, the preceding URLs are maintained at the discretion of the repository owners, so you should always ensure that they are the most current. However, having obtained the necessary repository setup files, it was then a matter of applying the following RPM-based command in order to unpack them, like so:

```
rpm -Uvh remi-release-6*.rpm epel-release-6*.rpm
```

Having done this, we were then required to open the relevant configuration files and enable them (by changing `enabled=0` to `enabled=1`) and setting a priority value (`priority=10`). While the former value will merely switch the repository on, the latter value would be used by Yum to correctly identify which repositories are the most appropriate when we called the `update` command.

As discussed in the previous recipe regarding Yum Priorites, the simple rule of thumb is based on remembering the phrase—the lower the number, the higher the priority.

This in itself (depending on your reasons) may not be a bad thing to do, but for the purpose of this recipe it is shown that the default CentOS repositories should take priority over all others. Of course, you may disagree with this and, yes, there is nothing stopping you from applying the same priority rule to a third-party supplier, but I do caution you before diving in, and this is particularly the case if this is for a mission-critical production server. Remember, if all the priority values were the same, then Yum will attempt to download the latest version by default.

The reason for setting both Remi and EPEL to a higher value than the existing CentOS-based repositories is based on the need to consider security updates. Unless you have determined otherwise, it is always advised that the base files should come from CentOS first. This includes, but is not limited to, Kernel updates, SELinux, and related packages. Third-party repositories should be used for additional packages that cannot be obtained from the original sources or for access to particular updates that may not be available to the base release of CentOS. This may include packages such as Apache, MySQL, or PHP.

As a final footnote, you will have noticed that both Remi and EPEL repositories shared the same priority value. This is by design as these repositories are often viewed as partners. However, if you decide to begin mixing repositories or use this recipe as a gateway to installing other repositories not mentioned here, then you should always do your research and evaluate every third-party on a case-by-case basis.

By completing this recipe you have discovered that adding a third-party repository is a relatively straightforward process. The Remi and EPEL repositories are very popular, so if you do intend to add more third-party resources, read around the subject, choose your repositories carefully, and stay loyal. Updates are released periodically and because the repositories are "run by a few but enjoyed by many", be patient, the next update will be with you very soon.

See also

> ▸ The EPEL/REMI repository home page:
> `http://blog.famillecollet.com/pages/Config-en`

> ▸ The official CentOS wiki on repositories:
> `http://wiki.centos.org/AdditionalResources/Repositories`

5
Securing CentOS

In this chapter, we will cover:

- ▶ Escalating user privilege with `sudo`
- ▶ Hardening the secure shell environment
- ▶ Configuring a firewall and working with IPTables
- ▶ Protecting SSH with fail2ban
- ▶ Preventing dictionary based attacks with DenyHosts
- ▶ Running antivirus scans with ClamAV

Introduction

This chapter is a collection of recipes that provides a solid approach to providing your server with a safer and more secure environment by guiding you through the process of escalating user privilege with `sudo`; hardening the secure shell environment; configuring a firewall and working with IPTables; protecting SSH with fail2ban; preventing dictionary-based attacks with DenyHosts; and running antivirus scans with ClamAV.

Escalating user privilege with sudo

In this recipe we will learn how to provide nominated users or groups the ability to execute a variety of commands with elevated privileges.

In a previous recipe we discovered how to create an administrative user that enables them to invoke the `su` command. Given that this provides full access to root user functionalities, this may suit your needs, but for those who want a greater degree of flexibility, a solid audit trail, and the ability to provide a limited array of administrative capabilities to a select number of trusted users, you have come to the right place. It is the purpose of this recipe to show you how to activate and configure the `sudo` (or superuser do) command.

Getting ready

To complete this recipe you will require a minimal installation of the CentOS 6 operating system with root privileges and a console-based text editor of your choice. It is assumed that your server maintains one or more users who qualify for this escalation in powers.

How to do it...

This recipe considers the act of providing a typical user with the option to invoke the sudo command. Otherwise known as the **superuser do** command, it enables a user to execute almost any command with elevated privileges. However, you should not confuse this with su, which is discussed elsewhere in this book.

1. To begin, log in as root and proceed to edit the /etc/sudoers file by typing:

   visudo

2. Scroll down this file until you find the following line:

   ```
   root    ALL=(ALL)ALL
   ```

3. Include a reference to your user by adding a new line, like so:

   ```
   root    ALL=(ALL)ALL
   user_name_here    ALL=(ALL)ALL
   ```

4. Now scroll down to the bottom of the file and add the following new line:

   ```
   Defaults syslog=local1
   ```

5. When finished, save the file in the usual way but when asked, remove the file extensions so that /etc/sudoers.tmp reads as follows:

   ```
   /etc/sudoers
   ```

6. When prompted, press *Y* to overwrite the existing file. We will now proceed to individualize the logging for any action performed when invoking the sudo command. To do this open the following file, like so:

   vi /etc/rsyslog

7. Scroll down and look for the following line:

   ```
   # The authpriv file has restricted access.
   authpriv.*
               /var/log/secure
   ```

8. And make it read:

   ```
   # The authpriv file has restricted access.
   local1.*
               /var/log/sudo.log
   authpriv.*
               /var/log/secure
   ```

9. Save and close the file and restart the system log by typing:

```
service syslog restart
```

How it works...

Unlike some Linux distributions, CentOS does not provide `sudo` by default. Instead, you are typically allowed to access the system as root or another valid user. This offers a certain degree of security, but for a multiuser server there is little to no flexibility unless you simply provide these individuals with root user access. This is not advisable, and for this reason, it was the purpose of this recipe to show you how to provide one or more users the right to execute commands with elevated privileges.

So what did we learn from this experience?

We started the recipe by issuing the `visudo` command like so:

```
visudo
```

The purpose of `visudo` is to enable safe updates, and it works by not only locking the `sudoers` file against multiple or simultaneous edits, but it also includes a series of basic validity checks.

Having done this, it is simply a matter of adding the appropriate user credentials to the file:

```
## Allow root to run any commands anywhere
root      ALL=(ALL)        ALL
user_name_here    ALL=(ALL)      ALL
```

This additional line simply states that the appointed user can use `sudo` from any host and execute any command. To finish this process, we then included an instruction to change the default logging behavior for the `sudo` function by adding the line:

```
Defaults syslog=local1
```

After saving the file, we proceeded to finalize our changes to the logging behavior by opening the systems log configuration file in order to add the following instruction:

```
# The authpriv file has restricted access.
local1.*
                /var/log/sudo.log
authpriv.*
                    /var/log/secure
```

By doing this, we are configuring the system log to send all `sudo` command-based reports to a unique log called `/var/log/sudo.log`. We then saved the file and restarted the system log service by typing:

```
service syslog restart
```

From now on, the nominated user can implement `sudo` in order to execute any command with elevated privileges. To do this, the user would be required to type the word `sudo` before any command, like so:

```
sudo root_user_action_or_command_here
```

For example, using the previous approach, they could run the following command:

```
sudo yum update
```

They will be asked to confirm their password, and after successful authentication, the `/etc/sudoers` file will check and confirm the relevant permissions. If allowed, the system will then invoke the requested action.

> The `sudo` (superuser do) command can provide nominated users or groups the ability to execute a variety of commands with elevated privileges. All actions are recorded, so there will be a log of all the commands and arguments used.
>
> This should not be confused with the `su` or switch user command, which was discussed earlier in this book, and which allows you to become another user. In the default instance, and unless you specify otherwise, this user will be root.

For additional information, you can refer to the `sudoers` manual by typing:

```
man sudoers
```

There's more...

For a server with a large user base, an alternative approach may be to consider providing group access. Thereby implying that access to the `sudo` command will be granted to a select group of users rather than a specific individual. In this way, you could consider it to be a shortcut method that saves having a very long list of usernames in the `sudoers` file.

To do this, log in as root and start by creating a new group by typing:

```
groupadd new_group_name
```

Now type:

```
visudo
```

Scroll down and locate the following lines:

```
    ## Allows people in group wheel to run all commands
    #%wheel  ALL=(ALL)   ALL
```

Now add the new group like so:

```
## Allows people in group wheel to run all commands
#%wheel     ALL=(ALL)     ALL
%new_group_name     ALL=(ALL)     ALL
```

Alternatively, if you have chosen to assign users to the wheel group, then you can provide access to sudo by uncommenting the group's reference, like so:

```
## Allows people in group wheel to run all commands
%wheel     ALL=(ALL)     ALL
```

Or you could employ both methods like this:

```
## Allows people in group wheel to run all commands
%wheel     ALL=(ALL)     ALL
%new_group_name     ALL=(ALL)     ALL
```

> The sudoers file does give you the option to enable sudo without requiring a password. However, given the security implications this method is best avoided.

Now save and close the file in the same way as you did for the main recipe and in the future, if you ever need to grant a new user access to sudo, instead of repeating the visudo process, simply add the new user to the relevant group like so:

usermod -a -G new_group_name username_here

For example, if you would like to add your user to the wheel group, use:

usermod -a -G wheel username_here

You can repeat this action for each user as and when required.

Change the default timeout

The default timeout for sudo to require a password again is estimated at around five minutes, but if you would like more control and want to alter this value, then add the following line at the top of the /etc/sudoers file:

```
Defaults timestamp_timeout=X
```

Where X is the number of minutes, this line should be read before any other default settings, so if you wanted to change the timeout to two minutes, then your file would look like:

```
Defaults timestamp_timeout=2
Defaults requiretty
```

The `Defaults requiretty` line instructs `sudo` that the user should be logged in to the console and it should not be changed.

Hardening the secure shell environment

In this recipe we will learn how to provide additional security measures in order to harden the secure shell environment.

The **secure shell (SSH)** is the basic toolkit that provides remote access to your server. The actual distance to the remote machine is negligible, but the shell environment enables you to perform maintenance, upgrades, install packages, transfer files, or facilitate whatever action you need to carry out as the administrator in a secure environment. It is an important tool, and as the gateway to your system, it is the purpose of this recipe to show you how to perform a few rudimentary configuration changes that will serve to deny root access, add a welcome banner, and protect your server from unwanted guests.

Getting ready

To complete this recipe you will require a minimal installation of the CentOS 6 operating system with root privileges and a console-based text editor of your choice. It is assumed that your server already maintains at least one, non-root based administration account that can use the new features provided by this recipe.

How to do it...

The role of SSH will be vital if you are forced to administer your server from a remote location and for this reason it is essential that a few basic steps are provided to keep it safe.

1. To begin, log in as root and create a backup of the original configuration file by typing the following command:

   ```
   cp /etc/ssh/sshd_config /etc/ssh/sshd_config.bak
   ```

2. Now open the `sshd_config` configuration file by typing:

   ```
   vi /etc/ssh/sshd_config
   ```

3. We shall begin by adjusting the time allowed to complete the login process, so scroll down and find the line that reads:

   ```
   #LoginGraceTime 2m
   ```

4. Uncomment this line and change the value to something more appropriate such as:

   ```
   LoginGraceTime 60
   ```

5. Now scroll down a couple of more lines and find the line that reads:

   ```
   #PermitRootLogin yes
   ```

6. Change this to:

   ```
   PermitRootLogin no
   ```

7. Find the following lines:

   ```
   #X11Forwarding no
   X11Forwarding yes
   ```

8. And change them to this:

   ```
   X11Forwarding no
   #X11Forwarding yes
   ```

9. Uncomment the following lines:

   ```
   PrintMotd yes
   PrintLastLog yes
   ```

10. Now save and close the `sshd_config` file before opening the following file to create your welcome banner:

    vi /etc/motd

11. Add your banner text to that file. For example, you could write:

    ```
    This computer system is for authorized users only. All activity
    is logged and regularly checked. Individuals using this system
    without authority or in excess of their authority are subject to
    having all their services revoked...
    ```

12. Again, save and close the file before restarting the `sshd` service like so:

    service sshd restart

13. The console should respond like so:

    ```
    Stopping sshd: [  OK  ]
    Starting sshd: [  OK  ]
    ```

14. At this stage you may want to consider creating a new SSH session using the new settings before exiting the current session. This is to ensure that everything is working correctly and to avoid locking yourself out of the server accidentally. If you have difficulty starting a new SSH session, then simply return to the original session window and make the necessary adjustments (followed by a restart of the SSH service). However, if no difficulties have been encountered and on a successful secondary login, you may close the original shell environment, by typing:

    exit

Remember, having followed this recipe, you should now find that root access to the shell is denied and you must log in using a standard user account. Any further work requiring root privilege will require the su or sudo command depending on your preferences. On your next login you will be greeted with your new welcome banner.

How it works...

SSH is a vital service that enables you to access your server remotely. A server administrator cannot work without it, and in this recipe you were shown how to make that service a little more secure.

So what did we learn from this experience?

We began the recipe by creating a backup of your original configuration file:

```
cp /etc/ssh/sshd_config /etc/ssh/sshd_config.bak
```

By definition SSH is the gateway to your system and if you ever encountered a problem, you would always have a backup of the original configuration file.

The next step was to open the main SSH configuration file:

```
vi /etc/ssh/sshd_config
```

The configuration file for sshd maintains a long list of settings that is ideal for most internal needs, but for a server in a production environment it is often advised that the default SSH configuration file will need to be changed to suit your particular needs.

In this respect, the first step was to make a recommended change to the login grace time:

```
LoginGraceTime 60
```

Instead of default two minutes, the preceding value will allow up to 60 seconds for an individual to complete the login process. You should customize this value to whatever suits your needs.

Following this, we then removed the ability for a remote user to log in as the root user by stating:

```
PermitRootLogin no
```

In most cases this is a must and a remote server should not allow a direct root login unless the server is in a controlled environment.

The next setting simply disabled X11 Forwarding:

```
X11Forwarding no
#X11Forwarding yes
```

In situations like these, it is often a good idea to apply the phrase "if you do not use it, disable it". In fact you could have simply removed the commented line, but if you ever intended to use X through a tunnel, then this alternative action would serve to reduce the amount of typing when re-editing the file at a later date.

The final changes to the SSH configuration were as follows:

```
PrintMotd yes
PrintLastLog yes
```

The first line tells the SSH server to activate the banner file while the second line re-enforces the need to print the last login details to the screen. None of these final modifications are required for security purposes, but they do allow you to open the /etc/motd file and create a welcome banner. A task that was achieved by opening the following file in your favorite text editor and adding your personalized message:

vi /etc/motd

To complete the recipe, you were required to restart the SSH server in order to allow the changes to take immediate effect and start a new SSH session with the intention of making sure that the modifications did indeed work as expected. No system is ever safe, but having done this you can now relax, safe in the knowledge of having made the SSH server a little bit safer.

There's more...

Most systems do not configure the server to keep SSH sessions alive, which implies that any break in connectivity will result in a lost session. You may feel that this is not applicable to you, but if your users are working via a mobile device, through an external connection of unknown origin, or on an external connection having a known history of intermittent connectivity, then it may be a good idea to plan for packet loss and prevent hanging sessions by setting the idle timeout interval on your server.

To do this, access your server with root privilege (by using sudo or su) and open the sshd_config configuration file with your favorite text editor like so:

vi /etc/ssh/sshd_config

Scroll down to find and uncomment the following lines like so:

```
ClientAliveInterval 60
ClientAliveCountMax 5
```

At this stage, you may want to change the numbers to something more suitable to your own needs, but here is what we have instructed the SSH server to do:

```
ClientAliveInterval 60
```

In the preceding line, we have told the SSH server to wait for a period of up to 60 seconds after receiving the last input before it will send a packet that requires a response.

```
ClientAliveCountMax 5
```

In the preceding line, we have set the number of missed or no-response intervals to 5, after this value the server will consider that the connection has been dropped.

Now find and uncomment the following line:

```
TCPKeepAlive yes
```

This will tell the SSH server to issue `TCPKeepAlive` packets to discover if the connection is still valid. Consequently, even if your session times out, this small feature will terminate the current session and prevent it from hanging and becoming a zombie.

Finally, to complete this process simply restart the SSH server like so:

```
service sshd restart
```

Your new settings will take effect on the next login.

Changing the SSH port number of your server

Port 22 is the default port used by all SSH servers and changing the port number used can go a small way in increasing the overall security of your server.

To do this, log in as root and type:

```
vi /etc/ssh/sshd_config
```

Now scroll down and locate the following line that reads:

```
#Port 22
```

Uncomment the line and change the port number to another value by replacing XXXX with an appropriate port number:

```
Port XXXX
```

You must ensure that the new port number is not already in use, and when complete, save the file and close the file before restarting the SSH service like so:

```
service sshd restart
```

It is important to remember that any changes made here are reflected in your firewall configuration.

Limiting SSH access by user or group

By default, all valid users on the system are allowed to log in and enjoy the benefit of SSH. However, a more secure policy is to only allow a predetermined list of users or groups to log in.

To do this, log in as root and open the SSH configuration file in your favorite text editor like so:

```
vi /etc/ssh/sshd_config
```

Now scroll down and locate the following line that starts with:

```
AllowUsers
```

When `henry`, `james`, and `helen` represent valid SSH users on the system, change this line to read as follows:

```
AllowUsers henry james helen
```

Alternatively, you can use the following method to enable any user that is a member of a valid administration group to log in:

```
AllowGroups
```

When `admin` represents a valid SSH group on the system, change this line to read as follows:

```
AllowUsers admin
```

When you have finished, save the file and close the file before restarting the SSH service, like so:

```
service sshd restart
```

See also

- ▶ The CentOS project wiki – securing OpenSSH: http://wiki.centos.org/HowTos/Network/SecuringSSH
- ▶ The OpenSSH project's home page: http://www.openssh.com/

Configuring a firewall and working with IPTables

In this recipe we will learn how to implement additional security measures by working with IPTables in order to configure the firewall.

By default, CentOS is made available with an extremely powerful firewall. More commonly known as **IPTables**, it is based on the use of IP addresses, protocols and ports, and provides you with the ability to manage all connection activity in and out of your server. Rules are based on chains (INPUT, OUTPUT, and FORWARD) and you maintain the ability to ACCEPT, DROP, or REJECT activity based on your criteria. IPTables will be the foundation of your server's security and for this reason, it is the purpose of this recipe to show you how to replace the pre-installed rule set and to build your own.

Getting ready

To complete this recipe you will require a minimal installation of the CentOS 6 operating system with root privileges and a console-based text editor of your choice.

How to do it...

Like most things in Linux as a whole, working with IPTables will require root privileges, so it will be assumed that your user account is able use the su command in order to become root and complete the following tasks:

1. Before we start, log in as root and use the following command to remove all the current rules:

   ```
   iptables --flush
   ```

2. To ensure we have no problems connecting, and as a temporary solution, type the following command:

   ```
   iptables -P INPUT ACCEPT && iptables -P FORWARD ACCEPT && iptables -P OUTPUT ACCEPT
   ```

3. Now save the current settings by typing the following command:

   ```
   service iptables save
   ```

4. To view the current rules use the following command:

   ```
   cat  /etc/sysconfig/iptables
   ```

5. Having completed this step, you will want to restart the service like so:

   ```
   service iptables restart
   ```

6. We are now ready to begin building the firewall. So first of all, we will want to allow unlimited traffic on the loopback in order to enable access from the localhost, like so:

```
iptables -A INPUT -i lo -j ACCEPT

iptables -A OUTPUT -o lo -j ACCEPT
```

7. If you use a static IP address to connect to your server, you can include your details by replacing XXX.XXX.XXX.XXX with the relevant values:

```
iptables -A INPUT -i lo -s XXX.XXX.XXX.XXX -d XXX.XXX.XXX.XXX -j
ACCEPT
```

8. To enable both STATE and ICMP packets, use:

```
iptables -A INPUT -p icmp --icmp-type any -j ACCEPT

iptables -A INPUT -m state --state ESTABLISHED,RELATED -j ACCEPT
```

9. And finally, to enable domain queries and SSH, we are going to add:

```
iptables -A INPUT -p tcp --dport 53 -j ACCEPT

iptables -A INPUT -p udp --dport 53 -j ACCEPT

iptables -A INPUT -p tcp -m tcp --dport 22 -j ACCEPT
```

10. Now alter the original chain policy that accepts all connections, like so:

```
iptables -P INPUT DROP && iptables -P FORWARD DROP && iptables -P
OUTPUT DROP
```

11. When finished, save your new settings like so:

```
service iptables save
```

12. Then restart the service:

```
service iptables restart
```

How it works...

IPTables is installed by default. It is a powerful tool and provides a chain-based mechanism that filters all inbound and outbound traffic. The configuration of IPTables can be challenging, particularly in view of the fact that familiarity with the command-line sequence is something that must be learned. However, by completing this recipe we did succeed in illustrating the basic processes involved, and with a little practice, everything else can begin to fall into line.

So what did we learn from this experience?

Before we started to add our firewall rules it was determined that we should flush the existing rule set and start from scratch. So we began by flushing the rules like so:

```
iptables --flush
```

As a temporary measure, to ensure that we will have no issues when trying to connect to the server, we then determined that the server could accept all incoming connections:

```
iptables -P INPUT ACCEPT&&iptables -P FORWARD ACCEPT&&iptables -P OUTPUT
ACCEPT
```

In the next step, we then save the rules:

```
service iptables save
```

Followed by restarting the service:

```
service iptables restart
```

As a result of this process, the new file will look something like this:

```
# Generated by iptables-save v1.4.7 on Sun Aug 26 16:39:43 2012
*filter
:INPUT ACCEPT [0:0]
:FORWARD ACCEPT [0:0]
:OUTPUT ACCEPT [0:0]
COMMIT
```

So having ensured that we cannot be disconnected, we began by adding a simple rule that would enable unlimited traffic on the loopback (`127.0.0.1`) in order to provide access from the localhost:

```
iptables -A INPUT -i lo -j ACCEPT
```

```
iptables -A OUTPUT -o lo -j ACCEPT
```

We followed this with an optional rule that would allow your static IP address:

```
iptables -A INPUT -i lo -s XXX.XXX.XXX.XXX -d XXX.XXX.XXX.XXX -j ACCEPT
```

The next step was to enable both `ICMP` and `STATE`. Where the former protocol is generally associated with diagnostics (that is, ping or trace route), or the task of network control and discovery, the latter enables IPTables to remember the status of any connection in conjunction with the protocols using the source and destination IP address.

```
iptables -A INPUT -p icmp --icmp-type any -j ACCEPT
```

```
iptables -A INPUT -m state --state ESTABLISHED,RELATED -j ACCEPT
```

Having done this, the next task was to open both the domain and SSH ports:

```
iptables -A INPUT -p tcp --dport 53 -j ACCEPT
```

```
iptables -A INPUT -p udp --dport 53 -j ACCEPT
```

```
iptables -A INPUT -p tcp -m tcp --dport 22 -j ACCEPT
```

Without these two lines there would be an impact on remote connections via SSH. You would still be able to use SSH, but if you try it, you will probably notice that the connection speed is that much slower because any calls to the domain name system are denied. For this reason we added port 53 to facilitate DNS queries, whereas port 22 was nominated as it represents the default port for SSH. So remember, if you have chosen to use a different port number for SSH, make this modification now.

At this stage the server is now ready, but before we finish, it is necessary to lock it down and deny unwanted access. We achieved this by using the following command that would serve to rewrite the current chain policy:

```
iptables -P INPUT DROP && iptables -P FORWARD DROP && iptables -P OUTPUT
ACCEPT
```

Remember, at this stage everything was loaded into memory and nothing was written to the main configuration file found at /etc/sysconfig/iptables. For this reason, our next task was to save our new configuration:

```
service iptables save
```

Followed by a command to restart the service:

```
service iptables restart
```

There is still much to be done and much more to learn, but having successfully configured your first set of firewall rules, you can be confident that IPTables is now working to protect your server.

There's more...

Having configured a basic firewall, you may want to consider opening a few additional ports in order to support features such as HTTPD, FTP, NTP, Mail, and other related services. Again, and like we saw in the recipe, doing this is relatively simple and it only involves extending your current rule set to provide each feature with a relevant input and output rule.

For example, to allow HTTP on ports 80 and 143, you would use:

```
iptables -A OUTPUT -p tcp --dport 80 -j ACCEPT
iptables -A INPUT -p tcp --dport 80 -j ACCEPT
iptables -A OUTPUT -p tcp --dport 143 -j ACCEPT
iptables -A INPUT -p tcp --dport 143 -j ACCEPT
```

To allow FTP on ports 20/21, you would use:

```
iptables -A OUTPUT -p tcp --dport 20:21 -j ACCEPT
iptables -A INPUT -p tcp --dport 20:21 -j ACCEPT
```

Similarly, to allow SMTP and POP3 on ports 25 and 110, you would use:

```
iptables -A INPUT -p tcp --dport 25 -j ACCEPT
iptables -A OUTPUT -p tcp --dport 25 -j ACCEPT
iptables -A INPUT -p tcp --dport 110 -j ACCEPT
iptables -A OUTPUT -p tcp --dport 110 -j ACCEPT
```

Finally, to allow NTP on port 123, you would use:

```
iptables -A OUTPUT -p udp --dport 123 -j ACCEPT
```

When you have finished, remember to save your new rules in the same way as we did in the original recipe and restart the IPTables service:

```
service iptables save
```

Then type:

```
service iptables restart
```

Allowing an IP address

If you have a list of IP addresses that represents a series of welcome guests, the root user can add them to the existing firewall rules and whitelist them by typing:

```
iptables -A INPUT -s XXX.XXX.XXX.XXX/32 -j ACCEPT
```

For example, if you wanted to whitelist the localhost, you could type:

```
iptables -A INPUT -s 127.0.0.1/32 -j ACCEPT
```

There is no limit to the number of IP addresses that can be listed, but remember to place these entries above any other rule, like so:

```
:INPUT DROP
:FORWARD DROP
:OUTPUT ACCEPT
-A INPUT -s XXX.XXX.XXX.XXX -j ACCEPT
-A INPUT -s XXX.XXX.XXX.XXX -j ACCEPT
```

When you have finished, save your new settings like so:

```
service iptables save
```

Then restart the service:

```
service iptables restart
```

Banning an IP address

If you have a list of IP addresses that represents a series of unwanted guests, the root user can add them to the existing firewall rules and effectively ban or blacklist them by typing:

```
iptables -A INPUT -s XXX.XXX.XXX.XXX -j DROP
```

There is no limit to the number of IP addresses you can ban, but these rules must appear before any other rule, like so:

```
:INPUT DROP
:FORWARD DROP
:OUTPUT ACCEPT
-A INPUT -s XXX.XXX.XXX.XXX -j DROP
-A INPUT -s XXX.XXX.XXX.XXX -j DROP
-A INPUT -s XXX.XXX.XXX.XXX -j DROP
```

In this way, rather than relying on another service to deal with unwanted visitors, denying them access to your server through the firewall would limit the size of your logfiles and reduce the burden on your server.

When you have finished, save your new settings like so:

```
service iptables save
```

Then restart the service:

```
service iptables restart
```

See also

- ▶ The Netfilter/IPTables project's home page: `http://iptables.org/`
- ▶ The CentOS project wiki: `http://wiki.centos.org/HowTos/Network/IPTables`

Protecting SSH with fail2ban

In this recipe we will learn how to implement additional security measures by protecting SSH server with a package called **fail2ban**.

Fail2ban is a tool that serves to protect a variety of services against unwanted visitors. It works by reading logfiles for patterns based on failed login attempts and deals with the offending IP addresses accordingly. Of course, you may have already hardened your SSH server and employed the necessary firewall rules, but it is the purpose of this recipe to show that when faced with the possibility of Brute Force Attacks, an added layer of protection is always useful.

Getting ready

To complete this recipe you will require a working installation of the CentOS 6 operating system with root privileges, a console-based text editor of your choice, and a connection to the Internet in order to facilitate the download of additional packages. In addition to this, it will be assumed that Yum is already configured to download packages from the EPEL repository.

How to do it...

Fail2ban is not installed by default, and for this reason we will need to invoke the Yum Package Manager and download the necessary packages.

1. To begin this recipe, log in as root and type the following command:

   ```
   yum install fail2ban
   ```

2. The recommended approach to using fail2ban is to consider placing all custom rules in a separate configuration file. For this reason, we will now make a copy the original file by typing:

   ```
   cp /etc/fail2ban/jail.conf /etc/fail2ban/jail.local
   ```

3. Now open the new configuration file in your favorite text editor, like so:

   ```
   vi /etc/fail2ban/jail.local
   ```

4. Scroll down and find the following line:

   ```
   ignoreip = 127.0.0.1
   ```

5. Replace 127.0.0.1 with your IP address like so:

   ```
   ignoreip = XXX.XXX.XXX.XXX
   ```

6. Scroll down and find the following line:

   ```
   bantime  = 600
   ```

7. The ban period is calculated in seconds, so adjust the time period to reflect a more suitable value. In this case we have chosen this as one hour:

   ```
   bantime  = 3600
   ```

8. Scroll down to find the following line:

   ```
   findtime  = 600
   ```

9. Now adjust the amount of time we have to log in to reflect a more suitable value:

   ```
   findtime  = 900
   ```

10. Now scroll down to find the following line:

    ```
    maxretry = 3
    ```

11. Again, adjust the maximum number of login attempts to to reflect a more suitable value:

```
maxretry = 5
```

12. Scroll down a little further until you find the following lines for SSH:

```
[ssh-iptables]
enabled   = true
filter    = sshd
action    = iptables[name=SSH, port=ssh, protocol=tcp]
            sendmail-whois[name=SSH, dest=root, sender=fail2ban@
example.com]
logpath   = /var/log/secure
maxretry = 5
```

13. Finally, replace the e-mail address `fail2ban@example.com` with something more appropriate to your own needs. In addition to this, you will notice that you now have the opportunity to adjust the `maxretry` value for the SSH server independently of the global value configured previously.

14. Now save and close the file in the usual way before proceeding to enable the `fail2ban` service at boot. To do this, type the following command:

```
chkconfig fail2ban on
```

15. To complete this recipe, you should now start the service by typing:

```
service fail2ban start
```

How it works...

Fail2ban is designed to monitor users who repeatedly fail to log in correctly on your server and its main purpose is to mitigate attacks designed to crack passwords and steal user credentials. It works by continuously reading logfiles, and if a logfile contains a pattern indicating a number of failed attempts, then it will proceed to act against the offending IP address. We all know that servers do not exist in isolation, and by using this tool, within a few minutes the server will be running with an additional blanket of protection.

So what did we learn from this experience?

Fail2ban is not available from the standard CentOS repositories and for this reason your server will need to have access to the EPEL repository. Installation of the fail2ban package was very simple, but by comparison to the many other services, we learned that local customization was best achieved by creating a replica `jail` file, like so:

```
cp /etc/fail2ban/jail.conf /etc/fail2ban/jail.local
```

We then proceeded to work through each line and make the necessary changes starting with the following global values:

```
ignoreip = XXX.XXX.XXX.XXX
```

This line enables you to whitelist certain IP addresses. So having included your own IP address, you can add additional IP addresses by separating the list with a single whitespace, like so:

```
ignoreip = XXX.XXX.XXX.XXX XXX.XXX.XXX.XXX/XX XXX.XXX.XXX.XXX/XX
```

 Make sure that there is a single whitespace between the different IP address. Remember, by doing this you will reduce the risk of accidentally banning yourself from the server.

Following this, we were asked to adjust the `bantime` value, which represents the total number of seconds a host will be blocked from accessing the server if they are found to be in violation of the rules. In this case it was simply a matter of adjusting the numeric value to something more appropriate to your own needs:

```
bantime  = 600
```

In the same way we were then asked to qualify the amount of time a user has when attempting to log in. This value is also measured in seconds and implies that if a user fails to log in within the maximum number of attempts during the designated period, then they are banned:

```
findtime = 600
```

Based on this, you were then asked to determine the maximum number of login attempts like so:

```
maxretry = 3
```

In the next phase we then scrolled down to review the individualized settings for our SSH server:

```
[ssh-iptables]
enabled  = true
filter   = sshd
action   = iptables[name=SSH, port=ssh, protocol=tcp]
           sendmail-whois[name=SSH, dest=root, sender=fail2ban@
example.com]
logpath  = /var/log/secure
maxretry = 5
```

By reading the file, it can be seen that SSH is already enabled by default. This area of the configuration not only shows us where fail2ban intends to log any violations, but it also presented us with the opportunity to set an independent number of login attempts. On the other hand, it is always nice to receive an e-mail when fail2ban has reported a violation, so our goal was to update the e-mail address.

For example, if your main e-mail address was `webmaster@theserver.com`, then your modified file will look like this:

```
[ssh-iptables]
enabled   = true
filter    = sshd
action    = iptables[name=SSH, port=ssh, protocol=tcp]
            sendmail-whois[name=SSH, dest=root, sender=webmaster@
theserver.com]
logpath   = /var/log/secure
maxretry = 5
```

So as we can see, fail2ban can be used to provide protection for any number of services including FTP, SMTP, Apache, and many more. The ability to set global options as opposed to application-specific options are just some of the features you may want to explore in the future; but until then, you now know that this very useful application is hard at work keeping your server safe.

There's more...

By default all fail2ban activity is logged in the system's log. For many this could represent the ideal location, but for those of you who prefer a separate logfile, we will now consider how this is achieved.

To begin, open the main configuration file in your preferred text editor:

vi /etc/fail2ban/fail2ban.conf

Scroll down to locate the following line:

```
logtarget = SYSLOG
```

Now modify the path to suit your needs:

```
logtarget = /var/log/fail2ban.log
```

You will see that other options are available, but when you have finished, simply save, and close the file before restarting the service, like so:

service fail2ban restart

As a result, all log activity can now be found at `/var/log/fail2ban.log`.

See also

> ► The fail2ban project's home page: `http://www.fail2ban.org/`

Preventing dictionary-based attacks with DenyHosts

In this recipe, we will learn how to protect the SSH server from dictionary-based attacks with DenyHosts.

Experienced administrators will tell you that that DenyHosts is a recommended tool that can provide an added layer of protection against dictionary-based attacks. It maintains a small footprint, requires minimal configuration, and by works to monitor invalid login attempts. It is the purpose of this recipe to show you how this essential application can go a long way to keep your server safe.

Getting ready

To complete this recipe, you will require a working installation of the CentOS 6 operating system with root privileges, a console-based text editor of your choice, and a connection to the Internet in order to facilitate the download of additional packages. In addition to this, it will be assumed that Yum is already configured to download packages from the EPEL repository.

How to do it...

DenyHosts is not installed by default, and for this reason we will need to invoke the Yum Package Manager and download the necessary packages.

1. Log in as root and install the DenyHosts package by typing:

   ```
   yum install denyhosts
   ```

2. We shall begin by creating a whitelist of allowed IP addresses. To do this, open the following file in your preferred text editor like so:

   ```
   vi /etc/hosts.allow
   ```

3. Now add the following IP addresses to the bottom of this file, but remember to include your own and any other IP address that requires access:

   ```
   ALL: 127.0.0.1
   ALL: 192.168.1.*
   ```

4. Now add the same list of IP addresses to the following file by typing:

   ```
   vi /var/lib/denyhosts/allowed-hosts
   ```

5. When complete, save and close the file before opening the main configuration file in your favorite text editor like so:

```
vi /etc/denyhosts.conf
```

6. Scroll down to locate the following line:

```
ADMIN_EMAIL = root
```

7. Change the e-mail address to reflect an appropriate value and scroll down a little further to ensure that the e-mail settings are correct for your system.

8. When you are finished, simply save and close the file before enabling the package to run at boot. To do this, type:

```
chkconfig denyhosts on
```

9. To complete this recipe, you should start the service like so:

```
service denyhosts start
```

How it works...

DenyHosts is a Python-based security tool that monitors server access logs to detect and mitigate dictionary-based attacks on a server. The package works by banning IP addresses that exceed a certain number of failed login attempts; and beyond the creation of a whitelist there is very little that needs to be done. DenyHosts is one of those packages that runs out of the box with very little effort.

So what did we learn from this experience?

We started the recipe by installing the necessary package:

```
yum install denyhosts
```

The first task was to provide a list of acceptable IP addresses and add them to the /etc/hosts.allow file. We did this by opening the required file like so:

```
vi /etc/hosts.allow
```

In order to build the list of IP addresses in the following way:

```
ALL: 127.0.0.1
ALL: 192.168.1.*
```

With this in mind, a complete and working example of `/etc/hosts.allow` will now look similar to the following:

```
#
# hosts.allow      This file contains access rules which are used to
#                  allow or deny connections to network services that
#                  either use the tcp_wrappers library or that have been
#                  started through a tcp_wrappers-enabled xinetd.
#
#                  See 'man 5 hosts_options' and 'man 5 hosts_access'
#                  for information on rule syntax.
#                  See 'man tcpd' for information on tcp_wrappers
#
ALL: 127.0.0.1
ALL: 192.168.1.*
```

At this point you were invited to repeat this step by adding the same list of addresses to the file found at `/var/lib/denyhosts/allowed-hosts`. This was achieved by opening the relevant file like so:

`vi /etc/denyhosts.conf`

In order to build the list of IP addresses in the following way:

`ALL: 127.0.0.1`

`ALL: 192.168.1.*`

With this in mind, a complete and working example of `/var/lib/denyhosts/allowed-hosts.allow` will now look similar to this:

```
# We mustn't block localhost
127.0.0.1
192.168.1.*
```

Following this you were asked to confirm the mail settings found in the main configuration file at `/etc/denyhosts.conf`. Of course, as the default settings send all e-mails to the root user, this modification is entirely optional, but it did provide you with the experience of reviewing this file for other options that may or may not be relevant to your circumstances.

For example, you could add multiple e-mail addresses by simply typing them in the following format:

`ADMIN_EMAIL = emailaddress1@domain.com, emailaddress2@domain.com`

Finally, we configured the service to start during the boot process and switched the service on. The result of these actions will provides us with a logfile, which is located at `/var/log/denyhosts`.

DenyHosts is an excellent example of how little effort can provide great returns. However, if you plan to test your server, make sure you run this test from a different IP address from where you intend to administer the server. If you have blocked your own IP address, then you will need to unblock it.

There's more...

There may come a time when you decide to simplify and personalize the DenyHosts configuration file. In many cases you could begin by simply removing the sections that are heavily commented and those which are not applicable. However, a better way to start will be to review some of the specific settings mentioned as follows.

To do this, open the main configuration file in your favorite text editor like so:

```
vi /etc/denyhosts.conf
```

Scroll down to find the following line which determines how long an IP address will remain on the denial list:

```
PURGE_DENY = 4w
```

For many a period of four weeks may be excessive, especially when you consider that the IP address could be dynamically assigned.

To remedy this, simply change the line to read:

```
PURGE_DENY = 2w
```

However, depending on your circumstances and if you do want to be very guarded, then simply changing this to an annual setting may prove to be a better solution:

```
PURGE_DENY = 1y
```

Now scroll down a little further and review the following lines:

```
# default: a denied host can be purged/re-added indefinitely
#PURGE_THRESHOLD = 0
```

By uncommenting this line you will be telling DenyHosts to repeatedly purge the offending IP address indefinitely. However, this approach may prove to be a little heavy-handed if you consider that a first-time visitor will tend to require a little more flexibility.

For this reason you should look at the alternative setting shown here:

```
# a denied host will be purged at most 2 times.
PURGE_THRESHOLD = 2
```

This makes far more sense, implying that any IP address added to the denial list will only be purged twice.

Finally, you should be aware that the default setting for DenyHosts is automatically set for SSH and you can see this in the following line:

```
BLOCK_SERVICE   = sshd
```

This may suit most servers, but if you want to tighten security even further, then you could simply change this to read as follows:

```
BLOCK_SERVICE = ALL
```

By making this simple change, you will be ensuring that any malicious attempts to access your server from an unrecognized host will be stopped immediately. Remember, it is far easier to whitelist an IP addresses rather than repair the damage done due to a compromised server.

Unblocking an IP address

If you want to remove an IP address that has been blocked by DenyHosts, then you should begin the process by accessing your server as an administrative user and stop DenyHosts.

To do this, log in as root and type:

```
service denyhosts stop
```

Now search and remove the relevant IP address from the following file:

```
vi /etc/hosts.deny
```

When you have finished, save and close the file before removing the IP address from all the files located in /var/lib/denyhosts.

This list is quite extensive and includes the following:

```
vi /var/lib/denyhosts/hosts
```
```
vi /var/lib/denyhosts/hosts-restricted
```
```
vi /var/lib/denyhosts/hosts-root
```
```
vi /var/lib/denyhosts/hosts-valid
```
```
vi /var/lib/denyhosts/users-hosts
```

However, rather than manually checking each file, you could try the following shortcut by substituting XXX.XXX.XXX.XXX with the IP address in question:

```
cd /var/lib/denyhosts
```
```
sed -i '/XXX.XXX.XXX.XXX/d' *
```

In addition to this, you may also want to consider adding this IP address to the following files in order that it will not be blocked again:

```
vi /etc/hosts.allow
```
```
vi /var/lib/denyhosts/allowed-hosts
```

When you have finished, remember to restart the service by typing:

```
service denyhosts start
```

See also

▶   The DenyHosts project's home page: `http://denyhosts.sourceforge.net/`

Running antivirus scans with ClamAV

In this recipe we will learn how to install, configure, and manage the **ClamAV** antivirus solution

Malware infections on Linux-based systems are rare, but with the passing of data from one machine to another it is possible that one of those machines may be sharing infected files through your server. So with this in mind, it is the purpose of this recipe to show you how to install and configure ClamAV and manage on-demand virus scans to ensure that your server can seek out and stop any threats before they spread.

Getting ready

To complete this recipe you will require a working installation of the CentOS 6 operating system with root privileges, a console-based text editor of your choice, and a connection to the Internet in order to facilitate the download of additional packages. In addition to this, it is assumed that Yum is already configured to download packages from the EPEL repository.

How to do it...

ClamAV is not installed by default, and for this reason we will need to invoke the Yum Package Manager and download the necessary packages.

1.   Log in as root and install the necessary packages by running:

```
yum install clamd
```

2.   To enable the ClamAV service during the boot process, type the following command:

```
chkconfig clamd on
```

3.   To start the ClamAV service, type the following command:

```
service clamd start
```

4.   To update the virus database/definitions in your console, type:

```
freshclam
```

5.   To run your first and any subsequent on-demand scan, type:

```
clamscan
```

6. Alternatively, you can customize and employ the following command:

```
clamscan --infected --remove --recursive /directory_name
```

7. Repeat the preceding step as and when required. The logfile for this service can be found at `/var/log/clamav/clamd.log`.

How it works...

Fast, free, and efficient, ClamAV is an open source antivirus engine that can be employed by CentOS to detect trojans, viruses, and other malicious software, malware, or threats. It is easy to install and as this recipe has shown, it is very simple to use.

So what did we learn from this experience?

We started by installing the package, enabling it during the boot process, switching the service on, and running a basic on-demand scan. This was a manual approach to using ClamAV and it allows you to re-run the command as often as you require by typing:

```
clamscan
```

As an alternative to this, you were also shown how the basic on-demand scan can be customized to suit a specific purpose:

```
clamscan --infected --remove --recursive /directory_name
```

Given that the `/directory_name` value indicates the target directory, you can quickly customize this instruction to scan a particular location, like so:

```
clamscan --infected --remove --recursive /home
```

Alternatively, to scan a specific user's home directory you can use:

```
clamscan --infected --remove --recursive /home/<username>
```

Following this, the recipe also showed you how to update the virus definitions by typing the following command:

```
freshclam
```

You will find that the scan report is succinct and for those who require additional details you can easily view the logfiles found at `/var/log/clamav/clamd.log` and `/var/log/clamav/freshclam.log`. Where the former shows all general activity, the latter confirms any updates to the package's virus database. You can always confirm the status of your antivirus tool by typing:

```
service clamd status
```

As you will discover, the output should report something similar to the following:

```
clamd (pid 1876) is running...
```

So as this recipe has shown, ClamAV is very quick to install and it can be used to afford a high degree of protection that not only makes your server feel safer, but it will work to protect your users. ClamAV is not intended to be complicated, but should you wish to learn more, simply visit the project's home page or read the manual by typing:

```
man clamd
```

There's more...

The manual approach to on-demand scans can be very useful, although we can alleviate some of the administrative burden by choosing to automate this process as a cron job.

To do this, log in as root and type the following command:

```
touch /root/bin/clamav.sh && vi /root/bin/clamav.sh
```

Now add the following lines:

```
#!/bin/bash
SCAN_DIR="/home"
LOG_FILE="/var/log/clamav/home.log"
/usr/bin/clamscan -i -r $SCAN_DIR >> $LOG_FILE
```

When you have finished, save and close the file in the usual way.

The purpose of this Bash Script is to require ClamAV to scan the /home directory and write the results to the logfile located at /var/log/clamav/home.log. Of course, you can always customize this code later on, but in order to complete this process we will need to provide the script with executable permissions.

To do this, type:

```
chmod +x /root/bin/clamav.sh
```

You can now test the script by running:

```
/root/bin/clamav.sh
```

Upon its completion you will find a new log entry at /var/log/clamav/home.log.

The result will look similar to this:

```
----------- SCAN SUMMARY -----------
Known viruses: 1297823
Engine version: 0.97.5
Scanned directories: 195
Scanned files: 131
Infected files: 0
Data scanned: 1.69 MB
Data read: 1.57 MB (ratio 1.08:1)
Time: 4.295 sec (0 m 4 s)
```

Having successfully tested our script, we will now create a new cron job by typing:

```
crontab -e
```

In the main editor screen, type the following line and customize the values shown (where XX is the exact minute and YY is the chosen hour to perform the task):

```
XX YY * * * /root/bin/clamav.sh
```

For example, if you want to run a scan at 13:00 hours daily, you can use:

```
00 13 * * * /root/bin/clamav.sh
```

Alternatively, you can choose a daily routine in which the script is run every week day at 3 A.M:

```
0 3 * * 1-5 /root/bin/clamav.sh
```

Once the cron job has been saved, simply type the following command to restart the crond service:

```
service crond restart
```

Of course, you can always embellish /root/bin/clamav.sh by reviewing the recipes provided throughout this book, but as a consequence of completing these steps, your antivirus solution will now automatically scan your system at a predetermined interval. Remember, it is relatively easy to modify the script file. You can also periodically review the logfile found at /var/log/clamav/home.log.

See also...

> ▸ The ClamAV project's home page: http://www.clamav.net/

6
Working with Samba

In this chapter, we will cover:

- ▶ Configuring Samba as a standalone server and enabling home directories
- ▶ Adding, deleting, and disabling a Samba user
- ▶ Providing a network recycle bin for Samba
- ▶ Hiding files and folders with Samba
- ▶ Creating a custom share folder for a specific user or a group of users

Introduction

This chapter contains a collection of recipes that focuses on the needs of today's file-sharing environment by simplifying the process of configuring Samba as a standalone server and enabling home directories; adding, deleting, and disabling a Samba user; providing a network recycle bin for Samba; hiding files and folders with Samba; and creating a custom share folder for a specific user or a group of users.

Configuring Samba as a standalone server and enabling home directories

In this recipe we will learn how to install and configure Samba as a standalone server in order to provide basic file-sharing services through the use of a user's home directory.

One of the most common ways to share files across different computer systems is to install and configure Samba as a standalone file server. Standalone servers are configured to provide local authentication and access control to all the resources they maintain. They are independent of all domain controllers and where a standalone server is expected to function like a workgroup server, they can use both, a simple or complicated configuration in order that all data served will be readily accessible to the entire user base. All-in-all every administrator knows that Samba remains a very popular open source distribution and it is the purpose of this recipe to show you how to deliver an instant approach to file sharing that provides seamless integration for any number of users on any type of modern computer across your entire working environment.

Getting ready

To complete this recipe you will require a working installation of the CentOS 6 operating system with root privileges, a console-based text editor of your choice, and a connection to the Internet in order to facilitate the download of additional packages. It is expected that your server will be using a static IP address.

If you are running a firewall, you will need to confirm that the firewall has been disabled, removed, or the appropriate ports are open. Similarly, if you are running SELinux, then you should confirm that it has been disabled or it is now running in permissive mode.

How to do it...

Samba is not installed by default, and for this reason we will begin by downloading and installing the required packages.

1. To do this, log in as root and type the following command in order to install the required packages:

   ```
   yum install samba samba-client samba-common
   ```

2. Having done this, the first step is to rename the original configuration file, like so:

   ```
   mv /etc/samba/smb.conf /etc/samba/smb.conf.bak
   ```

3. Now create a new configuration file in your preferred text editor by typing:

   ```
   vi/etc/samba/smb.conf
   ```

4. Begin building your new configuration by adding the following lines by substituting the values shown with values more representative of your own needs:

   ```
   [global]
   unix charset = UTF-8
   dos charset = CP932
   workgroup = <WORKGROUP_NAME>
   server string = <MY_SERVERS_NAME>
   ```

```
netbios name = <MY_SERVERS_NAME>
dns proxy = no
wins support = no
interfaces = 127.0.0.0/8 XXX.XXX.XXX.XXX/24 ethX
bind interfaces only = no
log file = /var/log/samba/log.%m
max log size = 1000
syslog only = no
syslog = 0
panic action = /usr/share/samba/panic-action %d
```

> MY_SERVERS_NAME refers to the name of your server. In most situations this could be in the form of FILESERVER or SERVER1 and so on.
>
> ethX refers to the name of your primary Ethernet interface. In most situations this could be eth0.
>
> XXX.XXX.XXX.XXX/XX refers to the primary network address. In most situations this could be 192.168.1.0/24.

5. We will now configure Samba as a standalone server. To do this, simply continue to add the following lines to your main configuration file:

```
security = user
encrypt passwords = true
passdb backend = tdbsam
obey pam restrictions = yes
unix password sync = yes
passwd program = /usr/bin/passwd %u
passwd chat = *Enter\snew\s*\spassword:* %n\n *Retype\snew\s*\
spassword:* %n\n *password\supdated\ssuccessfully* .
pam password change = yes
map to guest = bad user
usershare allow guests = no
```

6. For the purpose of this recipe we do not intend to configure Samba as a domain master or master browser. To do this, add the following lines:

```
domain master = no
local master = no
preferred master = no
os level = 8
```

7. We will now add support for home directory sharing by enabling valid users to access their home directories. This feature will support the appropriate read/write permissions and all folders will remain private from other users. To do this, add the following new lines:

```
[homes]
        comment = Home Directories
        browseable = no
        writable = yes
        valid users = %S
create mask =0755
        directory mask =0755
```

8. When you have finished, simply save and close the file before proceeding to ensure that the samba service will start during the boot process, like so:

```
chkconfig smb on && chkconfig nmb on
```

9. To complete this recipe, start the Samba server by typing:

```
service smb start && service nmb start
```

How it works...

Samba is a software package that enables you to share files, printers, and other common resources across a network. It is an invaluable tool for any working environment. By providing full connectivity across all modern computer systems, it was the purpose of this recipe to show you how to install and configure Samba as a standalone server using a tdbsam backend.

So what did we learn from this experience?

Having installed the necessary packages, we began this recipe by renaming the originally installed configuration file, like so:

```
mv /etc/samba/smb.conf /etc/samba/smb.conf.bak
```

In many respects you could have chosen to ignore this instruction and proceeded to make changes to the actual configuration file. However, where the depth of code-commenting can sometimes make this file a little cumbersome to navigate, the intention of this recipe was to show you that it is equally valid to start from scratch.

We achieved this by typing the following instruction:

```
vi /etc/samba/smb.conf
```

At this point in the recipe we now started to configure the Samba server. Beginning with the global configuration options, the first step was to declare compatibility with Unicode-based character sets:

```
[global]
unix charset = UTF-8
dos charset = CP932
```

You will need to be aware that the values can vary as a result of your circumstances. So depending on what type(s) of computers are on your network or what type(s) of languages you need to support, these values should be adjusted to meet your exact needs.

For example, when considering the use of Samba with Mac OS, you will not only need to consider modifying this section to reflect the appropriate values, but you will also want to apply a response object that Samba will use to print messages with:

```
[global]
unix charset = UTF-8-MAC
dos charset = 437
display charset = UTF-8-MAC
```

Having done this, we then proceeded to confirm the name of our server; declare the server string; specify the name of the workgroup; disable WINS, establish a Samba logfile, and register the network interface, like so:

```
#set a workgroup name
workgroup = WORKGROUP
#set a server string that will be visible
#in Windows Network Neighborhood
server string = MYSERVER
#set a netbios name for the server
netbios name = MYSERVER
#disable wins and dns features
dns proxy = no
wins support = no
#declare the Ethernet interface to which samba will respond
interfaces = 127.0.0.0/8 XXX.XXX.XXX.XXX/24 ethX
#disable binding the interface
bind interfaces only = no
#set a location for the log file
log file = /var/log/samba/log.%m
#declare the settings for the samba log file
max log size = 1000
syslog only = no
syslog = 0
#set the command to run if/when samba panics
panic action = /usr/share/samba/panic-action %d
```

Then, and in keeping with the spirit of this recipe, we elected the following standalone options by choosing a user-based security option, password encryption, and a tdbsam backend, like so:

```
security = user
encrypt passwords = true
passdb backend = tdbsam
obey pam restrictions = yes
unix password sync = yes
passwd program = /usr/bin/passwd %u
passwd chat = *Enter\snew\s*\spassword:* %n\n *Retype\snew\s*\
spassword:* %n\n *password\supdated\ssuccessfully* .
pam password change = yes
map to guest = bad user
usershare allow guests = no
```

The preferred mode of security is user-level security and using this approach implies that each share can be assigned to a specific user. Therefore, when a user requests a connection for a share, Samba authenticates this request by validating the given username and password with the authorized users in the configuration file and the Samba database.

The recipe then asked us to add the following lines:

```
domain master = no
local master = no
preferred master = no
os level = 8
```

In the case of a mixed operating system environment, a known conflict will result when a single client attempts to become the master browser. This situation may not disrupt the file-sharing service as a whole, but it will give rise to a potential issue being recorded by the Samba logfiles. So by configuring the samba server to not assert itself as the master browser, you will be able to reduce the chance of such issues being reported.

So having completed these steps, the recipe then considered the main task of enabling the home directory file-sharing in the following way:

```
[homes]
  #The following is used to describe the share.
  comment = Home Directories

  #The following value defines if the folder can be seen
  browseable = no

  #The following value defines if the folder
```

```
#has write permissions.
writable = yes


#The following value defines Which users
#are allowed to connect to the share.
valid users = %S


#The following values determine the
#relevant file permissions to mask against
#if a permission is not found.
create mask =0755


#The following values determine the
#relevant directory permissions to mask against
#if a permission is not found.
directory mask =0755
```

Of course, you can experiment with the options shown, but this simple set of instructions ensures that valid users will not only be able to access their home directory with the relevant read/write permissions, but by setting the browseable flag to no, you will be able to hide the home directory from public view and achieve a greater degree of privacy for the user concerned.

So having saved your new configuration file, the next step was to ensure that Samba and its related processes would be made available during the boot process:

chkconfig smb on && chkconfig nmb on

Samba requires two primary processes in order to work correctly. Beginning with smbd, it is the role of this service to provide file-sharing and printing services to Windows-based clients using the SMB (or CIFS) protocol. It achieves this through TCP ports 139 and 445 and its responsibilities include the need to manage user authentication, resource locking, and data sharing. At the same time, it is the role of the nmbd service to listen, understand, and reply to the NETBIOS name service's requests on UDP port 137. In this way the nmbd service provides a NetBIOS over IP-naming services while actively participating in the browsing protocols to give what Windows users will recognize as the Network Neighborhood.

Samba often includes another service call named winbindd, but it has been largely ignored because the intention to provide a WINS-based service (Windows Internetworking Name Server) or Active Directory Authentication requires additional consideration, which is beyond the scope of this recipe.

Consequently, our final task was to start both the Samba service (smbd) and the associated NetBIOS service (nmbd) by typing the following command:

```
service smb start && service nmb start
```

You now know how incredibly simple Samba is to install, configure, and maintain. There is always more to learn, and yet this simple introduction has served to illustrate Samba's relative ease of use, the simplicity of its syntax, and delivered a solution that has the ability to support a wide variety of different needs, a range of different computer systems, and one that will fulfill your file-sharing requirements for many years to come.

There's more...

You can test any configuration changes made to Samba by typing the following command:

```
testparm
```

The purpose of the `testparm` command is to parse the Samba configuration in order to validate the syntax and report any known errors. This tool is provided by default with the Samba package and it can be used to confirm your configuration without being required to run the Samba service.

Disable printing support in Samba

Samba provides support for printing by default and it will try to connect to a printer regardless as to whether a printer is connected to your server or not. So, unless you are intending to install CUPS, then you should consider the act of disabling printer sharing in order to avoid any unnecessary error messages being recorded in the Samba logfiles.

To do this, log in as root and open the main Samba configuration file in your favorite text editor like so:

```
vi/etc/samba/smb.conf
```

Scroll down to the end of the global section and comment out all lines associated with printer support:

```
load printers = no
printing = bsd
printcap name = /dev/null
disablespoolss = yes
show add printer wizard = no
```

For those of you who are using the default Samba configuration, comment out the following lines:

```
;load printers = yes
;printing = cups
;printcap name = cups
```

Then remove or comment out the [printers] section, like so:

```
;[printers]
;comment = All Printers
;path = /var/spool/samba
;browseable = no
;public = yes
;guest ok = no
;writable = no
;printable = yes
;printer admin = root
```

When you have finished, save and close the configuration file in the usual way before restarting the Samba service, like so:

```
service smb restart && service nmb restart
```

Relaxing the rules for SELinux

By default, SELinux will prevent users from accessing their home directory. There is always the option to disable SELinux, but if you do intend to keep this service running you will be required to begin by relaxing the conditions that SELinux employs on your server.

To do this, log in as the root user and begin by checking the mode SELinux is currently using; type the following command:

```
getenforce
```

 If SELinux is currently enforcing, then it must be set to the permissive mode by typing the setenforce 0 command.

Now type the following command to enable the home directories:

```
sudo setsebool samba_enable_home_dirs on
```

In addition to this, if you are trying to enable Samba as a domain controller, then you should use the following command:

```
setsebool -P samba_domain_controller on
```

Remember, if SELinux is enabled and you do not execute the preceding commands, your users will continue to experience errors when trying to access the server.

Opening the firewall

If you are running IPTables, you will need to configure your firewall in order to allow access to your Samba server. To do this, log in as root and type the following commands to open ports `137`, `138`, `139`, and `445`:

```
iptables -A INPUT -s XXX.XXX.XXX.0/24 -m state –state NEW -p udp --dport
137 -j ACCEPT
iptables -A INPUT -s XXX.XXX.XXX.0/24 -m state –state NEW -p udp --dport
138 -j ACCEPT
iptables -A INPUT -s XXX.XXX.XXX.0/24 -m state –state NEW -p tcp --dport
139 -j ACCEPT
iptables -A INPUT -s XXX.XXX.XXX.0/24 -m state –state NEW -p tcp --dport
445 -j ACCEPT
```

Now save your new rules by typing:

```
service iptables save
```

Finally, restart IPTables:

```
service iptables restart
```

Assigning the master browser

In a mixed operating system environment it is not always advisable to make Samba the master browser, but it may be the case that this small addition may serve to improve the overall performance of both CentOS and your network in general.

To do this, log in as root and open the main Samba configuration file in your favorite text editor, like so:

```
vi/etc/samba/smb.conf
```

Now scroll down to the global section and make the following changes:

```
    domain master = no
    local master = yes
    preferred master = yes
    wins support = no
    os level = 65
```

Having completed the preceding changes, simply save and close your file before proceeding to restart the Samba service in the following way:

```
service smb restart && service nmb restart
```

Remember, if you have more than one Samba server running on your network, then only one server should be elected as the primary master browser and given the `os` level stated earlier.

See also

- ▶ The Samba project's home page: `http://www.samba.org/samba/`
- ▶ The official Samba guide:
  `http://www.samba.org/samba/docs/man/Samba3-HOWTO/`
- ▶ SELinux project – Samba recipes:
  `http://selinuxproject.org/page/SambaRecipes`
- ▶ The CentOS wiki –SELinux: `http://wiki.centos.org/HowTos/SELinux`
- ▶ The Samba project's man pages: `http://www.samba.org/samba/docs/man/`
  `Samba-HOWTO-Collection/NetworkBrowsing.html`

Adding, deleting, and disabling a Samba user

In this recipe we will learn how to add, delete, and disable a Samba user.

Samba is a popular open source program that provides file and print services to all modern operating systems. Configured as a standalone file-sharing environment, Samba employs the use of a local user database called the **Trivial Database** (**tdb**) in order to store passwords and manage access. This database is entirely separate from your server and for this reason it is the purpose of this recipe to show you how to add, delete, and disable a Samba user.

Getting ready

To complete this recipe you will require a working installation of the CentOS 6 operating system with root privileges. It is assumed that Samba is already running and it is configured to run as a standalone server.

How to do it...

Configured as a standalone server, Samba's resources will be made available in either share mode or in user mode. This will imply that all passwords are associated with an existing system account and for this reason we must begin by creating a new CentOS user.

1. To do this, log in as root and create a new system group by typing:

   ```
   groupadd <sambausers>
   ```

   > Adding all Samba users to a single group is entirely optional, but it can serve to simplify the process of managing access and file permissions.

2. Now create a new system user and add them to the new group, like so:

```
useradd <username> -m -G <sambausers>
```

3. This command will not only serve to create a new user profile, but it will also establish an associated user ID, make the relevant home directory (-m), set the default shell to bash, and add them to a group called sambausers. However, because we do not want to provide this user with general system access, we will not give them a system password at this present time.

> However, if you do want to offer them a system password, then simply type the passwd <username> command at any time.

4. To create a Samba password for the new user, type:

```
smbpasswd -a <username>
```

> In this instance, username relates to the CentOS username created earlier.

5. When prompted, enter a password for the new user. Having completed these steps, the new user will be able to access the server with the CentOS username and the associated Samba password.

How it works...

Managing Samba is all about managing accesses and it was the purpose of this recipe to illustrate how to create a Samba user.

So what did we learn from this experience?

Samba does not manage usernames, but it does enable you to create a password for a valid system user account. The Samba user is inextricably tied to this account and for this reason we began the recipe by creating a new CentOS group in the following way:

```
groupadd <sambausers>
```

It is an accepted convention that all system users should belong to a group and in this instance you were directed to create a group called sambausers.

We all know that servers can maintain any number of users, but by creating a relationship between them, you can provide a common rule that will enable the members of the same group to read, write, and execute specific files and directories.

In many respects, groups represent the principle component of an organization, and this not only makes the task of administration much easier, but it also enables you to develop a subset of user-based rights that is based on a group privilege.

Having done this, we then proceeded to create a new CentOS user and assign them to the new group, like so:

```
useradd <username> -m -G <groupname>
```

Used in this way, the `useradd` command required us to provide a suitable username in order to (–m) create the users home directory if it does not exist and (–g) elect the relevant `groupname` value for the purpose of membership.

For the purpose of this recipe, the term "user" remains non-specific, and it can be tied to a physical user, a workstation, or to an account that exists for a specific task or application and for this reason you were given the option to provide this user with shell access.

This can be achieved by typing the following command:

```
passwd <username>
```

However, for the purpose of file sharing it was determined that shell access would not be required so that no further actions would be performed in relation to the creation of a new CentOS user.

In the final phase we then proceeded to create a Samba password for a specific username by typing the following command:

```
smbpasswd -a <username>
```

The consequence of this action is to enable the CentOS user to access the Samba server and begin sharing files. It works by identifying users and associating them with a valid username and group. It will authenticate them by checking the associated passwords, and then control any access to the resources concerned by comparing the relevant access rights to the permissions on files and directories.

Samba supports multiple operating systems and having completed this recipe your server can now deploy the benefits of standalone Samba server.

There's more...

Managing Samba users is simply a matter of managing a password. You have the power to disable or to delete an account, but it does not involve any username as these are always attributed and managed by the server itself.

If you would like to disable a samba user, log in as root and type:

```
smbpasswd -d <username>
```

If you would like to delete a Samba user, log in as root and type:

```
smbpasswd -x <username>
```

Remember, by deleting the password you will not be removing the associated user profile (username) from the server or affecting the relevant home directory and its contents. So there is always an option of re-enabling the account at any time. However, if you would like to delete these items permanently, then you must use the following command:

```
userdel -r <username>
```

By using the -r flag, this command will not only delete the user, but it will also remove the associated home directory and mail spool.

Providing a network recycle bin for Samba

In this recipe we will learn how to enable a network recycle bin for Samba.

A network does not have a recycle bin and the action of deleting a file from a shared folder on your network will always result in the permanent loss of that data. So an approach to fix this issue could imply the use of a third-party tool, educating your users, or consider performing a complex workaround. It is the purpose of this recipe to provide your server with a holding area for files and folders and enable you to recover data that was accidentally deleted.

Getting ready

To complete this recipe you will require a working installation of the CentOS 6 operating system with root privileges. It is assumed that Samba is already installed and it is configured to run as a standalone server.

How to do it...

The purpose of this recipe is to provide a holding area for files and folders that are deleted by users across the network. So you will need to account for the additional storage required to facilitate this feature.

1. To begin, log in as root and create a folder called recycle-bin in your home directory by typing the following command:

   ```
   mkdir /home/recycle-bin
   ```

2. You may also want to assign the correct permissions to this folder, like so:

   ```
   chmod 0775 /home/recycle-bin
   ```

3. Now open you current samba configuration file by typing:

   ```
   vi/etc/samba/smb.conf
   ```

4. Scroll down and before the end of the [global] section and the beginning of the [homes] section, add the following lines:

```
vfs object = recycle
recycle:repository = /home/recycle-bin/%U
recycle:keeptree = Yes
recycle:touch = Yes
recycle:versions = Yes
recycle:maxsize = 0
recycle:exclude = *.tmp
recycle:exclude_dir = /tmp, /recycle-bin
recycle:noversions = *.tmp, *.temp
```

5. Finally, at the end of the configuration file add the following lines in order to make your recycle bin available to your network users:

```
[recycle-bin]
path = /home/recycle-bin
public = yes
writable = yes
browsable = yes
```

6. Now save and close the file before restarting Samba like so:

```
Service smb restart && service nmb restart
```

How it works...

Accidentally deleting files from a network share is almost as common as file-sharing itself. It can happen to all of us and at any time, but as this recipe has shown, through a simple implementation of Samba's recycling process, CentOS will treat those files in the same way as though you were deleting a file on your desktop.

So what did we learn from this experience?

Having initially created a folder at /home/recycle-bin, we then began to update the current Samba configuration file with the following new settings:

```
vfs object = recycle
recycle:repository = /home/recycle-bin/%U
```

By invoking the vfs object = recycle line within the [global] section of the main configuration, we not only activated the recycling module but we did it on the behalf of every user with an array of features based on setting either a Yes or No value.

We started by determining as to whether we would like to maintain the original directory structure:

```
recycle:keeptree = Yes
```

It was then decided that the file's last modified date should be updated when the file is recycled by declaring:

```
recycle:touch = Yes
```

The final feature then confirmed as to whether the filename should be modified:

```
recycle:versions = Yes
```

If `Yes`, the preceding instruction determines that two files with the same name will not only be stored in the recycle bin, but—and should this event take place—you will notice that the later file will be appended as `copy of...`.

Having completed these steps, we then proceeded to determine a maximum size for the `recycle-bin` folder. Calculated in bytes, any file smaller than the numeric value shown will not be recycled:

```
recycle:maxsize = 0
```

Following this, it was determined that the following list of files and folders should not be recycled:

```
recycle:exclude = *.tmp
recycle:exclude_dir = /tmp, /recycle-bin
```

Fortunately, this feature supports the use of wildcard which can also be used in the following feature that simply states that when `recycle:versions` is enabled, here is the list of paths that will not be supported:

```
recycle:noversions = *.tmp, *.temp
```

At this stage it is important to notice that a comma-separated list is supported when listing directories. However, you should be aware that Samba will not implement any form of cleaning or compression for recycled files. For this reason you may want to consider creating another type of process that removes these files and directories after a certain period of time in order to save disk space.

With this in mind, your final Samba configuration may look similar to this:

```
[global]
unix charset = UTF-8
dos charset = CP932
workgroup = WORKGROUP
server string = MY_SERVERS_NAME
netbios name = MY_SERVERS_NAME
```

```
dns proxy = no
interfaces = 127.0.0.0/8 XXX.XXX.XXX.XXX/24 ethX
bind interfaces only = no
log file = /var/log/samba/log.%m
max log size = 1000
syslog only = no
syslog = 0
panic action = /usr/share/samba/panic-action %d
security = user
encrypt passwords = true
passdb backend = tdbsam
obey pam restrictions = yes
unix password sync = yes
passwd program = /usr/bin/passwd %u
passwd chat = *Enter\snew\s*\spassword:* %n\n *Retype\snew\s*\
spassword:* %n\n *password\supdated\ssuccessfully* .
pam password change = yes
map to guest = bad user
usershare allow guests = no
domain master = no
local master = no
preferred master = no
os level = 0
load printers = no
printing = bsd
printcap name = /dev/null
disablespoolss = yes
show add printer wizard = no

vfs object = recycle
recycle:repository = /home/recycle-bin/%U
recycle:keeptree = Yes
recycle:touch = Yes
recycle:versions = Yes
recycle:maxsize = 0
recycle:exclude = *.tmp
recycle:exclude_dir = /tmp, /recycle-bin
recycle:noversions = *.tmp,*.temp

[homes]
    comment = Home Directories
    browseable = no
    writable = yes
    valid users = %S
```

```
          valid users = MYDOMAIN\%S
   create mask =0755
       directory mask =0755


[recycle-bin]


path = /home/recycle-bin
public = yes
writable = yes
browsable = yes
```

So in conclusion, we have not only discovered that implementing such a feature is very simple, but by completing this recipe you can see how easily the process of adding a network recycle bin can be customized to suit your needs.

There's more...

In this recipe you must have noticed that we added the recycling module to the [global] section of the Samba configuration file. This would imply that all shared objects would be subject to the recycling regardless of the location pertaining to the original source directory. This is a great feature, but what if you would prefer to restrict this function to recycle the contents of the user's home directories only? To do this, you would simply remove the module from the [global] section and insert this function within the [homes] section as follows:

```
[homes]
    comment = Home Directories
    browseable = no
    writable = yes
    valid users = %S
      valid users = MYDOMAIN\%S
create mask =0755
       directory mask =0755
vfs object = recycle
recycle:repository = /home/recycle-bin/%U
recycle:keeptree = Yes
recycle:touch = Yes
recycle:versions = Yes
recycle:maxsixe = 0
recycle:exclude = *.tmp
recycle:exclude_dir = /tmp, /recycle-bin
recycle:noversions = *.tmp,*.temp,*.o,*.obj,*.TMP,*.TEMP
```

If you are intending to make this change, you could also use this opportunity to customize the values used. For example, you could expand the types of files you do not wish to recycle, like so:

```
recycle:exclude = *.tmp,*.temp,*.o,*.obj,*.TMP,*.TEMP
```

When you have finished, simply save your configuration file and restart Samba by typing the following command:

servicesmb restart && service nmb restart

Hiding folders and files with Samba

In this recipe we will learn how to hide files and folders with Samba.

Managing a network often implies the need to hide files and folders from users for a wide variety of reasons. It is the purpose of this recipe to show you how easily this can be achieved.

Getting ready

To complete this recipe you will require a working installation of the CentOS 6 operating system with root privileges. It is assumed that Samba is already installed and it is configured to run as a standalone server.

How to do it...

The typical method of hiding files is to use a dot (.) as the first character in the filename. However, in circumstances where a user has specified the option to see such files, then our intentions can be circumvented. It is for this reason that we will also be using the veto files option.

1. To begin, log in as root and simply open your current Samba configuration file by typing:

    vi /etc/samba/smb.conf

2. Within the [global] section of the Samba configuration file, add the following line in order to hide all dot (.) files:

    hide dot files = yes

3. Having done this, you should now include the veto files option. To do this, add the following lines but remember to customize the values shown to suit your needs:

    ```
    veto files = /.*/foldername/filename.txt/filename.???/
    delete veto files = yes
    ```

4. When you have finished, simply save the file before restarting the Samba server like so:

```
service smb start && service nmb start
```

How it works...

Samba is a highly customizable tool that enables you to determine the type of network service you wish to provide and as this recipe has shown, the addition of a few small lines will not only hide .dot files, but they will ensure that a full range of other files and directories are removed from view in order to provide a fully customized file-sharing experience.

So what did we learn from this experience?

We began by opening the Samba configuration file and adding the following instruction:

```
hide dot files = yes
```

By doing this, Samba is instructed to set the hide attribute to any file beginning with a period. However, this action was then followed with an instruction to veto a particular range of files and folders:

```
veto files = /.*/foldername/filename.txt/filename.???/
```

In this instance, Samba has now been told to place a veto flag on any file or folder that not only starts with a period (.*), but one that may have been called foldername, filename. txt, or any item that simply starts with the word "filename" regardless of the file type in question. As a result, the user will not be able to see or access those files regardless as to whether their local settings will permit this or not.

It should be noted that when dealing with more than one pattern, each pattern type must be preceded and followed with a slash (/). Wildcards can be used and in places where you may not know the actual file type, the use of question marks can come in handy. For example, if you used the recipe exactly as shown and created a file called filename.jpg, then the file would not be seen.

Finally, you were asked to write the following line:

```
delete veto files = yes
```

The purpose of this line is to protect any folder whose sole content consists of hidden files. In other words, if a user saw a directory that looks empty, then they may try to delete it. So by setting this instruction, you will be able to ensure that such directories also remain hidden in order to avoid this from happening.

So as we can see, the ability to hide files and folders within Samba is very powerful and it can be used to avoid one of the many issues faced when serving a cross-platform network. This recipe may have concentrated on a selection of key functions, but overall, I think you would agree that in terms of convenience alone, this recipe provides an excellent starting point on which you can build and develop your very own rules.

There's more...

You may enhance this recipe by simply taking the example shown and extending the act of hiding and vetoing files and directories to any share folder that may require specific needs.

For example, to hide a chosen range of patterns within the home folders only, simply start with the following template to determine the level of control you need:

```
[homes]
comment = Home Directories
browseable = no
writable = yes
valid users = %S
valid users = MYDOMAIN\%S
create mask =0755
directory mask =0755
hide dot files = yes
veto files = /.*/
delete veto files = yes
```

Based on this, you can now extend the virtue of hiding files and folders to any type of custom share on your server.

Creating a custom share folder for a specific user or a group of users

In this recipe we will learn how to create a custom share folder for a specific user or a group of users for use with Samba.

Sharing a home directory with Samba has its advantages, but it cannot fulfill every need. You may want to create a shared folder that is used by one or more users to store documents, images, or to act as a repository for your media files. You may want to designate limited permissions, provide read-only access, or provide a global directory for an entire group of users. The options are endless, and it is the purpose of this recipe to show you how to create a custom share folder that can be used to augment your networking environment.

Getting ready

To complete this recipe you will require a working installation of the CentOS 6 operating system with root privileges and a console-based text editor of your choice. It is assumed that Samba is already installed and that it is configured to run as a standalone server.

How to do it...

During the course of this recipe we will consider both individual access and group access to a customized share folder of your choice. However, in this first exercise we will consider the needs of a specific user before we return to the subject of group access a little later on.

1. To begin, log in as root and create a new directory by typing the following command:

   ```
   mkdir/home/<foldername>
   ```

2. Now assign the ownership of this folder to a particular user and group. Define the necessary permissions by typing the following command and substituting the values shown with those that suit your own needs:

   ```
   chown <username> /home/<foldername> && chgrp <groupname> /
   home/<foldername> && chmod 0770 /home/<foldername>
   ```

3. When you have finished, open the Samba configuration file with your preferred text editor like so:

   ```
   vi/etc/samba/smb.conf
   ```

4. Now scroll down to the bottom of the file and add the following lines. Again, remember to customize the comment, the `foldername` value, and replace `username` and `groupname` with the same values as used in the previous step:

   ```
   [foldername]
           comment = your foldername description
           path = /home/foldername/
           browseable = yes
           guest ok = no
           writable = yes
           create mask =0666
           directory mask =0770
           valid users = username
   force group = groupname
   forceuser = username
   ```

The purpose of this recipe is to serve as an introduction, so you should consider customizing the preceding values to reflect your own needs. Additional customization options will be discussed later on in this recipe, but in the preceding example, any new directory created will be given the permissions of `0770`, while any new file added will have the permissions set to `0666`. The only valid users that can connect to this share folder are defined by the `username` value while all files and directories will have the group name of `groupname` applied to it.

5. When you have finished, simply save the configuration file before restarting the Samba server like so:

```
service smb start && service nmb start
```

How it works...

Samba is very simple. In fact, its simplicity can be mildly confusing and having completed this recipe you now know how to deploy an unlimited amount of assets for any specific user or user group.

So what did we learn from this experience?

During the initial stages the recipe showed you how to create a working directory, assign the relevant permissions, and determine the ownership of a new shared folder that will be used to enhance your current file sharing services.

To create a new folder for sharing, it was simply a matter of typing:

```
mkdir/home/<foldername>
```

To assign the correct features to this directory, it was simply a matter of substituting the appropriate values and typing:

```
chown <username> /home/<foldername> && chgrp <groupname> /
home/<foldername> && chmod 0770 /home/<foldername>
```

The recipe illustrated this as a single-line command, but for future reference, you could expand the entire process into multiple lines like so:

```
chown <username> /home/<foldername>
chgrp <groupname> /home/<foldername>
chmod 0770 /home/<foldername>
```

We then modified the current Samba configuration to reflect the availability of this new directory by using the following characteristics:

```
[foldername]
     comment = your foldername description
     path = /home/foldername/
     browseable = yes
     guest ok = no
     writable = yes
     create mask =0666
     directory mask =0770
     valid users = username
force group = groupname
forceuser = username
```

Starting with a share name, comment, and path, the preceding characteristics enable us to manage the folder's behavior by simply calling on a few basic functions.

We started by assigning a name for the asset by typing:

```
[foldername]
```

You should always begin by providing a suitable title for your share folder. The name will appear in brackets as shown. Always try to keep it simple. For example, if your shared folder was called `files`, then you will want to use:

```
[files]
```

In the next step you were required to add a brief description for the asset, like so:

```
comment = your foldername description
```

For example, if your shared folder was called `files`, then you will want to use the following description:

```
comment = my shared files
```

Following this, you were then required to supply a full path to the shared folder:

```
path = /home/foldername/
```

Based on our previous examples, if the shared folder was called `files`, then your configuration may reflect the following:

```
path = /home/files/
```

At this point we then ensured that the folder would be seen, that it is write-enabled while ensuring that guest access would be denied:

```
browseable = yes
guest ok = no
writable = yes
```

Having done this, we then wanted to ensure that any new file will have the permissions set to `0666`:

```
create mask =0666
```

That a new directory will be given the permissions of `0770`:

```
directory mask =0770
```

That the only valid users who can connect to this share folder are defined by the `username` value:

```
valid users = @username
```

While all files and directories will have the group name of `groupname` and `username` applied to it, like so:

```
force group = groupname
forceuser = username
```

Finally, you were asked to save your work and restart the Samba service in the following way:

`service smb start && service nmb start`

By completing this recipe, you should realize that it was not intended to serve as the ultimate guide to providing a shared folder on Samba. Instead, its purpose is to serve as an introduction with the primary intention to get you up and running in no time at all. It has already been said that Samba can be as simple or as complicated as you want it to be, so remember to apply and adapt the recipe as necessary, as it is expected that Samba will play a significant role in your day-to-day responsibilities as a server administrator.

There's more...

In the main recipe we saw how easily access could be given to a single user. However if you are intending to enable multiple user access, then you can enhance this to include more users by listing the relevant usernames, like so:

```
valid users = username1, username2, username3
```

On the other hand, an alternative solution can be achieved by specifying the @ parameter like so:

```
valid users = @groupname
```

This implies that anyone who is a member of `groupname` is a valid user for the share folder concerned. With this in mind, your modified configuration statement could look similar to this:

```
[folder_name]
        comment = folder_name description
        writable = yes
        valid users = @groupname
        path = /home/samba/folder_name
        create mode = 0660
        directory mode = 0770
```

Furthermore, if you wanted a particular share to be accessible by the users of multiple groups, then the code would look more like this:

```
[folder_name]
        comment = folder_name description
        writable = yes
        valid users = @groupname1, @groupname2, @groupname3
        path = /home/samba/folder_name
        create mode = 0660
        directory mode = 0770
```

 To use the group access feature, users must be members of the same group as Samba cannot overrule the existing rules implied by CentOS.

Remember, whenever you make any changes to your Samba configuration file, always restart the service in the following way:

```
service smb start && service nmb start
```

Controlling access and enabling a write list for specific users or groups

Instead of making your custom folders writeable to all who can access them, Samba provides the ability to define a writelist in order to restrict the number of users who are able to utilize these permissions. To do this, log in as root, and open the main Samba configuration file like so:

```
vi /etc/samba/smb.conf
```

If your intention is to create a rule set for individual users, scroll down to your custom share folder settings and delete the following lines:

```
writable = yes
valid users = username
```

Now add the following lines by substituting the values shown with those of valid users on your system:

```
read only = yes
valid users = username1 username2
write list = username1 username2 username3
```

As you can see from the preceding example, you have now established a read-only folder for username1, username2, and username3; but by adding the write list option you have restricted write permissions to username1 and username2 only.

Alternatively, we could invoke the @ parameter to provide group access rules in the following way:

```
read only = yes
valid users = @groupname1, @groupname2, @groupname3
write list = @groupname1
```

As you can see from the preceding example, you have now established a read only folder for the user groups groupname1, groupname2, and groupname3; but by adding the write list option you have restricted write permissions to groupname1 only.

In terms of the time taken to provide group access, the second approach is easier to achieve, but whatever approach you have taken, when you have finished, simply save the configuration file before restarting the Samba server like so:

```
service smb start && service nmb start
```

Remember, the use of write list cannot override the permissions imposed by CentOS. So if you have created a series of users without giving them the relevant group permissions, they will be denied access.

Enabling guest-only access to a custom share folder

Samba provides you with the ability to specify guest-only access to a share.

For example, if you have created a custom folder called documents and you wish to restrict access in this share to guests only, then the following configuration may prove useful:

```
[documents]
comment = guest only access share folder
path = /home/documents
writable = yes
guest ok = yes
guest only = yes
guest account = nobody
deadtime = 10
max smbd processes = 500
```

 Because the preceding directive implies that guest only = yes, then valid Samba users with existing access will be forced to relogin using the guest account. A password is not required as we have set the guest ok value to yes. You can customize the guest account used, but always state yes for both guest only and guest ok otherwise, Samba will not use the guest account value that you specify.

Finally, you can manage the use of this folder by limiting the number of concurrent connections with max smbd processes and by specifying the deadtime, or number of minutes before an unused connection will be terminated. This will serve to preserve the status of your Samba server and reduce the risk of degrading the service as a whole.

See also

▸ The Samba project's man pages:
http://www.samba.org/samba/docs/man/Samba-HOWTO-Collection/

7
Working with Domains

In this chapter, we will cover:

- ▶ Building a caching-only nameserver with BIND
- ▶ Writing zone files for BIND
- ▶ Adding zones to BIND
- ▶ Deploying a local nameserver with dnsmasq
- ▶ Logging events with dnsmasq and combining this with logrotate
- ▶ Enabling domain name wildcards with dnsmasq
- ▶ Hardening BIND with chroot and providing better security measures

Introduction

This chapter contains a collection of recipes that explores the task of handling domain names, domain resolution, and DNS queries by showing you the methods and approaches associated with building a caching-only nameserver with BIND; writing zone files for BIND; adding zones to BIND; deploying a local nameserver with dnsmasq; logging events with dnsmasq and combining this with logrotate; enabling domain name wildcard with dnsmasq; and hardening BIND with chroot and providing better security measures.

Building a caching-only nameserver with BIND

In this recipe we will learn how to install and configure a caching-only nameserver with BIND.

BIND is the classic domain name solution used by servers all over the world. Otherwise known as the **Berkeley Internet Name Domain**, it represents an implementation of the DNS protocols that offers a comprehensive array of features that are suitable for any environment. BIND is a big subject, and it is the purpose of this recipe to provide the perfect starting point by showing you how to install BIND and use it as a simple IPv4-based caching-only nameserver that will not only provide caching services for the entire local network, but will also serve to forward all queries to a remote DNS with the intention of speeding up general access to the Internet.

Getting ready

To complete this recipe you will require a working installation of the CentOS 6 operating system with root privileges, a static IP address, and a console-based text editor of your choice. An Internet connection will be required to download additional packages.

If you are running a firewall, you will need to confirm that the firewall has been disabled, removed, or the appropriate ports are open. Similarly, if you are running SELinux, then you should confirm that it has been disabled or it is now running in permissive mode.

How to do it...

In this recipe we will consider the role of BIND as a caching-only nameserver. It will not provide domain name resolution, but it will use the default root servers in order to cache the results of any query that has been performed, while all external domain queries will be resolved on third-party DNS servers. With this in mind, any workstation using this service should experience a significant improvement to all DNS requests.

1. To begin, log in as root and install the required packages by typing:

   ```
   yum install bind bind-utils
   ```

2. Now open the main configuration file with your favorite text editor:

   ```
   vi /etc/named.conf
   ```

3. Scroll down to find the following line:

   ```
   allow-query { localhost; };
   ```

4. At this stage we are going to disallow zone transfers and enable all hosts to make queries. So change this line to read:

   ```
   allow-transfer{ "none";};
   ```

5. Then add this line:

```
allow-query      { any; };
```

6. Now find the following line:

```
listen-on-v6 port 53 { ::1; };
```

7. Change it to read:

```
listen-on-v6 port 53 { none; };
```

> Due to limited support we are going to disable IPv6. However, if you would like to keep the functionality of IPv6, then simply change this line to read as `listen-on-v6 port 53 { any; };`.

8. We will now list the forwarders we have permission to query and determine that they should be checked first. Do this by substituting the relevant IP address values and type:

```
forwarders {XXX.XXX.XXX.XXX;XXX.XXX.XXX.XXX;};
forward first;
```

9. Now scroll down and find the following line to make sure that the server will always provide a recursive query behavior:

```
recursion yes;
```

10. Having done this, we will now enhance this feature by making it read as follows:

```
recursion yes;
allow-recursion { any ; };
allow-query-on {any;};
allow-query-cache { any; };
```

> As an option you can use the following query statement to define the server interface from which queries are accepted: `allow-query-on {XXX.XXX.XXX.XXX;};`. This can be useful if the server spans more than one network or has multiple IP addresses.

11. When you are finished, save and close the file in the usual way, before finalizing the configuration process by ensuring that IPv6 is no longer required. To do this, type:

```
echo 'OPTIONS="-4"' >> /etc/sysconfig/named
```

[If you are intending to use or keep the IPv6 functionality, you should skip this step.]

12. We now want to set the value of the nameserver. To do this, open the following file with your favorite text editor:

```
vi /etc/resolv.conf
```

13. Now remove all current nameserver references and replace the current values with the following:

```
nameserver 127.0.0.1
```

[If you have already set a static IP address using a similar method to that described in a previous recipe found within this book, you will want to review the /etc/sysconfig/network-scripts/ ifcfg-eth0 file and modify the current DNS reference to read as DNS1=127.0.0.1.]

14. Now ensure the service will be available at boot by typing:

```
chkconfig named on
```

15. To finish, start the service like so:

```
service named start
```

How it works...

By using BIND as a caching nameserver, it will serve to improve the responsiveness of your overall network by caching the answer to any name-based queries. Using such a process will shorten the waiting time on any visits to the same location. It is a feature that is particularly useful if you happen to be managing a large and busy network, or if you are using a slow connection.

So what did we learn from this experience?

We started by installing the necessary packages. This included a reference to bind-utils, a small package that enables you to run many different network tasks such as dig, nslookup, and host, and for this reason it represents the preferred way to install BIND.

To complete this task, it was simply a matter of typing:

```
yum install bind bind-utils
```

The name of the DNS daemon in the BIND package is called `named`, and for this reason the next step was to begin making the necessary configuration changes by editing the following file:

```
vi /etc/named.conf
```

Our purpose is to build a caching-only nameserver and so we began this process by disallowing zone transfers and ensuring that the server would listen on all interfaces like so:

```
allow-transfer{ "none";};
allow-query    { any; };
```

The next step involved disabling IPv6, and our reason behind this action is purely based on the fact that we are configuring a forwarding nameserver with caching properties that will be used to improve our connectivity to the World Wide Web. We completed this step by typing:

```
listen-on-v6 port 53 { none; };
```

Where IPv6 may work well within a local network, in the wider world, support for IPv6 on many of the major DNS servers is limited and for this reason the decision to disable it will reduce the number of error messages you will find in BIND's logs.

These logfiles are located at `/var/named/data`, and if you decide not to disable IPv6 or reactivate IPv6 at a later date, then a typical error message will look like this:

```
error (network unreachable) resolving 'ns2.p34.dynect.net/AAAA/IN':
2001:500:90::100#53
```

To ensure that you are able to resolve all DNS queries, it is always a good idea to include the `forwarders` option in order that all external queries can be resolved. We are telling BIND to use this option first, and in most cases you will be able to use the DNS nameservers provided by an external server or an external third-party.

 A forward first server will send all queries to the forwarder. If they are not answered, it will attempt to answer the query locally.

We completed this step by typing:

```
forwarders {XXX.XXX.XXX.XXX;XXX.XXX.XXX.XXX;};
forward first;
```

Based on this you could easily employ the use of Google's Public DNS, like so:

```
forwarders { 8.8.8.8; 8.8.4.4; };
forward first;
```

Following this, it was simply a matter of maintaining the recursive qualities of BIND and recursion determining which IP address(es) are allowed to issue recursive queries to the server, by setting the following statements:

```
recursion yes;
allow-recursion { any ; };
allow-query-on {any;};
```

For the purpose of this recipe the `allow-query` and `allow-recursion` lines have been used to permit queries from any source. However, you can restrict this to only permit local machines by using the following syntax: `allow-query { localhost; 192.168.0.0/24; };`. Moreover, where the use of `allow-query-cache` can be employed to determine access to the server's cache, you can use this statement to imply additional limits to the recursive behavior by defining a list of IP addresses that are allowed to issue queries to the server's cache.

So instead of using this:

```
allow-query-cache { any; };
```

You could use this:

```
allow-query-cache { 127.0.0.1; 192.168.1.0/24; };
```

 If a value for `allow-query-cache` is not present and recursion is enabled, then this value will default to `allow-query-cache {localnets; localhost;};`.

So having saved your revised configuration file, it may look something like this:

```
options {
// make the server listen on all interfaces
// This will specify on which interface the server will listen for
incoming queries.
listen-on port 53 { any; };
    // disable IPv6 as it is not supported by most servers or
networks.
    listen-on-v6 port 53 { none; };
    directory    "/var/named";
    dump-file    "/var/named/data/cache_dump.db";
statistics-file "/var/named/data/named_stats.txt";
memstatistics-file "/var/named/data/named_mem_stats.txt";

// disables all zone transfer requests
allow-transfer{"none";};
// allow the query range from any source on our network
allow-query     { any; };
```

```
// list the DNS servers you have permission to query
forwarders {XXX.XXX.XXX.XXX;XXX.XXX.XXX.XXX;};
// enable forwarders first
forward first;
//maintain this feature and allow recursion
// set recursion in order that the server will always provide
recursive query behaviour
recursion yes;
// allow-recursion determines which IP address(es) which are allowed
to
// issue recursive queries to the server.
allow-recursion { any ; };
allow-query-on {any;};
allow-query-cache { any; };

    // DNSSEC (DNS Security Extensions) is a technology that was
developed to
// address certain vulnerabilities in the Domain Name System by
digitally
// signing data so you can be assured it is valid.
dnssec-enable yes;
    dnssec-validation yes;
    dnssec-lookaside auto;

    /* Path to ISC DLV key */
    bindkeys-file "/etc/named.iscdlv.key";
    managed-keys-directory "/var/named/dynamic";
};
```

So having saved the file, we then proceeded to complete the configuration by typing the following expression in order to tell BIND not to invoke IPv6:

```
echo 'OPTIONS="-4"' >> /etc/sysconfig/named
```

 If you are intending to use or keep IPv6 functionality, you should skip this step.

At this point it was then necessary to confirm that /etc/resolv.conf was configured correctly before proceeding to activate the BIND at boot and start the service like so:

```
chkconfig named on && service named start
```

As mentioned, starting BIND for the first time can result in what seems to be a relatively long waiting process. It will take a few moments to complete but with final confirmation comes the chance to review the status of BIND by issuing the following command at any time:

```
service named status
```

This will result in the following output:

```
version: 9.8.2rc1-RedHat-9.8.2-0.10.rc1.el6_3.5
```

```
CPUs found: 2
```

```
worker threads: 2
```

```
number of zones: 19
```

```
debug level: 0
```

```
xfers running: 0
```

```
xfers deferred: 0
```

```
soa queries in progress: 0
```

```
query logging is OFF
```

```
recursive clients: 0/0/1000
```

```
tcp clients: 0/100
```

```
server is up and running
```

```
named (pid  1177) is running...
```

Of course, to complete this recipe you will now want to modify the DNS settings of your local workstations to use your server as the primary source, but before doing this, you may want to run a simple dig command-based experiment in order to utilize the bind-utils package and to see how BIND will perform.

To do this, simply elect a target website and type:

```
dig www.your_chosen_website.com
```

In this instance you may choose to type:

```
dig www.packtpub.com
```

Having run this test, you may see a query time that results in something like this:

```
;; Query time: 39 msec
```

Now repeat this exercise again by re-testing the same URL. Depending on your networking environment this may produce the following result:

```
;; Query time: 12 msec
```

Now do it again for another website, and on every repeat of the preceding command you should not only see a reduced query time, but you should also experience a faster response time in delivering the output. This same result will be evident in the browser refresh rate and as a result, we could say that this simple exercise has not only introduced you to BIND, but it will ultimately serve to improve the speed of your local network when surfing the World Wide Web.

There's more...

It is entirely optional, but you can configure a namesever to run in the `forward only` mode.

Unlike `forward first`, the action of `forward only` will imply that all queries will be sent to one or more predetermined DNS servers and no other nameservers will be used. In the `forward only` mode, the use of these external forwarders will greatly improve the performance of any DNS query.

To do this, simply open the following configuration file in your favorite text editor like so:

```
vi /etc/named.conf
```

Now apply the following settings to your existing options section:

```
forwarders {
# the following IP addresses will be used for looking
# up ALL hostnames.
XXX.XXX.XXX.XXX;      # Primary Master
XXX.XXX.XXX.XXX;      # Secondary Slave
};
forward only;
```

As working example, you could use Google's Public DNS like so:

```
options {
forwarders {8.8.8.8;8.8.4.4;};
forward only;}
};
```

When you have finished, remember to save and close the file in the usual way before restarting the named service like so:

```
service named restart
```

Enabling access to a DNS server from behind a firewall

If you are running a firewall on the nameserver system, you will need to configure your firewall in order to open port 53 and allow both TCP and UDP traffic.

To do this, log in as root and type:

```
iptables -A INPUT -m state —state NEW -m tcp -p tcp —dport 53 -j ACCEPT
iptables -A INPUT -m state —state NEW -m udp -p udp —dport 53 -j ACCEPT
```

Now save your new rules by typing:

```
service iptables save
```

Finally, restart IPTables:

```
service iptables restart
```

Cleaning expired records

The cache is stored in memory and you can schedule the cleaning of expired records which may be useful if the server is handling a limited amount of requests.

To do this, open the main configuration for BIND in your favorite text editor:

```
vi /etc/named.conf
```

Now scroll down to the bottom of the `options` section and add the following line:

```
cleaning-interval 40320;
```

The `cleaning-interval` line defines the number of minutes when all expired records will be deleted and by adding this line you will be asking BIND to clear the cache every 28 days. This is the maximum value that can be used with the default being set at 60 minutes.

When you have finished, remember to save and close the file in the usual way before restarting the `named` service like so:

```
service named restart
```

See also

> ▶ The official BIND home page: `https://www.isc.org/software/bind`
> ▶ The *DNSSEC – What Is It and Why Is It Important?* article in the ICANN home page: `http://www.icann.org/en/about/learning/factsheets/dnssec-qaa-09oct08-en.htm`

Writing zone files for BIND

In this recipe we will learn how to write both the forward and reverse zone files for BIND.

Having already configured a caching-only nameserver, we will now approach the subject of zone files in order that you can provide name resolution across a local network. BIND is complicated, but as it represents the industry standard when building a nameserver solution of choice. It is the purpose of this recipe to introduce you to the process of writing zone files.

Getting ready

To complete this recipe you will require a working installation of the CentOS 6 operating system with root privileges, a static IP address, and a console-based text editor of your choice. It is assumed that you have already installed BIND.

How to do it...

Zone files are simple text files that contain pertinent information regarding the configuration of our DNS-based data. They contain directives, resources, user-based administrative comments, and they are used to describe part of the overall domain name system. All zone files should be created within the server's working directory, and because they are also known as db (database) files, it is an accepted convention that a zone file is typically prefixed or appended in the appropriate way.

1. To begin, log in as root and type the following command in order to create your forward zone file. As shown, name the file after the zone whose resource records it will contain:

    ```
    vi /var/named/<domain>.<top-level domain>.db
    ```

    > For example, if you were creating a forward zone for centos.home, you should name the file centos.home. db by substituting the value <domain> with centos and <top-level domain> with home. You should remember to keep the dots (.) at all times throughout this recipe.

2. Now add the following lines by customizing the values shown:

    ```
    $TTL XXXXX
    @    IN   SOA <primary-name-server>.   < hostmaster-email.primary-
    name-server >. (
            YYYYMMDDVV; serial-number
            XXXX; time-to-refresh in seconds
            XXXX; time-to-retry in seconds
    ```

```
        XXXXXX; time-to-expire in seconds
        XXXXX; minimum-TTL in seconds
)
IN  NS                  <primary-name-server>.
IN  NS                  <primary-name-server>.
IN  A                   XXX.XXX.XXX.XXX

IN  MX   10      <primary-name-server>.

<hostname>              IN  A      XXX.XXX.XXX.XXX
<primary-name-server>.  IN  A      XXX.XXX.XXX.XXX
localhost               IN  A      127.0.0.1
<domain.tld>.           IN  A      XXX.XXX.XXX.XXX
ftp                     IN  A      XXX.XXX.XXX.XXX
smtp                    IN  A      XXX.XXX.XXX.XXX
pop                     IN  A      XXX.XXX.XXX.XXX
mail                    IN  A      XXX.XXX.XXX.XXX
www                     IN  A      XXX.XXX.XXX.XXX
```

3. When you have finished, simply save and close the file before proceeding to create the reverse zone file:

   vi /var/named/<hostname>.<domain>.<top-level domain>.db

4. Based on the values added to the forward zone, simply add the following lines:

```
$TTL XXXXX
@   IN  SOA <primary-name-server>.  < hostmaster-email.primary-
name-server >. (
        YYYYMMDDVV; serial-number
        XXXX; time-to-refresh in seconds
        XXXX; time-to-retry in seconds
        XXXXXX; time-to-expire in seconds
        XXXXX; minimum-TTL in seconds
)
IN          NS  <primary-name-server>.
IN          NS  <primary-name-server>.

XXX         IN  PTR    <hostname>.<domain.tld>.
XXX         IN  PTR    ftp.<domain.tld>.
XXX         IN  PTR    mail.<domain.tld>.
XXX         IN  PTR    pop.<domain.tld>.
XXX         IN  PTR     smtp.<domain.tld>.
XXX         IN  PTR     www.<domain.tld>.
```

How it works...

The purpose of this recipe was to introduce you to the methods and approaches used when creating both a forward and reverse zone file. A zone file is a simple text file that consists of directives and resource records, they can look quite complicated. But by considering the universal requirements of a zone file, it is possible to make what is often considered to be a daunting task that much easier.

So what did we learn from this experience?

We began the recipe by creating and customizing the following file:

```
vi /var/named/<domain>.<top-level domain>.db
```

This file is opened with the `$TTL` control statement. Known as the **time to live**, this provides other nameservers with a time value that determines how long they can cache the records from this zone. The format of this statement is very succinct, the actual value is calculated in seconds and it is often used in the following way:

```
$TTL 86400
```

Alternatively, you can provide a shortened statement like so:

```
$TTL 1d
```

 The value of one day is typical for this value whether it is represented as seconds (`86400`) or shown as `1d`.

Following this we then provided a **Start of Authority** record:

```
@   IN  SOA <primary-name-server>.  < hostmaster-email.primary-name-
server >.
```

More commonly referred to as the **SOA**, this record contains specific information about the zone as a whole. This begins with the zone name (@), a specification of the zone class (`IN`), a value for the primary name server in the format `hostname.domain.TLD.`, and an e-mail address of the zone administrator. This latter value is typically in the form `hostmaster.` `hostname.domain.TLD.` and it is formed by replacing the typical @ symbol with a dot (`.`). Having done this, it was then a matter of opening the brackets to assign the zone's serial number, refresh value, retry value, expire value, and negative caching time-to-live value in the following way:

```
(
        YYYYMMDDVV; serial-number
        XXXX; time-to-refresh in seconds
        XXXX; time-to-retry in seconds
        XXXXXX; time-to-expire in seconds
        XXXXX; minimum-TTL in seconds
)
```

These directives can be summarized as follows:

▶ The `serial-number` value is a numeric value, typically taking the form of the date in reverse (`YYYYMMDD`) with an additional value (`VV`), which is incremented every time the zone file is modified or updated in order to indicate it is time for the named service to reload the zone. The value `VV` typically starts at `00`, and the next time you modify this file, simply increment it to `01`, `02`, `03`, and so on.

▶ The `time-to-refresh` value determines how frequently secondary or slave nameservers will ask the primary nameserver if any changes have been made to the zone. Again, this value is calculated in seconds, but time values between one to three hours are common.

▶ The `time-to-retry` values determines how frequently secondary or slave nameservers should check the primary server after the serial number has failed. If a failure has occurred during the time frame specified by the `time-to-expire` value elapses, the secondary nameservers will stop responding as an authority for requests. The `time-to-retry` value is calculated in seconds, but time values between 15 minutes to 1 hour are common, where the `time-to-expire` value should be set to a longer period (calculated in weeks or months).

▶ The `minimum-TTL` value determines how long other name servers can cache negative responses. This value is calculated in seconds, but time values between 15 minutes and 3 hours are common.

Remember, when you are configuring your zones, all times are specified in seconds. However, it is possible to use abbreviations when specifying units of time other than seconds, such as minutes (`M`), hours (`H`), days (`D`), and weeks (`W`).

Having completed this section and closed the corresponding bracket, we then proceeded to add the authoritative nameserver information like so:

```
IN   NS          <primary-name-server>.
IN   NS          <primary-name-server>.
```

Typically speaking, you will have at least two—if not three—nameservers. Each will carry a unique IP address and in most circumstances the format of these lines may look similar to this:

```
IN   NS          ns1.domian.com.
IN   NS          ns2.domian.com.
```

However, it is possible to set only one nameserver which is particularly useful if you are running the server in an office or a home environment and would like to enjoy the benefit of local name resolution such as `.home`, `.lan`, or `.dev`.

For example, if your primary server was called `centos.centos.lan`, the administrator's e-mail was `hostmaster`, and the IP address of your server was `192.168.1.100`, then try experimenting with the following settings by ensuring you provide an `A` record, like so:

```
$TTL 86400
@   IN  SOA centos.centos.lan. hostmaster.centos.centos.lan. (
2012060101  ;serial
        3600        ;refresh
        1800        ;retry
        604800   ;expire
        86400      ;minimum-TTL
)
;define your nameserver here.
IN      NS      centos.centos.lan.
;add the internal IP address of name server here
IN      A       192.168.1.100
```

The next stage then required us to include a reference for the **Mail eXchanger** records in order that we can specify a mail server for the zone, like so:

```
IN   MX   10        <primary-name-server>.
```

The `MX` value indicates priority—the lower the number, the higher the priority. In this respect, a secondary mail server should have a higher value.

Depending on your needs, you may intend to use the primary server as your mail server, although you may have another server dedicated to that role. So if you have more than one mail server, you can add several MX records, like so:

```
;define the mail exchanger here
IN      MX       10            mail.primary-server.lan.
IN      MX       20            mail.secondary-server.lan.
```

Following this, it was then a matter of creating the appropriate `A` records and assigning the appropriate IP address (that of your primary server) to the values shown. Initially, we would begin with our primary server or primary nameserver, defining the localhost, and the domain name like so:

```
<hostname>                      IN  A       XXX.XXX.XXX.XXX
<primary-name-server>.          IN  A       XXX.XXX.XXX.XXX
localhost                       IN  A       127.0.0.1
<domain.tld>.                   IN  A       XXX.XXX.XXX.XXX
```

A task that would be enhanced by creating the relevant values for our remaining services:

```
ftp                          IN   A      XXX.XXX.XXX.XXX
smtp                         IN   A      XXX.XXX.XXX.XXX
pop                          IN   A      XXX.XXX.XXX.XXX
mail                         IN   A      XXX.XXX.XXX.XXX
www                          IN   A      XXX.XXX.XXX.XXX
```

An A record is used for linking a fully qualified domain name or FQDN to an IP address, but much of the preceding settings will be based on your exact needs. You should not forget that there is an opportunity to use a CNAME (Canonical Name) record, which is used to assign an alias to an existing A record like so:

```
servername      IN   A       XXX.XXX.XXX.XXX
ftp             IN   CNAME   servername
mail            IN   CNAME   servername
mail2           IN   CNAME   servername
www             IN   CNAME   servername
```

For example, and by extending the earlier example, because my mail and web server is also my domain server, the resulting configuration shows that a CNAME value has been assigned in order that both the www and mail references points at centos:

```
centos                       IN   A       XXX.XXX.XXX.XXX
centos.centos.lan.           IN   A       XXX.XXX.XXX.XXX
localhost                    IN   A       127.0.0.1
centos.lan.                  IN   A       XXX.XXX.XXX.XXX
ftp                          IN   A       XXX.XXX.XXX.XXX
mail                         IN   CNAME       centos.lan.
www                          IN   CNAME       centos.lan.
```

Arguably CNAME values make your DNS data easier to manage by pointing back to an A record. So if you ever consider the need to change the IP address of the A record, all your CNAME records pointed to that record automatically. However, and as this recipe has tried to show, the alternative solution is to have multiple A records which implies the need for multiple updates in order to change the IP address. You could say that this will increase the risk of error, but you could also say that because CNAME values are difficult to set up, the role of personal preference will probably play the greater part in determining your choice.

At this stage of the recipe, we then turned our attention towards the reverse DNS zone; and here you will find some similarities between the directives and resources used. However, it is important to remember that reverse DNS is wholly separate and distinct from forward DNS.

The reverse DNS zone is designed to assist in the conversion of an IP address to a domain name. This process is referred to as a **reverse DNS lookup**, and it works in the reverse to your forward zone. For this reason, you must ensure that a unique `PTR` record exists for every `A` record, as shown in the following:

```
XXX             IN   PTR     ftp.<domain.tld>.
XXX             IN   PTR     mail.<domain.tld>.
```

The IP address value for the first column should only show the last octet. So by advancing our earlier examples, your reverse DNS may look like this:

```
100             IN   PTR     ftp.centos.lan.
100             IN   PTR     mail.centos.lan.
100             IN   PTR     www.centos.lan.
```

Alternatively, you could establish a `PTR` record for every workstation in your network in the following way:

```
101             IN   PTR     workstation1.centos.lan.
102             IN   PTR     workstation2.centos.lan.
103             IN   PTR     workstation3.centos.lan.
```

We will return to the concept of reverse DNS in the subsequent recipe but until then, you now have a better understanding of how to write a zone file. BIND is a big subject and there is a lot more to learn as this recipe has only served to introduce you to the subject. In most cases, you may even find that your initial learning period will become known as a process of trial and error, but it will improve. Remember, practice makes perfect and if you do create additional forward zones, always reference them in the reverse zone file.

See also

- The official BIND home page: `https://www.isc.org/software/bind`

- *Red Hat Enterprise Linux 4: Reference Guide, Chapter 12. Berkeley Internet Name Domain (BIND)*: `http://www.centos.org/docs/4/html/rhel-rg-en-4/s1-bind-zone.html`

- *Red Hat Enterprise Linux Deployment Guide, Chapter 17. Berkeley Internet Name Domain (BIND)*: `http://www.centos.org/docs/5/html/5.1/Deployment_Guide/ch-bind.html`

- *Red Hat Linux 7.2: The Official Red Hat Linux Reference Guide, Chapter 14. Berkeley Internet Name Domain (BIND)*: `http://www.centos.org/docs/2/rhl-rg-en-7.2/ch-bind.html`

Adding zones to BIND and configuring a nameserver

In this recipe we will learn how to add zones to BIND in order to finalize the configuration of a nameserver.

BIND performs name-resolution services through the `named` daemon, and having already created your forward and reverse zone files, you are now in a position to complete the configuration of the `named` service in order to implement a fully qualified domain name service across your local network.

Getting ready

To complete this recipe you will require a working installation of the CentOS 6 operating system with root privileges, a static IP address, and a console-based text editor of your choice. It is expected that BIND has been installed, that it is already running, and that you have prepared the required forward and reverse zone files.

How to do it...

As a continuation from your work with the associated zone files, we will now begin to make certain modifications to the `named` configuration in order to augment its functionality with a series of zone statements.

1. To begin, log in as root and open the following configuration file in your favorite text editor, like so:

   ```
   vi /etc/named.conf
   ```

2. Now scroll down and locate the following line:

   ```
   include "/etc/named.rfc1912.zones";
   ```

3. Immediately following this line, create a space for your work and add the appropriate zone statement to enable your reverse zone, like so:

   ```
   include "/etc/named.rfc1912.zones";
   zone "XXX.XXX.XXX.in-addr.arpa" IN {
   type master;
   file "/var/named/hostname.domainname.lan.db";
   allow-update { none; };
   };
   ```

Remember to substitute the values shown with something more relevant to suit your own needs.

4. Having done this, you can now proceed to add a zone statement for your forward zone, like so:

```
zone "primary-domain-name.lan" IN {
type master;
file "/var/named/primary-domain-name.lan.db";
allow-update { none; };
};
```

Remember to substitute the values shown with something more relevant to suit your own needs.

5. Now repeat the previous step for any remaining forward zones, like so:

```
zone "another-domain-name.lan" IN {
type master;
file "/var/named/another-domain-name.lan.db";
allow-update { none; };
};
```

6. When you have finished, simply save and close the file before proceeding to restart the named service by typing:

```
service named restart
```

How it works...

All DNS servers are configured to perform caching functions, but where a caching-only server is restricted in its ability to answer queries, a nameserver is a DNS server that maintains the master zone for a particular record. It is the definitive record holder that is responsible for answering all DNS queries related to that zone, and for this reason adding your zone files to named.conf represents the final stage in building a fully comprehensive domain name solution for your network.

So what did we learn from this experience?

We began the recipe by opening named.conf in your favorite text editor in order that you could begin adding the relevant zone information:

```
vi /etc/named.conf
```

Starting with the reverse zone file, you then proceeded to create the appropriate entry in the following way:

```
# create a zone entry statement for the reverse zone
zone "XXX.XXX.XXX.in-addr.arpa" IN {
        #tell the server that it holds the master record
type master;
#confirm a path to the zone data
file "/var/named/hostname.domainname.lan.db";
#disable updates from other servers
allow-update { none; };
#close the entry
};
```

The reverse zone file is designed to assist in the conversion of an IP address to a domain name. This process is often referred to as a reverse DNS lookup, and it works in the opposite direction to your forward zone. For example, if you were to type XXX.XXX.XXX.XXX in a browser, the process of IP address to domain name mapping would enable you to view your website at http://domain name.com.

Reverse DNS is principally associated with the task of discovery (that is, where an e-mail message came from, where a visitor came from, and so on) While it is not seen to be critical to the role of website hosting, it does play a very important part in the life of a mail server. For example, many mail servers are now configured in such a way that they will reject any incoming mail from a server that does not have a reverse DNS.

Of course, there is still a lot more to learn about this subject, but based on this information, you now know that if your server has an IP address of 192.168.1.100, the hostname of servername, and the full domain name of domain.com, then you can use the following syntax in order to add your reverse DNS entry to named.conf:

```
zone "1.168.192.in-addr.arpa" IN {
type master;
file "/var/named/servername.domain.com.db";
allow-update { none; };
};
```

So having successfully created your reverse DNS entry, you then proceeded to create the entries for the forward zones in the following way:

```
#create a zone entry statement for the forward zone
zone "primary-domain-name.lan" IN {
#tell the server that it holds the master record
type master;
#confirm a path to the zone data
file "/var/named/primary-domain-name.lan.db";
#disable updates from other servers
allow-update { none; };
#close the statement
};
```

Unlike reverse DNS, the forward zone file is designed to assist in the conversion of a FQDN to an IP address. For example, if you were to ping `domain name.com`, the process of domain name mapping would enable you to identify the appropriate IP address as `XXX.XXX.XXX.XXX`.

You may add unlimited forward zones, but each must be given a single entry like so:

```
zone "primary-domain-name-1.lan" IN {
type master;
file "/var/named/primary-domain-name.lan.db";
allow-update { none; };
};

zone "primary-domain-name-2.lan" IN {
type master;
file "/var/named/another-domain-name.lan.db";
allow-update { none; };
};

zone "primary-domain-name-3.lan" IN {
type master;
file "/var/named/another-domain-name.lan.db";
allow-update { none; };
};
```

 In order to keep this file tidy, it is often a good idea to add your forward zones in an alphabetical order.

Having completed these actions, you were then required to save and close the configuration file before restarting the `named` service by typing:

`service named restart`

Well done! As a consequence of completing this recipe, you will not only have a working installation of BIND that acts as a caching nameserver, but one that will provide a comprehensive domain name system that can grow to support all your needs.

There's more...

Having added your zones and enabled BIND, you are now able to test your configuration.

To do this, simply return to your console and type the following command:

`host domain-name-here`

Alternatively, you can use:

```
host XXX.XXX.XXX.XXX
```

In this instance, the IP address used should correspond to the domain for which you have configured reverse DNS.

For example, if your domain name was `domain-name.lan` and your server was known as `hostname.domain-name.lan` with an IP address of `192.168.1.100`, you would use:

```
host domain-name.lan
```

This function will not only confirm the IP address, but it will also provide full feedback for the MX (mail exchanger) record like so:

```
host domain-name.lan
domain-name.lan has address 192.168.1.100
domain-name.lan mail is handled by 10 hostname.domain-name.lan.
```

In addition to this—and in a similar manner—you can also use `dig`, as shown here:

```
dig <domain-name>
```

See also

▶ The official BIND home page: `https://www.isc.org/software/bind`

▶ *Red Hat Enterprise Linux 4: Reference Guide, Chapter 12. Berkeley Internet Name Domain (BIND)*: `http://www.centos.org/docs/4/html/rhel-rg-en-4/s1-bind-zone.html`

▶ *Red Hat Enterprise Linux Deployment Guide, Chapter 17. Berkeley Internet Name Domain (BIND)*: `http://www.centos.org/docs/5/html/5.1/Deployment_Guide/ch-bind.html`

▶ *Red Hat Linux 7.2: The Official Red Hat Linux Reference Guide, Chapter 14. Berkeley Internet Name Domain (BIND)*: `http://www.centos.org/docs/2/rhl-rg-en-7.2/ch-bind.html`

Deploying a local nameserver with dnsmasq

In this recipe we will learn how to deploy a local nameserver with dnsmasq.

Dnsmasq is designed for a smaller network that loosely consists of no more than 1000 computers. It is often used as a domain name server, as a NAT forwarder, or as an alternative to many common DHCP servers. Dnsmasq isn't BIND—and it isn't intended to be—but this lightweight package is an exceptional alternative for those who would prefer a fast and capable solution that is a lot simpler to configure and maintain.

Getting ready

To complete this recipe you will require a working installation of the CentOS 6 operating system with root privileges, a static IP address, and a console-based text editor of your choice. An Internet connection will be required to download additional packages.

If you are running a firewall, you will need to confirm that the firewall has been disabled, removed, or the appropriate ports are open. Similarly, if you are running SELinux, then you should confirm that it has been disabled or it is now running in permissive mode.

How to do it...

In this recipe we will consider the role of dnsmasq as a nameserver. This solution will provide domain name resolution for both local and Internet-based domain names, support local workstations, and it will work without the need to configure zone files.

1. To begin, log in as root and type the following command to install the required packages:

   ```
   yum install dnsmasq bind-utils
   ```

2. Having installed the required package, the first step is to open the following file with your favorite text editor:

   ```
   vi /etc/resolv.conf
   ```

3. Our intention is to use dnsmasq for domain name resolution, and for this reason you should remove all current nameserver references and replace those values with the following:

   ```
   search home
   nameserver 127.0.0.1
   ```

   > If you have already set a static IP address using a similar method found within this book, you should review the file located at `/etc/sysconfig/network-scripts/ifcfg-eth0` and modify the current DNS reference to read as `DNS1=127.0.0.1`.
   >
   > If your network settings have been changed, remember to reboot or type `service network restart` to ensure that the changes take immediate effect.

4. Before we begin making any configuration changes to dnsmasq itself, rename the original file by typing:

   ```
   mv /etc/dnsmasq.conf /etc/dnsmasq.conf.bak
   ```

5. Now create a new configuration file with your favorite text editor, like so:

vi /etc/dnsmasq.conf

6. Add the following lines, but remember to substitute the relevant values to suit your own needs:

```
domain-needed
bogus-priv
no-hosts
dns-forward-max=150
cache-size=1000
neg-ttl=3600
resolv-file=/etc/dnsmasq-resolver
addn-hosts=/etc/dnsmasq-hosts
no-poll
```

7. Now save and close the file in the usual way before proceeding to create a nameserver resolution file, like so:

vi /etc/dnsmasq-resolver

8. Add one or more nameservers:

```
nameserver XXX.XXX.XXX.XXX
nameserver XXX.XXX.XXX.XXX
```

 For example, you could use the Google Public DNS facilities by typing:

```
nameserver 8.8.8.8
nameserver 8.8.4.4
```

9. Now save and close the file in the usual way before proceeding to create the hosts file with your favorite text editor:

vi /etc/dnsmasq-hosts

10. Add your local domain name(s) in full with a relevant IP address. To get you started, here are a few examples:

```
XXX.XXX.XXX.XXX    www.domain1.lan
XXX.XXX.XXX.XXX    www.domain2.lan
XXX.XXX.XXX.XXX    www.domain3.lan
XXX.XXX.XXX.XXX    www.domain4.lan
XXX.XXX.XXX.XXX    www.domain5.lan
XXX.XXX.XXX.XXX    www.domain6.lan
```

11. When you have finished, save and close the file in the usual way before ensuring that the service will start at boot by typing:

chkconfig dnsmasq on

12. To finish, start the `dnsmasq` service like so:

```
service dnsmasq start
```

13. Having installed `bind-utils`, you can now test domain name resolution with `dig` using:

```
dig <domainname>
```

How it works...

Dnsmasq is lightweight, easy to configure and maintain. It is designed to provide DNS-based services to a small network and it represents an excellent choice for anyone who wants a fast and flexible alternative to BIND. Dnsmasq is a very flexible solution, and by completing this recipe, we have just seen how quickly it can be used to provide a comprehensive domain name resolution service across your local network.

So what did we learn from this experience?

We began the recipe by installing the required packages and setting `/etc/resolv.conf` to ensure that dnsmasq will be used for all domain name resolution.

In this instance the local network is called `home` and `nameserver` is `127.0.0.1`:

```
search home
nameserver 127.0.0.1
```

 If your network settings have been changed, remember to reboot or type `service network restart` to ensure that the changes take immediate effect.

Following this, we then proceeded to rename the original dnsmasq configuration in order that we could create a new configuration file, like so:

```
vi /etc/dnsmasq.conf
```

Having completed these steps, we then started to make some basic changes to dnsmasq in order to confirm the required functionality:

```
# require dnsmasq to prevent forwarding plain names
# (a name without dots) or addresses in the non-routed
# address space to the parent nameservers.
domain-needed
bogus-priv


# do not read the hostnames in /etc/hosts.
no-hosts
```

```
# set the maximum number of concurrent DNS queries to 150
dns-forward-max=150

# set the size of dnsmasq's cache to 1000.
#The default is 150 names, but setting this value to 0 will disable
the cache
cache-size=1000

#set a timeout for to receive Time To Live values from the SOA records
neg-ttl=3600
```

In the subsequent steps we then added a reference to our external or parental nameserver file and followed this with a reference to our local domain name list:

```
#read the specified file for local domain names
addn-hosts=/etc/dnsmasq-hosts

#get the IP addresses of the upstream nameservers from
#the named file instead of /etc/resolv.conf
resolv-file=/etc/dnsmasq-resolver
```

We then ensured that dnsmasq would not poll /etc/resolv.conf for any changes:

```
no-poll
```

So having completed the main configuration file, we then proceeded to create the nameserver resolution file by typing:

vi /etc/dnsmasq-resolver

You have the option to choose your own nameservers, but during the course of this recipe you were shown how to use Google's Public DNS:

```
nameserver    8.8.8.8
nameserver    8.8.4.4
```

Following this, and having saved your work, we then proceeded to create a new hosts file like so:

vi /etc/dnsmasq-hosts

This file is used to list any local domain names and as you can see, the format of this file is a lot simpler than you would expect:

```
<XXX.XXX.XXX.XXX>        <domainname>
```

For example, your settings could look like this

```
192.168.1.100          www.domain1.lan
192.168.1.100          www.domain2.lan
192.168.1.100          www.domain3.lan
192.168.1.101          www.domain4.lan
192.168.1.102          www.domain5.lan
192.168.1.103          www.domain6.lan
```

Finally, we then made the service available at boot:

chkconfig dnsmasq on

Before starting the service like so:

service dnsmasq start

Of course, the list of domain names can be as long as you need and you can test your new configuration by using dig, like so:

dig www.domain1.lan

Alternatively you can try:

dig www.google.com

In order to experience this to full effect and to see the caching feature in action, the more times the site is visited, the quicker the response will be.

For example, the first attempt at using dig www.google.com shows the following result:

```
;www.google.com.       IN     A


;; ANSWER SECTION:
www.google.com.    300    IN    A    173.194.47.84
www.google.com.    300    IN    A    173.194.47.81
www.google.com.    300    IN    A    173.194.47.82
www.google.com.    300    IN    A    173.194.47.83
www.google.com.    300    IN    A    173.194.47.80
```

Repeating this same experiment 10 seconds later results in:

```
;www.google.com.          IN      A


;; ANSWER SECTION:
www.google.com.    290    IN     A       173.194.47.84
www.google.com.    290    IN     A       173.194.47.81
www.google.com.    290    IN     A       173.194.47.82
www.google.com.    290    IN     A       173.194.47.83
www.google.com.    290    IN     A       173.194.47.80
```

While the third attempt around 20 seconds later shows:

```
;www.google.com.          IN      A


;; ANSWER SECTION:
www.google.com.    278    IN     A       173.194.47.84
www.google.com.    278    IN     A       173.194.47.81
www.google.com.    278    IN     A       173.194.47.82
www.google.com.    278    IN     A       173.194.47.83
www.google.com.    278    IN     A       173.194.47.80
```

Dnsmasq may not be the definitive domain name system, but do not underestimate it. Having completed this recipe, you now have a fully functioning DNS that can serve in excess of 1000 workstations without the complexity of zone files. So remember, the next time you decide to establish a new network infrastructure, why not give dnsmasq a try, it could prove to be a pleasant surprise.

See also

> ▸ The dnsmasq project's home page:
>   http://www.thekelleys.org.uk/dnsmasq/doc.html
> ▸ The dnsmasq man page:
>   http://www.thekelleys.org.uk/dnsmasq/docs/dnsmasq-man.html

Logging events with dnsmasq and combining this with logrotate

In this recipe we will learn how to log events with dnsmasq and provide for log rotation using logrotate.

Without any additional configuration dnsmasq will send all log messages to the generic system log. However, where convenience and simplicity marks the road to success, it is the purpose of this recipe to show you how the log facility in dnsmasq can not only support the use of a standalone logfile, but how you can add dnsmasq to logrotate with the help of a new system user.

Getting ready

To complete this recipe you will require a working installation of the CentOS 6 operating system with root privileges, a static IP address, and a console-based text editor of your choice. It is assumed that you have already installed dnsmasq as a result of the advice provided by the previous recipe.

If you are running a firewall, you will need to confirm that the firewall has been disabled, removed, or the appropriate ports are open. Similarly, if you are running SELinux, then you should confirm that it has been disabled or it is now running in permissive mode.

How to do it...

By default, the output of any log activity will be sent to `/var/log/messages`, however, during the course of this recipe we will learn how to customize this behavior, create an individual logfile in `/var/log` and then add dnsmasq to logrotate to ensure that the practice of automated log rotation is observed. We will start by creating a new system user for the sole purpose of running dnsmasq.

1. To begin, log in as root and type the following command to create a new system group:

    ```
    groupadd -r dnsmasq
    ```

2. Now type the following command to create the new user account:

    ```
    useradd -r -g dnsmasq dnsmasq
    ```

3. Having completed these steps, we will now open the dnsmasq configuration file in order to apply our new user. To do this, simply open the following file in your favorite text editor:

    ```
    vi /etc/logrotate.d/dnsmasq
    ```

4. At the top of this file, add the following lines:

```
user=dnsmasq
group=dnsmasq
pid-file=/var/run/dnsmasq.pid
```

5. Now scroll down to the bottom of the file and add the following lines in order to activate logging:

```
log-queries
log-facility=/var/log/dnsmasq.log
```

6. When you have finished, save and close the file in the usual way before proceeding to restart dnsmasq, like so:

service dnsmasq restart

> At this stage you will now find a dnsmasq-dedicated logfile located at `/var/log/dnsmasq.log`, which will record all server and workstation activity.

7. The next step is to add dnsmasq to logrotate and we will do this by using a simple script. To do this, we will create a new file in your favorite text editor by typing:

vi /etc/logrotate.d/dnsmasq

8. Now add the following lines:

```
/var/log/dnsmasq.log {
missingok
notifempty
delaycompress
sharedscripts
size 200M
weekly
create 0640 dnsmasq dnsmasq
postrotate
       [ ! -f /var/run/dnsmasq.pid ] || kill -USR2 `cat /var/run/
dnsmasq.pid`
endscript}
```

9. Having completed these steps, you can now test your script with the following command:

logrotate -d -f /etc/logrotate.conf

How it works...

Logfiles are always useful, and as this recipe has shown, you can easily enhance your existing dnsmasq service with a customized logfile that not only records the activity of the server and any associated workstations, but one that also will enjoy the benefits of log rotation with logrotate.

So what did we learn from this experience?

We began by creating an unprivileged system user called dnsmasq, which would belong to a new system group called dnsmasq:

```
useradd -r -g dnsmasq dnsmasq
```

The reasons for doing this are purely in order to satisfy the needs of logging; a process that requires dnsmasq to change its identity from the role of root to another known user.

The action of writing logfiles requires permissions and in the case of dnsmasq, when initially run as the root user, the service is then required to drop these initial privileges and run as an unprivileged user. If a known user does not exist, then this new user is nobody, an account that maintains no permissions and owns no files. However, by creating a known user, we can then provide consistency and ensure that the entire process is moderated:

```
#specify the user to which dnsmasq will change after start-up
user=dnsmasq
#specify the group to which the above user belongs
group=dnsmasq
#provide a unique process id
pid-file=/var/run/dnsmasq.pid
```

Having done this, the next step was to activate logging within dnsmasq by adding the following lines:

```
#activate the need to log the results
log-queries
#log all information to the following file
log-facility=/var/log/dnsmasq.log
```

The next step was to save our work and restart the dnsmasq service, like so:

```
service dnsmasq restart
```

At this stage you will now find a dnsmasq-dedicated logfile located at /var/log/dnsmasq.log, which has already started to record all server and workstation activity. But in order to complete the recipe, we took the final steps towards creating a script that will automate the entire process of log rotation with logrotate. To do this, we created the following file:

```
vi /etc/logrotate.d/dnsmasq
```

To which, we then added the following lines:

```
/var/log/dnsmasq.log {
    missingok
    notifempty
    delaycompress
    sharedscripts
    size 200M
    weekly
    create 0640 dnsmasq dnsmasq
    postrotate
        [ ! -f /var/run/dnsmasq.pid ] || kill -USR2 `cat /var/run/
dnsmasq.pid`
    endscript}
```

The preceding script applies similar convention to those found throughout this book and simply implies the need for logrotate to rotate the log `weekly`; over rule this period if the size exceeds `200 MB`; delay compression until rotation is complete; use the required permissions; use the appropriate username and group to apply those permissions; and issue the correct `kill` signal through the registered process `dnsmasq.pid`.

Finally, having saved your work you can now consider testing log rotation by typing:

```
logrotate -d -f /etc/logrotate.conf
```

And should you wish to force a full rotation of all the files, then simply use the following variation:

```
logrotate -f /etc/logrotate.conf
```

So as you can see, with a few minor changes dnsmasq will support all your needs for logging. It is a great package and going beyond personal preferences, for those who want simplicity, it is a far easier tool to use by comparison to setting up a BIND server.

See also

- ▶ The dnsmasq project's home page:
  `http://www.thekelleys.org.uk/dnsmasq/doc.html`

- ▶ The dnsmasq man page:
  `http://www.thekelleys.org.uk/dnsmasq/docs/dnsmasq-man.html`

Enabling domain name wildcards with dnsmasq

In this recipe we will learn how to enhance dnsmasq with domain name wildcards.

Having successfully deployed a local nameserver that supports domain lists, it is the purpose of this recipe to expand on our previous success by establishing a system of automatic domain name creation based on a predefined set of values.

Getting ready

To complete this recipe you will require a working installation of the CentOS 6 operating system with root privileges, a static IP address, and a console-based text editor of your choice. It is assumed that you have already installed dnsmasq as a result of the advice provided by the previous recipes found within this chapter, namely *Deploying a local nameserver with dnsmasq* and *Logging events with dnsmasq and combining this with logrotate*.

If you are running a firewall, you will need to confirm that the firewall has been disabled, removed, or the appropriate ports are open. Similarly, if you are running SELinux, then you should confirm that it has been disabled or it is now running in permissive mode.

How to do it...

In this recipe we will consider expanding the features of dnsmasq as a local nameserver by enabling the use of wildcards for automated domain population.

1. To begin, log in as root and open the configuration file for dnsmasq in your favorite text editor, like so:

   ```
   vi /etc/dnsmasq.conf
   ```

2. By substituting the relevant IP address (XXX.XXX.XXX.XXX) with those most suitable to your own needs, add the following new lines:

   ```
   address=/lan/XXX.XXX.XXX.XXX
   address=/home/XXX.XXX.XXX.XXX
   ```

3. When you have finished, save and close the file in the usual way before proceeding to remove those files that are no longer required:

   ```
   rm /etc/dnsmasq-resolver
   ```

4. To finish, restart the service like so:

   ```
   service dnsmasq restart
   ```

5. To test your new settings, type the following command but take the time to experiment with a random value for both `<sub-domain>` and `<domain>`:

```
dig <sub-domain>.<domain>.lan
```

6. Alternatively, using the same random values for both `<sub-domain>` and `<domain>` you can try:

```
dig <sub-domain>.<domain>.home
```

How it works...

Dnsmasq is without doubt a very simple alternative to BIND, and by completing this recipe you have successfully reduced the burden of managing a list of domain names that may require frequent updates.

So what did we learn from this experience?

We began by editing the dnsmasq configuration file to reflect the following revised settings:

```
user=dnsmasq
group=dnsmasq
pid-file=/var/run/dnsmasq.pid
domain-needed
bogus-priv
no-hosts
dns-forward-max=150
cache-size=1000
neg-ttl=3600
resolv-file=/etc/dnsmasq-resolver
address=/lan/XXX.XXX.XXX.XXX
address=/home/XXX.XXX.XXX.XXX
no-poll
log-queries
log-facility=/var/log/dnsmasq.log
```

As many of the preceding values have accumulated as a result of previous recipes found within this chapter, the main purpose of showing this example was to illustrate the structure of the overall configuration file in order to confirm that the following reference was removed:

```
addn-hosts=/etc/dnsmasq-hosts
```

Next, an action that enabled us to issue a command that would delete the file as it was no longer required:

```
rm /etc/dnsmasq-resolver
```

The next step was to add the following lines by replacing XXX.XXX.XXX.XXX with an IP address used by your server:

```
address=/lan/XXX.XXX.XXX.XXX
address=/home/XXX.XXX.XXX.XXX
```

For example, if your server's IP address was 192.168.1.100, then the preceding lines may look like this:

```
address=/lan/192.168.1.100
address=/home/192.168.1.100
```

Alternatively, you could implement various IP addresses, like so:

```
address=/lan/192.168.1.101
address=/home/192.168.1.100
```

The preceding lines represent the heart of the wildcard feature. By enabling these lines, your server will be able to automatically pass any domain that followed the appropriate naming schema:

```
<any_value>.lan
<any_value>.<any_value>.lan
<any_value>.home
<any_value>.<any_value>.home
```

Based on this, and having issued the following command, a list of domain names would no longer be required.

service dnsmasq restart

To test your new settings, simply nominate a combination of words and letters for any_value (and do try something unusual) and use dig to check the results.

```
dig <any_value>.lan
dig <any_value>.<any_value>.lan
dig <any_value>.home
dig <any_value>.<any_value>.home
```

As you will see, the server will now respond with by providing you with a relevant answer and question section, like so:

```
;; QUESTION SECTION:
;any_value.any_value.          IN      A

;; ANSWER SECTION:
any_value.any_value.    0    IN    A    192.168.1.100
```

In fact, whatever you try, (as long as it ends in either `.lan` or `.home`) it will be shown to function as if you had spent time configuring the zone file or domain list. Moreover, you can expand this criterion by simply adding a new reference in the form of:

```
address=/<top-level-domain>/<server_ip_address>
```

In this instance, the choice of a `top-level-domain` name will determine the naming schema of your dynamic domains and to avoid confusion you should restrict your additions to one of the following: `.home`, `.lan`, `.dev`, or similar.

 Remember, it is important that you do not use `.com`, `.net`, `.co.uk`, `.org` or other values typically associated with the world-wide web. For similar reasons you should also avoid `.local`, which is known to be a reserved name for many packages.

So having completed this recipe, you will now have a fully functioning dynamic DNS system without the complexity of zone files, host files, reverse-DNS, and even domain lists. In fact, every name using the preconfigured `top-level-domain` name will be passed to your server and for this reason it represents a time-saving solution that can be enjoyed by any local network.

See also

▶ The dnsmasq project's home page:
http://www.thekelleys.org.uk/dnsmasq/doc.html

▶ The dnsmasq man page:
http://www.thekelleys.org.uk/dnsmasq/docs/dnsmasq-man.html

Hardening BIND with chroot and providing better security measures

In this recipe we will learn how to harden the basic installation of BIND with a chroot (change root) environment and providing better security measures.

BIND is a service that is in constant communication with the Internet at large and for this reason it remains vulnerable to abuse. Securing BIND can be difficult, but it is the purpose of this recipe to provide a series of configuration changes that will make your server much harder to compromise.

Getting ready

To complete this recipe you will require a working installation of the CentOS 6 operating system with root privileges, a static IP address, and a console-based text editor of your choice. An Internet connection will be required in order to install additional packages. Moreover, it will be assumed that you have already installed BIND as a result of the advice provided by a previous recipe found within this chapter (see *Building a caching-only nameserver with BIND*).

If you are running a firewall, you will need to confirm that the firewall has been disabled, removed, or the appropriate ports are open. Similarly, if you are running SELinux, then you should confirm that it has been disabled or it is now running in permissive mode.

How to do it...

We will begin this recipe by configuring BIND in a chroot (change root) environment. This will require the installation of an additional package known as `bind -chroot`, which will make a permanent change to the location of your zone files.

1. To do this, log in as root and type:

   ```
   yum install bind-chroot
   ```

2. Having installed the relevant package, the first step is to make some basic changes to `/etc/named.conf` in order to provide some additional security measures. To do this, open the following file in your favorite text editor:

   ```
   vi /etc/named.conf
   ```

3. Scroll down to the `options` section and add the following lines:

   ```
   version "Not available";
   fetch-glue no;
   ```

4. At this point you may consider removing recursive queries; although doing this will affect the caching service offered to your workstations. If you would like to proceed, simply make the following modification to your configuration file:

   ```
   recursion no;
   ```

5. Now look for the line that reads:

   ```
   listen-on port 53 { any; };
   ```

6. In this instance we want to bind all activity to a particular IP address. Where `XXX.XXX.XXX.XXX` is your server's IP address, replace the `any` value and make this line read as follows:

   ```
   listen-on port 53 { 127.0.0.1; XXX.XXX.XXX.XXX; };
   ```

7. For additional security measures you may wish to reduce the range of queries from any source to that of your local network only. To do this, find the line that reads:

```
allow-query       { any; };
```

8. Where XXX.XXX.XXX.XXX/24 is your server's IP address, replace the any value and make this line read as follows:

```
allow-query       { 127.0.0.1; XXX.XXX.XXX.0/24; };
```

9. When you have finished, simply save and close the file before proceeding to restart the service, like so:

```
service named restart
```

How it works...

The purpose of this recipe was to show you how quickly you can make a few simple changes that will ultimately serve to harden the basic installation of BIND. Of course, no security measure is considered to be definitive and there is always more that can be done, but during the course of this recipe your attention was drawn to the basic principles of providing better security measures and considering the need for ongoing management.

So what did we learn from this experience?

We started the recipe by installing bind-chroot. To do this, it was simply a matter of typing the following command:

```
yum install bind-chroot
```

Having done this, we have effectively placed BIND in a jail with the intention to employ the principle of damage limitation. In simple terms, this is a process that limits access to other system resources in order to reduce the amount of harm that can be done to a compromised system.

The consequence of running the change root (chroot) package on BIND means that your old files have not been modified, but from this point on, you will need to access /var/named/chroot/ in order to manage your new and existing zone files.

 So remember, the next time you access your system with the intention to manage your new or existing zone files, your working directory has been moved to /var/named/chroot/.

Following this, the next step was to make a few modifications to `named.conf` as detailed here:

```
options {
//make the server listen on local interfaces only
listen-on port 53 { 127.0.0.1; XXX.XXX.XXX.XXX; };

listen-on-v6 port 53 { none; };
directory          "/var/named";
dump-file          "/var/named/data/cache_dump.db";
statistics-file "/var/named/data/named_stats.txt";
             memstatistics-file "/var/named/data/named_mem_stats.txt";

             //allow the queries from local network only
             allow-query     { localhost; XXX.XXX.XXX.0/24; };

//do not display the version number
             version "Not available";

             //disable recursive queries to stop spoofing attacks
             fetch-glue no;
             //keep recursive queries for a caching nameserver
recursion yes;

             //optional, disable recursion if this is a pure domain
name service
             //recursion no;

             dnssec-enable yes;
             dnssec-validation yes;
             dnssec-lookaside auto;

             /* Path to ISC DLV key */
             bindkeys-file "/etc/named.iscdlv.key";
             managed-keys-directory "/var/named/dynamic";
};
```

As shown in the preceding code snippet, disabling `recursion` is optional; and for those of you who want your server to remain a caching nameserver, it is necessary to keep this feature enabled. Based on this, your version of the preceding file will look similar to this:

```
options {
//make the server listen on local interfaces only
listen-on port 53 { 127.0.0.1; XXX.XXX.XXX.XXX; };

listen-on-v6 port 53 { none; };
directory "/var/named";
dump-file "/var/named/data/cache_dump.db";
```

```
statistics-file "/var/named/data/named_stats.txt";
          memstatistics-file "/var/named/data/named_mem_stats.txt";

          //allow the queries from local network only
          allow-query     { localhost; XXX.XXX.XXX.0/24; };

//do not display the version number
          version "Not available";

          //disable recursive queries to stop spoofing attacks
            fetch-glue no;
          //keep recursive queries for a caching nameserver
recursion yes;

          //optional, disable recursion if this is a pure domain
name service
          //recursion yes;

          dnssec-enable yes;
          dnssec-validation yes;
          dnssec-lookaside auto;

          /* Path to ISC DLV key */
          bindkeys-file "/etc/named.iscdlv.key";
          managed-keys-directory "/var/named/dynamic";
};
```

The prospect of hardening your server against a determined third-party will always remain an ongoing challenge, but as a result of this recipe you can now consider that your installation of BIND is a lot harder to compromise.

See also

- ▶ The official BIND home page: `https://www.isc.org/software/bind`
- ▶ *Red Hat Enterprise Linux 4: Reference Guide, Chapter 12. Berkeley Internet Name Domain (BIND)*: `http://www.centos.org/docs/4/html/rhel-rg-en-4/s1-bind-zone.html`
- ▶ *Red Hat Enterprise Linux Deployment Guide, Chapter 17. Berkeley Internet Name Domain (BIND)*: `http://www.centos.org/docs/5/html/5.1/Deployment_Guide/ch-bind.html`
- ▶ *Red Hat Linux 7.2: The Official Red Hat Linux Reference Guide, Chapter 14. Berkeley Internet Name Domain (BIND)*: `http://www.centos.org/docs/2/rhl-rg-en-7.2/ch-bind.html`

8
Working with Databases

In this chapter, we will cover:

- ▶ Installing and hardening MySQL server with `mysql_secure_installation`
- ▶ Creating a MySQL database, adding a MySQL user, and assigning user privilege from the command line
- ▶ Installing PostgreSQL, adding a user, and creating your first database
- ▶ Configuring remote access to PostgreSQL server

Introduction

This chapter is a collection of recipes that delivers the necessary steps that will enable you to deploy the most common database systems by showing you how to consider installing and hardening MySQL server with `mysql_secure_installation`; creating a MySQL database, adding a MySQL user and assigning user privilege from the command line; installing PostgreSQL, adding a user and creating your first database; and configuring remote access to PostgreSQL server.

Installing and hardening MySQL server with mysql_secure_installation

In this recipe we will learn how to install and harden MySQL server by using the `mysql_secure_installation` script that implements the necessary recommendations that will serve to improve the security of your server.

Supporting over 70 collations, more than 30 character sets, multiple storage engines and deployment in virtualized environment; MySQL is a mission-critical database server that is used by production servers all over the world. It is capable of hosting a vast number of individual databases and it can provide support for various roles across your entire network. MySQL server has become synonymous with the World Wide Web(WWW), it is used by desktop software, extends local services and is one of the world's most popular relational database systems. The purpose of this recipe is to show you how to download, install, and lockdown this powerful database server.

Getting ready

To complete this recipe you will require a working installation of the CentOS 6 operating system with root privileges, a console based text editor of your choice and a connection to the Internet in order to facilitate the download of additional packages. It is expected that your server will be using a static IP address.

If you are running a firewall, you will need to confirm that the firewall has been disabled, removed, or the appropriate ports are open. Similarly, if you are running SELinux, then you should confirm that it has been disabled or it is now running in permissive mode.

How to do it...

During the course of this recipe we will employ the recognized installation routine to ensure that the process of installing MySQL server remains safe and secure. Moreover, by using this approach we will not only ensure that this process remains relatively simple, but it will also serve to limit the amount of steps required to complete the overall recipe:

1. To begin, log in as root and type the following command to install the required packages:

    ```
    yum install mysql-server
    ```

2. When complete, ensure the service starts at boot by typing:

    ```
    chkconfig mysqld on
    ```

3. Now start the MySQL service as follows:

    ```
    service mysqld start
    ```

4. Finally, begin the secure installation process with the following command:

    ```
    mysql_secure_installation
    ```

5. When you first run the previous command you will be asked to provide a password, but as this value has not been set, press the *Enter* key to represent the value (blank or) none.

6. Having been asked to `Set root password?`. Choose `Y` and confirm your password. The process will look like this:

```
Set root password? [Y/n] y

New password:

Re-enter new password:

Password updated successfully!

Reloading privilege tables..

    ... Success!
```

7. At the next prompt you will be asked if you would like to remove anonymous users. Unless you require this feature, choose `Y` to proceed.

8. You will then be asked if you wish to disallow remote logins by the root user. Unless you require this feature, choose `Y` to proceed.

9. At the next prompt you will be asked if you wish to remove the test database. Again, unless you need it, choose `Y` to proceed.

10. Finally, you will be asked if you would like to reload the privilege tables. Choose `Y` to complete the installation process which will respond with the following message:

```
All done! If you've completed all of the above steps, your MySQL
installation should now be secure.


Thanks for using MySQL!
```

How it works...

MySQL is a fast, efficient, multithreaded, and robust SQL database server. It supports multiple users, provides access to a number of storage engines and by following a few short steps you now know how to download, install, and lockdown MySQL server by implementing the highly recommended `mysql_secure_installation` script.

So what did we learn from this experience?

We started the recipe by installing the necessary packages by typing the following command:

```
yum install mysql-server
```

Having done this, we then proceeded to ensure that the MySQL deamon (`mysqld`) would start during the boot process:

```
chkconfig mysqld on
```

Before starting the `mysqld` service as follows:

```
service mysqld start
```

At this point we now have a working installation but in order to ensure that our installation was safe we then invoked the secure installation script in order to guide us through a few simple steps that would serve to harden our basic installation.

We did this by typing:

```
mysql_secure_installation
```

As the basic installation process does not enable you to set a default password for the root user, when asked you were simply required to press the *Enter* key.

And for this reason, the first step is to set the root password by choosing Y to proceed:

```
Set root password? [Y/n] y
```

The process was simply a matter of completing the prompts and by doing this you can be certain that no one can access the MySQL root user account without the required authorization:

```
New password:
Re-enter new password:
```

The result of which would result in the following response:

```
Password updated successfully!
Reloading privilege tables..
 ... Success!
```

We then discovered that a typical MySQL installation maintains an anonymous user. The purpose of this is to allow anyone to log into your MySQL server without having to have a valid user account. It is typically used for testing purposes only and unless you are in unique circumstances that require this facility it is always advisable to remove this feature.

Following this, and to ensure that the root user cannot access your MySQL server installation we then opted to disallow remote root access before removing the test database and performing a reload of the privilege tables.

Having completed this recipe we have learned that the process of downloading, installing and locking down MySQL server was very simple. Of course, there are always more things that can be done in order to make the installation useful but the purpose of this recipe was to show you that the most important part of installing your new database system was to make it secure.

Remember, the act of running the `mysql_secure_installation` is recommended for all MySQL servers and it is advisable regardless as to whether you are building a development server or one that is used in a production environment. As a server administrator, security should always remain your top priority.

There's more...

In order to access your MySQL server from the terminal you will need to type the following command:

```
mysql -u root -p
```

The previous command will require a password, so provide the administration password created during the previous stages and you will be greeted as follows:

```
# mysql -u root -p
Enter password:
Welcome to the MySQL monitor.  Commands end with ; or \g.
Your MySQL connection id is 11
Server version: 5.1.61 Source distribution


Copyright (c) 2000, 2011, Oracle and/or its affiliates. All rights
reserved.


Oracle is a registered trademark of Oracle Corporation and/or its
affiliates. Other names may be trademarks of their respective
owners.


Type 'help;' or '\h' for help. Type '\c' to clear the current input
statement.


mysql>
```

Following this, you now have complete access to your MySQL server installation as the root user. For example, to show all databases you would type:

```
show databases;
```

This would result in the following response:

```
mysql> show databases;
+--------------------+
| Database           |
+--------------------+
| information_schema |
| mydbb              |
```

```
| mysql              |
+--------------------+
3 rows in set (0.01 sec)
```

 If you would prefer to use a graphical tool installed on a local workstation then I would suggest looking at MySQL Workbench. It is available for free, it supports various operating systems and you can learn more by reviewing the link at the bottom of this recipe.

In order to exit the MySQL interface at any time you should use the following command:

```
exit
```

See also

> ▸ MySQL Project Homepage: `http://www.mysql.com`
> ▸ MySQL Workbench Project Homepage. A comprehensive visual tool that provides for data modeling, SQL development, server configuration, user administration, and more: `https://www.mysql.com/products/workbench/`

Creating a MySQL database, adding a MySQL user, and assigning user privilege from the command line

In this recipe we will learn how to create a database and a database user for MySQL server.

MySQL server is fast, efficient, and supports a full range of open source solutions. It can be used in conjunction with a wide variety of graphical tools, but in situations where you simply need to create a database and provide an associated user it is often useful to perform this task from the command line. Known as the MySQL Shell, this simple command line facility supports the full range of SQL commands and affords both local and remote access to your database server. It is text based, but the MySQL Shell provides you with complete control over your database server, and for this reason it represents the perfect tool that will enable you to create a new database, add a new database user, and assign the correct permissions in order that you can start your MySQL work.

Getting ready

To complete this recipe you will require a working installation of the CentOS 6 operating system with root privileges. It is expected that MySQL server is already installed and running.

How to do it...

Having successfully installed your MySQL database server, this recipe will consider the need to create a new database, add a new database user and enable the correct permissions in order that the new user account can perform the expected duties. We will achieve this by using the MySQL Shell but in order to complete this task you will need root access to your server.

1. To begin, log in as the root user and type the following command in order to access the MySQL server:

```
mysql -u root -p
```

2. On a successful login you will now be greeted with the MySQL Terminal interface. This feature is signified by the MySQL Shell:

```
mysql>
```

3. In this first step we will create a new database. To do this, simply customize the following command by substituting an appropriate value for the new `<database-name>` value and type:

```
CREATE DATABASE <database-name>;
```

 If this is your first introduction to the MySQL Shell, remember to end each line with a semi-colon (;) and press the *Enter* key after typing each command.

4. Having created your database we will now create a MySQL user. Each user will consist of a username and password that is completely independent of the operating system and a single system user can have multiple MySQL accounts. For reasons of security we will ensure that access is restricted to `localhost`. To proceed, simply customize the following command by changing the values `<username>`, `<password>`, and `<database-name>` to reflect your needs:

```
GRANT ALL PRIVILEGES ON <database-name>.* TO
'<username>'@'localhost' IDENTIFIED BY '<password>' WITH GRANT
OPTION;
```

5. Now enter the following line to complete this process:

   ```
   FLUSH PRIVILEGES;
   ```

6. When you have finished, simply type the following command to exit the MySQL Shell:

   ```
   exit;
   ```

7. Finally, you can test the `<username>` by accessing the MySQL Shell in the following way:

   ```
   mysql -u <username> -p
   ```

How it works...

MySQL is an open source database management system that facilitates the ability to store, organize, and retrieve data. It has become the world's most popular open source database system and during the course of this recipe you were not only shown how to create a database, but you were also shown how to create a database user.

So what did we learn from this experience?

We started the recipe by accessing the MySQL Shell as the root user:

```
mysql -u root -p
```

By doing this, we were then able to create a database with a simple SQL function in the following way:

```
CREATE DATABASE <database-name>;
```

 You can enhance this command by electing to use the full command in the following way:
```
SHOW CREATE DATABASE <database-name>;
```

However, this command can be modified to invoke the need to check if a database name is already in use by using:

```
CREATE DATABASE IF NOT EXISTS <database-name>;
```

In this way, you can then DROP or remove a database by using the following command:

```
DROP DATABASE IF EXISTS <database-name>;
```

The recipe expected that you would customize the actual `<database-name>` value, and having done that it was simply a matter of adding a new database user with the appropriate permissions:

```
GRANT ALL PRIVILEGES ON <database-name>.* TO '<username>'@'localhost'
IDENTIFIED BY '<password>' WITH GRANT OPTION;
```

The use of GRANT OPTION allows the <username> option to grant or remove other user privileges, while the use of ALL PRIVILEGES and <database-name>.* allows that user complete access to a designated <database-name> and all the tables (.*).

In this way, and by running the previous command, you would be providing <username> with full privileges via a defined <password> from localhost.

As a specific <database-name> was elected, then this level of permission would be restricted to that particular database, but as an alternative, you can always decide to minimize the privileges offered in the following way:

```
GRANT SELECT, INSERT, DELETE ON <database-name>.* TO
'<username>'@'localhost' IDENTIFIED BY '<password>' WITH GRANT OPTION;
```

So remember, in order to provide a chosen user with specific permission, you can use the following approach:

```
GRANT [type of permission] ON <database name>.<table
name> TO '<username>'@'localhost';
```

Using the previous technique, here is a summary of the permissions that can be employed:

- CREATE: allows the <username> value to create new tables or databases
- DROP: allows the <username> value to delete tables or databases
- DELETE: allows the <username> value to delete rows from tables
- INSERT: allows the <username> value to insert rows into tables
- SELECT: allows the <username> value to use the Select command to read through databases
- UPDATE: allows the <username> value to update table rows

However, once the privileges have been granted the recipe then showed you that we must FLUSH the system in order to make our new settings available to the system itself.

To do this, it is simply a matter of typing:

```
FLUSH PRIVILEGES;
```

It is important to note that all commands within the MySQL Shell should end in a semicolon (;) and having completed our task we simply exit the console as follows:

```
exit;
```

So having completed this recipe, not only have we learned how to create a MySQL database and user, but we have also been introduced to the concept of assigning privilege. MySQL is an excellent database system but like all services, it can be abused. So remain vigilant at all times, and by considering the previous advice you can be confident that your MySQL installation will remain safe and secure.

There's more...

Creating a restricted user is one way of providing database access but if you have a team of developers who require constant access to a development server you may wish to consider providing a universal user who maintains super user privilege.

To do this, simply access the MySQL Shell in the following way:

```
mysql -u root -p
```

Then create a new user in the following way:

```
GRANT ALL PRIVILEGES ON *.* TO '<username>'@'%' WITH GRANT OPTION;
```

By doing this, you will enable <username> to add, delete, and manage databases across your entire MySQL server, but given the range of administrative features this new user account will have, you may wish to restrict all activity to localhost in the following way:

```
GRANT ALL PRIVILEGES ON *.* TO '<username>'@'localhost' IDENTIFIED BY
'<password>' WITH GRANT OPTION;
```

As it was stated previously, the use of ALL PRIVILEGES allows a MySQL user all access to a designated database, but because there was no specific database name given this would provide them with full server rights.

> So in simple terms, if you wanted to provide <username> with access to any database or to any table, always use an asterisk (*) in the place of the database name or table name.

Finally, every time you update or change a user permission always be sure to use the FLUSH PRIVILEGES command as follows:

```
FLUSH PRIVILEGES;
```

Before exiting the MySQL Shell in the following way:

```
exit;
```

Reviewing and revoking permissions or dropping a user

It is never a good idea to keep user accounts active unless they are used, so your first consideration would be to review their current status by typing:

```
SELECT * FROM mysql.user WHERE USER='<username>';
```

Having done this, if you intend to `revoke` permission(s) or remove that user with the `drop` command you would begin by accessing your MySQL database in the usual way:

```
mysql -u root -p
```

First of all you should review what privileges they have by running:

```
show grants for '<username>'@'localhost';
```

You now have two options, starting with the ability to revoke the user's privileges as follows:

```
revoke all privileges, grant option from '<username>'@'localhost';
```

You may either reallocate privilege using the formula provided in the main recipe:

```
GRANT <type of permission> ON<database name>.<table name> TO
'<username>'@'localhost';
```

Alternatively, you can decide to remove the user by typing:

```
drop user 'username'@'localhost';
```

Finally, and regardless of which option you choose, you should exit the MySQL Shell by using the following command:

```
exit
```

See also

- MySQL Project Homepage, Official Documentation: http://dev.mysql.com/doc/
- MySQL Reference Manual, *MySQL User Account Management*: http://dev.mysql.com/doc/refman/4.1/en/user-account-management.html
- MySQL Project Homepage, *SQL Statement Syntax*: http://dev.mysql.com/doc/refman/5.5/en/sql-syntax.html

Installing PostgreSQL, adding a user, and creating your first database

In this recipe we will not only learn how to install PostgreSQL, but we will discover how to add a new user and create your first database.

PostgreSQL is considered to be the most advanced open source database system in the world. It is known for being a solid, reliable, and well-engineered system that is fully capable of supporting high-transaction, mission-critical applications. PostgreSQL is a descendant of Ingres database, it is community driven, maintained by a large collection of contributors from all over the world but unlike MySQL, it comes in one free flavor. It may not be as flexible or as pervasive as MySQL, but because PostgreSQL is a very secure database system that excels in data integrity, it is the purpose of this recipe to show you how to begin exploring this forgotten friend.

Getting ready

To complete this recipe you will require a working installation of the CentOS 6 operating system with root privileges, a console based text editor of your choice and a connection to the Internet in order to facilitate the download of additional packages. It is expected that your server will be using a static IP address and that you have already configured an appropriate user account.

If you are running a firewall, you will need to confirm that the firewall has been disabled, removed, or the appropriate ports are open. Similarly, if you are running SELinux, then you should confirm that it has been disabled or it is now running in permissive mode.

How to do it...

PostgreSQL (also known as Postgres) is an object-relational database management system. It supports a large part of the SQL standard and it can be extended by the server administrator in many ways. However, in order to begin, we must start by installing the necessary packages:

1. To do this, log in as root and type:

   ```
   yum install postgresql postgresql-server
   ```

2. Having installed the database system we must now enable the database server at boot by typing:

   ```
   chkconfig postgresql on
   ```

3. When you have finished, initialize the database system as follows:

   ```
   service postgresql initdb
   ```

4. Now complete this process by starting the database server by typing:

```
service postgresql start
```

5. We will now assign your current CentOS user account as a database user. To begin, connect to the database server using the following command:

```
su - postgres
```

6. A new database will be created by cloning the standard system database template, so launch the `psql` command-line utility by typing:

```
psql template1
```

7. We will now issue a command to create a database, so by substituting the relevant values with those associated with your system user account type:

```
CREATE USER <username> WITH PASSWORD '<password>';
```

8. Create your first database, replacing the `<database-name>` value with something more appropriate to your needs:

```
CREATE DATABASE <database-name>;
```

9. Now complete the user setup by assigning the correct privileges, substituting the relevant values with those used previously:

```
GRANT ALL PRIVILEGES ON DATABASE <database-name> to <username>;
```

10. When finished, quit the current facility by typing:

```
\q
```

11. And then quit the Postgres console as follows:

```
exit
```

How it works...

PostgreSQL is an Object-Relational Database Management System and it is available to all CentOS servers. Postgres may not be as common as MySQL, but its architecture and large array of features do make it an attractive solution for many companies who are concerned with data integrity. We have discovered that Postgres is an easy-to-install database system; that databases are created by using a system of templates; that it supports a large part of the SQL standard; and because of these features it can be extended by the server administrator.

So what did we learn from this experience?

We began the recipe by installing the necessary packages:

```
yum install postgresql postgresql-server
```

Having done this, we then proceeded to make the system available at boot by typing:

```
chkconfig postgresql on
```

Before initializing the database system:

```
service postgresql initdb
```

We completed this process by starting the database service:

```
service postgresql start
```

In the next stage we were required to connect to the database server in order that we could create our first database. By default, the `postgresql` package creates a new system user called `postgres` and by using this account we were able to access the `psql` command-line facility as follows:

```
su - postgres
-bash-4.1$
```

Following this, we then launched template1, the boilerplate (or default template) that is used to start building databases:

```
psql template1
```

> Unlike MySQL, the following CREATE DATABASE command works by copying the standard system database named template1. In this way you are able to extend PostgreSQL by adding objects to template1, or by creating a new template, and as a result, these objects will be copied into any subsequent user databases.

`psql` is the primary command-line tool for entering SQL queries, and by using this tool we were able to create our first database user that was based on a current system user account as follows:

```
CREATE USER <username> WITH PASSWORD '<password>';
```

Followed by the instruction to create a database:

```
CREATE DATABASE <database-name>;
```

And the option to grant all privileges on the recently created database to the new user:

```
GRANT ALL PRIVILEGES ON DATABASE <database-name> to <username>;
```

Having completed this task we simply exited the `psql` command-line tool using the following command:

`\q`

Before exiting the main console as follows:

`exit`

Of course, there is always more to learn and it is true to say that there are many different approaches to install PostgreSQL. However, having completed this recipe you could say that you not only know how to install PostgreSQL, but this process has served to highlight some simple architectural differences between this database system and MySQL.

There's more...

Having installed and configured your PostgreSQL database server you may wish to alter the logging parameters in order that you can customize the recorded values.

To do this, open the main configuration by typing:

`vi /var/lib/pgsql/data/postgresql.conf`

Scroll down and find the following line that starts with the following:

`log_line_prefix`

Now change this line to read something like the following:

`log_line_prefix = '%d %u %t'`

The previous commands will use the database name, username, and timestamp format when writing the `log` files, and when complete, simply save the file and restart the database server by typing the following command:

`service postgresql restart`

Connecting to PostgreSQL

PostgreSQL is not MySQL and connecting using `psql` is very different, so having completed the previous recipe you may be wondering how you can access your database(s).

To begin, simply issue the following command:

`su - postgres`

Access the interactive screen by typing:

`psql template1`

Depending on the type of connection method you are using you may be asked to supply your password, but on success you will be greeted as follows:

```
# su - postgres
-bash-4.1$ psql template1
Password:
psql (8.4.13)
Type "help" for help.


template1=#
```

From this point on you can use SQL to complete any template related task, but when your duties are complete, you can quit the terminal by typing:

```
\q
```

This command will return you to the `postgres` user prompt, which you can close at any time by issuing the following command:

```
exit
```

Accessing a PostgreSQL database using psql

If you wish to access a specific database as a specific user you would begin by accessing the main terminal with the `postgres` user as follows:

```
su - postgres
```

Having done this you would access the relevant database by using the appropriate user in the following way:

```
psql -d <database-name> -U <username> -W
```

Complete this process by submitting your password when requested and you will be greeted appropriately.

The entire process may look similar to this:

```
su - postgres
-bash-4.1$ psql -d <database-name> -U <username> -W
Password for user <username>:
psql (8.4.13)
Type "help" for help.


<database-name>=>
```

Creating a copy of a database in PostgreSQL

Postgres allows the use of any existing database on the server as a template when creating a new database. To do this, simply access the `psql` console using the previously mentioned `postgres` user and use the following command:

```
CREATE DATABASE <new-database-name> WITH TEMPLATE <original-database-
name> OWNER <username>;
```

You should be aware that the original database should be idle in order for this command to work without error.

See also

- ▶ PostgreSQL Project Homepage: `http://www.postgresql.org/`
- ▶ PostgreSQL Manuals: `http://www.postgresql.org/docs/manuals/`
- ▶ Learn more at Planet PostgreSQL: `http://planet.postgresql.org/`
- ▶ PostgreSQL Wiki: `http://wiki.postgresql.org/wiki/FAQ`
- ▶ PostgreSQL Project, Administration pages: `http://www.postgresql.org/docs/8.4/static/admin.html`

Configuring remote access to PostgreSQL

In this recipe we will learn how to configure local and remote access to PostgreSQL.

PostgreSQL can be configured to allow remote access and yet it is not always obvious how this can be achieved. PostgreSQL employs a method called Host Based Authentication and it is the purpose of this recipe to show you how to troubleshoot client authentication in order to provide the access rights you need to run a safe and secure database server.

Getting ready

To complete this recipe you will require a working installation of the CentOS 6 operating system with root privileges and a text editor of your choice. It is expected that PostgreSQL is already installed and running.

How to do it...

The PostgreSQL client authentication is controlled using a system known as host-based authentication and to make any changes we will need to access the main configuration file:

1. To do this, log in as root and open the Host Based Authentication configuration file in your favorite text editor by typing:

    ```
    vi /var/lib/pgsql/data/pg_hba.conf
    ```

2. Scroll down and locate the following section at the bottom of this file:

    ```
    # "local" is for Unix domain socket connections only
    ```

3. By replacing the XXX.XXX.XXX.XXX/XX value with a value more suitable to your own needs, make these lines read as follows:

    ```
    local   all         all                                  trust
    # IPv4 local connections:
    host    all         all         127.0.0.1/32             trust
    host    all         all         XXX.XXX.XXX.XXX/XX        md5
    ```

     If the IP address of your server was 192.168.1.100 then the value used in the previous example would be 192.168.1.0/24.

4. When you have finished, simply save and close the file in the usual way before typing:

    ```
    vi /var/lib/pgsql/data/postgresql.conf
    ```

5. And make the following adjustments:

    ```
    listen_addresses = '*'
    port = 5432
    ```

     Instead of applying a wildcard, you can also set listen_address to a specific IP address or a pre-determined range of IP addresses using a comma separated list.

6. When you have finished, simple save the file in the usual way before restarting the database server by typing the following command:

    ```
    service postgresql restart
    ```

How it works...

PostgreSQL is a safe and secure database system but where we access it (either remotely or locally) can often become a cause of confusion. It was the purpose of this recipe to lift the lid on Host Based Authentication and provide an easy to use solution that will enable you to get your system up and running.

So what did we learn from this experience?

We began the recipe by opening the Host Based Authentication configuration file with your favorite text editor in the following way:

```
vi /var/lib/pgsql/data/pg_hba.conf
```

We then located the relevant section and made the appropriate changes to enable easy access both locally and remotely:

```
# TYPE   DATABASE      USER          CIDR-ADDRESS          METHOD
# "local" is for Unix domain socket connections only
local    all           all                                 trust
# IPv4 local connections:
host     all           all           127.0.0.1/32          trust
host     all           all           XXX.XXX.XXX.XXX/XX   md5
# IPv6 local connections:
host     all           all           ::1/128               ident
```

Each of the previous records specifies a connection type, database name, a user name, a client IP address range, and the authentication method. Of course, an IP address range may not always be relevant but PostgreSQL will read this file in order and if a single record indicates that access is not allowed, then access will be denied.

Many of the previous commands may already be understood but it is important to realize that there are several different methods of authentication:

- ▶ `trust`: allows the connection unconditionally and it enables anyone to connect with the database server without the need for a password.
- ▶ `reject`: allows the database server to reject a connection unconditionally. A feature that remains useful when filtering certain IP addresses or certain hosts from a group.
- ▶ `md5`: implies that the client needs to supply an MD5-encrypted password for authentication.

Having completed this task, we then saved and closed the file before opening the main PostgreSQL configuration file located at `/var/lib/pgsql/data/postgresql.conf` to make the following adjustments:

```
listen_addresses = '*'

port = 5432
```

As you may or may not be aware, remote connections will not be possible unless the server is started with an appropriate value for `listen_addresses`, and where the default setting placed this on a local loopback address it was necessary to allow the database server to listen to all IP addresses (signified by the use of a star symbol or `*`) on the `5432` port.

When you were finished, we simply saved the file and restarted the database server by typing the following command:

```
service postgresql restart
```

There is always much more to learn, but as a result of completing this recipe you not only have a better understanding of Host Based Authentication but you will have the ability to access your PostgreSQL database server both locally and remotely.

See also

> ▸ PostgreSQL Project Homepage: `http://www.postgresql.org/`

9
Providing Mail Services

In this chapter, we will cover:

- ▶ Enabling a domain-wide **Mail Transport Agent** (**MTA**) and testing your SMTP configuration with Telnet
- ▶ Building a local POP3/SMTP server with Postfix and Dovecot
- ▶ Closing the open relay, enabling SMTP authentication and dealing with Spam by configuring SASL, and enabling Postfix header and body checks
- ▶ Using Postfix and Dovecot to serve e-mail across virtual domains

Introduction

Providing mail services contains a series of recipes that provides an introduction to build your very own CentOS based mail server solution. This guide is suitable for any local network and can be used as a starting point for taking your mail server online. However, unlike previous sections of this book, it is recommended that you work through this chapter, recipe by recipe in the order they are presented with the intention to enable a domain-wide MTA and test your SMTP configuration with Telnet, building a local POP3/SMTP server with Postfix and Dovecot, closing the open relay, enabling SMTP authentication, dealing with spam by configuring SASL, enabling the postfix header and body checks, and using Postfix and Dovecot to serve e-mail across virtual domains.

Enabling a domain-wide Mail Transport Agent (MTA) and testing your SMTP configuration with Telnet

In this recipe, we will learn how to configure Postfix as a domain-wide MTA and test your SMTP configuration with Telnet.

Postfix is now the default MTA for CentOS but by default it does not accept network connections from any host other than the localhost. This is quite restrictive. So the purpose of this recipe is to show you how to configure Postfix to accept incoming connections on all interfaces, to setup a mailbox for each user, to enable a domain-wide MTA, and to test your resulting SMTP configuration with Telnet.

Getting ready

To complete this recipe you will require a working installation of the CentOS 6 operating system with root privileges, a console based text editor of your choice and a connection to the Internet in order to facilitate the download of additional packages. It is expected that your server will be using a static IP address that it maintains on one or more system user accounts and that it employs a FQDN. It is also assumed that you are working through this chapter, recipe by recipe in the order that they appear.

If you are running a firewall, you will need to confirm that the firewall has been disabled, removed, or the appropriate ports are open. Similarly, if you are running SELinux, then you should confirm that it has been disabled or it is now running in permissive mode.

How to do it...

Postfix is installed by default and it should be in a running state. However, before we begin modifying the MTA it is important that we install the Telnet service in order that we can test the resulting configuration changes:

1. To do this, log in as root and type the following command to install the Telnet service:

   ```
   yum install telnet
   ```

2. Now open the main Postfix configuration file by typing:

   ```
   vi /etc/postfix/main.cf
   ```

3. First of all we will want Postfix to listen on all interfaces. So scroll down and update the following line that starts with `inet_interfaces` to read:

   ```
   inet_interfaces = all
   ```

4. With the intention that this server may become a domain-wide mail server you should now update the following line that starts with `mydestination` to read:

   ```
   mydestination = $myhostname, localhost.$mydomain, localhost,
   $mydomain
   ```

5. We now need to specify the pathname of a mailbox file relative to a user's home directory. To do this, scroll down and locate the line that begins with `home_mailbox` and uncomment the following option:

   ```
   home_mailbox = Maildir/
   ```

6. Now scroll down and make sure that the following line remains commented out:

   ```
   #mail_spool_directory = /var/spool/mail
   ```

7. Now save and close the file in the usual way before restarting the Postfix service as follows:

   ```
   service postfix restart
   ```

8. Having finished the basic configuration of Postfix we will now proceed to test the MTA with Telnet. To do this, we will begin by opening a Telnet session in the following way:

   ```
   telnet localhost smtp
   ```

9. Having done this, your server should respond as follows:

   ```
   Trying 127.0.0.1...

   Connected to localhost

   Escape character is '^]'

   220 servername.localdomain ESMTP Postfix
   ```

10. Now type the following:

    ```
    ehlo localhost
    ```

11. Having done this, your server should respond as follows:

    ```
    250-servername.localdomain
    250-PIPELINING
    250-SIZE 10240000
    250-VRFY
    250-ETRN
    250-ENHANCEDSTATUSCODES
    250-8BITMIME
    250 DSN
    ```

12. We will now send a message. So replace the `<username>` value with a valid system account and type the following command:

    ```
    mail from:<username>
    ```

13. Now press the *Enter* key and the terminal will respond in the following way:

    ```
    250 2.1.0 Ok
    ```

14. Now replace the `<recipient>` value with either a valid user account or a third party e-mail address and type the following command:

    ```
    rcpt to:<recipient>
    ```

15. Press the *Enter* key to continue and the terminal should respond as follows:

    ```
    250 2.1.5 Ok
    ```

16. Now type the following command in order that we can create a simple message:

    ```
    data
    ```

17. The terminal will now respond as follows:

    ```
    354 End data with <CR><LF>.<CR><LF>
    ```

18. Now type your message. Remember to keep it simple, so you could type:

    ```
    Hello, this is a test message.
    ```

19. When you complete typing, press the *Enter* key and use a . key to finish the process as follows:

    ```
    .
    ```

20. On success, the terminal should respond in the following way:

    ```
    250 2.0.0 Ok: queued as 6A35D19F61A
    ```

21. To quit the Telnet session, type:

    ```
    quit
    ```

22. At this stage your first e-mail should be on route to its destination, meanwhile the terminal will now respond as follows:

    ```
    221 2.0.0 Bye
    Connection closed by foreign host.
    ```

How it works...

Having successfully completed this recipe you now have the ability to send basic e-mail messages from a CentOS server and by completing this recipe you have seen how quickly the initial installation of Postfix can be modified to support this task. Of course, this is only the first stage of developing a mail server solution and some restrictions are still enforced, but with the help of Telnet, you can now test your settings and remain confident that you are moving in the right direction.

So what did we learn from this experience?

At the beginning of this recipe you were shown how to install Telnet and make a few simple adjustments to the main Postfix configuration file which can be summarized as follows:

```
#set the network interface that Postfix can send email on.
inet_interfaces = all
```

```
#set the list of domains that will be managed by this server.
mydestination = $myhostname, localhost.$mydomain, localhost, $mydomain
```

```
#set the path of the mailbox relative to the users home directory.
home_mailbox = Maildir/
```

We also ensured that the `mail_spool_directory` lines were commented out in order that they do not override the `home_mailbox` settings as follows:

```
#mail_spool_directory = /var/spool/mail
```

Postfix is already configured to start at boot but to complete this part of the recipe we then restarted the Postfix service in order that it would accept the new configuration settings.

To do this, we simply typed:

```
service postfix restart
```

At this stage the process of configuring Postfix was complete, but to test the changes made, we then used a Telnet session to confirm that Postfix was indeed working as required.

The Telnet session was started by typing as follows:

```
telnet localhost smtp
```

Telnet has been around for quite a long time, but it is an extremely useful tool for troubleshooting issues related to SMTP. For example, it can be use to verify that SMTP is installed properly and that your server is accessible over the Internet, it can be used to attempt mail delivery directly over the TCP port, to determine that your server is accepting connections, to determine if a firewall is blocking a connection, and ensure that a single user domain not can only send mail but they can also receive mail.

A detailed description of how Telnet works is beyond the purpose of this recipe, but a full transcript of your session would look similar to this:

```
Trying 127.0.0.1...
Connected to localhost.
Escape character is '^]'.
220 <servername>.localdomain ESMTP Postfix
ehlo localhost
250-<servername>.localdomain
250-PIPELINING
250-SIZE 10240000
250-VRFY
250-ETRN
250-ENHANCEDSTATUSCODES
250-8BITMIME
250 DSN
mail from:<username>
250 2.1.0 Ok
rcpt to:<recipient>
250 2.1.5 Ok
data
354 End data with <CR><LF>.<CR><LF>
Hello, this is a test message.
.
250 2.0.0 Ok: queued as 6BD9019F61A
quit
221 2.0.0 Bye
Connection closed by foreign host.
```

Having done this, you should have received a test message and as a result you will be happy to know that everything is working correctly. However, if you did happen to encounter any errors you should always refer to the `log` file located at `/var/log/maillog`.

There's more...

Having completed the above recipe you would have noticed that your message may have been issued from `username@servername.domainname`. However, as it is expected that you are using a fully qualified domain name you may be wondering how to update these settings to reflect a more friendly form such as `username@mail.domain.home`.

To do this, simply open the main configuration file by typing:

```
vi /etc/postfix/main.cf
```

First of all we would like to update the Internet-based hostname of the mailing system. So simply scroll down and update the following line to reflect your needs:

```
myhostname = hostname.domain-name.tld
```

We now need to set the `domain-name` of the mail server. We can do this by updating the next line with your `domain-name` only:

```
mydomain = domain-name.tld
```

Now uncomment the following line to determine the origin:

```
myorigin = $myhostname
```

Finally, and depending on the role of your mail server, you can modify the trust and relay controls to reflect your local conditions. This is a list of trusted IP addresses that may or may not send e-mail, which is always useful for an internal network. To do this, find the following lines:

```
#mynetworks = 168.100.189.0/28, 127.0.0.0/8
#mynetworks = $config_directory/mynetworks
#mynetworks = hash:/etc/postfix/network_table
```

And add the following new line by customizing the IP value `XXX.XXX.XXX.XXX/XX` as required:

```
mynetworks = XXX.XXX.XXX.XXX/XX, 127.0.0.0/8
```

For example, if your server IP address was 192.168.1.100, then you could use the following settings:

```
mynetworks = 192.168.1.0/24, 127.0.0.0/8
```

Now, before trying a new Telnet session to review your work, remember to restart Postfix with the following command in order that your changes take immediate effect:

```
service postfix restart
```

Now test your settings using Telnet using the method outlined in the main recipe. Again, if you experience any difficulties, simply check the `log` file located at `/var/log/maillog`.

See also

- ▸ Postfix Project Homepage: `http://www.postfix.org`
- ▸ Postfix Project Documentation, *Postfix Basic Configuration*: `http://www.postfix.org/BASIC_CONFIGURATION_README.html`
- ▸ CentOS Project Postfix HowTo: `http://wiki.centos.org/HowTos/Postfix`

Building a local POP3/SMTP server with Postfix and Dovecot

In this recipe we will learn how to configure Postfix to work with Dovecot in order to provide a basic POP3/SMTP service.

In a previous recipe you were shown how to configure Postfix as a domain-wide MTA and test your settings with Telnet. As a MTA, Postfix does a remarkable job but by working together with Dovecot, you are able to allow users to access their email by using the typical POP3 or IMAP protocols. Most professional server administrators would agree that Postfix and Dovecot are perfect partners and it is the purpose of this recipe to show you how to configure Dovecot in order that you can provide an industry standard mail service for your users across the local network.

Getting ready

To complete this recipe you will require a working installation of the CentOS 6 operating system with root privileges, a console-based text editor of your choice and a connection to the Internet in order to facilitate the download of additional packages. It is expected that your server will be using a static IP address; that it maintains one or more system user accounts; and that it employs a FQDN. It is also assumed that you are working through this chapter, recipe by recipe in the order that they appear and for this reason it is expected that Postfix has been configured as a domain-wide MTA.

 This recipe serves as a guide to setting up a basic POP3/SMTP service for trusted users on a local network. It is not suitable for general Internet use without applying additional security measures.

How to do it...

Dovecot is not installed by default and for this reason we must begin by installing the necessary packages by following the given steps:

1. To do this, log in as root and install Dovecot by typing the following command:

   ```
   yum install dovecot
   ```

2. Once installed, enable the Dovecot service at boot by typing:

   ```
   chkconfig dovecot on
   ```

3. Now open the main Dovecot configuration file in your favorite text editor by typing:

   ```
   vi /etc/dovecot/dovecot.cf
   ```

4. Begin by confirming the protocols we want to use by un-commenting the following line:

   ```
   protocols = imap pop3 lmtp
   ```

5. Now save and close the file in the usual way before opening the following file in your favorite text editor:

   ```
   vi /etc/dovecot/conf.d/10-mail.conf
   ```

6. Scroll down and uncomment the following line:

   ```
   mail_location = maildir:~/Maildir
   ```

7. Again, save and close the file in the usual way before opening the following file in your favorite text editor:

   ```
   vi /etc/dovecot/conf.d/20-pop3.conf
   ```

8. Start by uncommenting the following line:

   ```
   pop3_uidl_format = %08Xu%08Xv
   ```

9. Now scroll down and amend the following line:

   ```
   pop3_client_workarounds = outlook-no-nuls oe-ns-eoh
   ```

10. Save and close the file in the usual way. In our final configuration setting we will now allow for plain text logins. To do this, open the following file in your favorite text editor:

    ```
    vi /etc/dovecot/conf.d/10-auth.conf
    ```

11. Change the following line to state:

    ```
    disable_plaintext_auth = no
    ```

12. Now scroll down and ensure the following line reads:

    ```
    auth_mechanisms = plain
    ```

13. Now, save and close the file before starting the Dovecot service:

```
service dovecot start
```

How it works...

Unless your server is on the Internet and maintains a registered domain name, the activity of sending e-mail messages will be restricted to your local area network but having successfully completed this recipe you have just created a basic POP3/SMTP service for all valid server users. Of course, there is still much more that can be done to enhance the service, but you can now enable all local system account holders to configure their desktop software to send e-mail messages using your server.

So what did we learn from this experience?

We started the recipe by installing Dovecot:

```
yum install dovecot
```

Having done this, we then enabled Dovecot to run at boot before proceeding to make a few brief changes to series configuration files.

Starting with the need to determine which protocol would be used in /etc/dovecot/ dovecot.cf these initial changes were as follows:

```
protocols = imap pop3 lmtp
```

We then confirmed the mail directory location in /etc/dovecot/conf.d/10-mail.conf:

```
mail_location = maildir:~/Maildir
```

Following this, we then opened the POP3 protocol in /etc/dovecot/conf.d/20-pop3. conf by adding a fix relating to various e-mail clients:

```
pop3_uidl_format = %08Xu%08Xv
pop3_client_workarounds = outlook-no-nuls oe-ns-eoh
```

Finally, we enabled plain text authorization by making several changes to /etc/dovecot/ conf.d/10-auth.conf. We did this by applying the following rule set:

```
disable_plaintext_auth = no
auth_mechanisms = plain login
```

SMTP provides an access control mechanism that enables you to manage how users may access an account, but because we were concentrating on a local area network (for a group of trusted server users) then by allowing plain login we should not necessarily see this as a risk. Remember, if you happen to encounter any errors you should always refer to the log file located at /var/log/maillog.

There's more...

In the main recipe you were shown how to install Dovecot in order to enable trusted local users with system accounts to send and receive e-mails. Users will be able to use their existing username for the basis of their e-mail address, but by making a few enhancements you can quickly enable aliases.

To start building a list of user aliases you would begin by opening the following file in your favorite text editor:

```
vi /etc/aliases
```

Now add your new identities, where `<username>` would be the name of the actual system account:

```
#users aliases for mail

newusernamea:    <username>

newusernameb:    <username>
```

For example, if you had a user called `henry` who currently (only) accepted e-mail at `henry@domain-name.home`, but you wanted to create a new alias for `henry` called `marketing@domain-name.home` you would write:

```
#users aliases for mail

marketing:    henry
```

Repeat this action for all aliases, but when you have finished, remember to save and close the file in the usual way before running the following command:

```
newaliases
```

Again, if you experience any difficulties, simply check the `log` file located at `/var/log/maillog`.

Setting up e-mail software

There are a vast number of e-mail clients on the open market and by now, you will want to start setting up your local users to be able to send and receive e-mail. This isn't complicated by any means, but in order to give you a good starting point you will want to consider the following principles.

The format of the e-mail address will be `system_username@domain-name.home`.

The incoming POP3 settings will be similar to the following:

```
mail. domain-name.home
Port 110
Username: system_username
Connection Security: None
Authentication: Password/None
```

The outgoing SMTP settings will be similar to the following:

```
mail. domain-name.home
Port 25
Username: system_username
Connection Security: None
Authentication: None
```

Depending on your network conditions your users should now be able to send e-mails to third-party servers such as Hotmail, Google Mail, or any other domain on the World Wide Web. However, do not consider using this recipe for use on a server located beyond the boundary of a trusted network (that is on the World Wide Web). For that purpose you will need to consider using a registered domain name, enabling incoming connections from an external source, and SMTP-Authorization (that is discussed later in this chapter).

See also

▶ Postfix Project Homepage : `http://www.postfix.org`

▶ CentOS Project Postfix, HowTo: `http://wiki.centos.org/HowTos/Postfix`

Closing the open relay, enabling SMTP authentication and dealing with Spam by configuring SASL, and enabling Postfix header and body checks

In this recipe we will learn how to configure Postfix to work with Dovecot in order to provide a local POP3/SMTP service that can support SMTP authentication and serve to reduce spam.

In today's world, running a mail server can be a hazardous occupation. Spam is always a consideration, whether you are receiving this type of unwanted mail or worried that your server may be assisting spammers to distribute this type of content. It is the purpose of this recipe to provide a starting point that shows you how to set up and configure your mail server in such a way that it will not only make you feel more confident, but it will also provide a safer and more secure approach to manage mail across any network.

Getting ready

To complete this recipe you will require a working installation of the CentOS 6 operating system with root privileges and a console based text editor of your choice. It is expected that your server will be using a static IP address that maintains one or more system user accounts; and employs a FQDN. It is also assumed that you are working through this chapter, recipe by recipe in the order that they appear.

If you are running a firewall, you will need to confirm that the firewall has been disabled, removed, or the appropriate ports are open. Similarly, if you are running SELinux, then you should confirm that it has been disabled or it is now running in permissive mode.

How to do it...

SMTP Authentication is an extension to the SMTP and simply requires the user to log in using an authentication process chosen by you. Most professional administrators would argue that this is without doubt a highly recommended way of running your mail services and this is where we will begin:

1. Log in as root and open the following file with your preferred text editor:

   ```
   vi /etc/dovecot/conf.d/10-master.conf
   ```

2. Scroll down and find the following lines:

   ```
   # Postfix smtp-auth
    #unix_listener /var/spool/postfix/private/auth {
    #   mode = 0666
    #}
   ```

3. Change them as follows:

   ```
   # Postfix smtp-auth
    unix_listener /var/spool/postfix/private/auth {
       mode = 0666
       user = postfix
       group = postfix
    }
   ```

4. Now save and close the file in the usual way before opening the following file in your favorite text editor:

   ```
   vi /etc/dovecot/conf.d/10-mail.conf
   ```

5. Ensure the following lines read as follows:

   ```
   disable_plaintext_auth = no
   auth_mechanisms = plain login
   ```

6. Now save and close the file before opening the main Postfix configuration file:

   ```
   vi /etc/postfix/main.cf
   ```

7. Scroll down and find the following line and change it to read:

   ```
   mynetworks = 127.0.0.0/8
   ```

8. Now scroll down to the bottom of the file and add the following lines:

   ```
   smtpd_sasl_type = dovecot
   smtpd_sasl_path = private/auth
   smtpd_sasl_auth_enable = yes
   smtpd_recipient_restrictions = permit_mynetworks, permit_sasl_
   authenticated, reject_unath_destination
   broken_sasl_auth_clients = yes
   ```

9. Again, save and close the file in the usual way before ensuring that the SASL service will start at boot with the following command:

   ```
   chkconfig saslauthd on
   ```

10. At this stage you can now start the SASL daemon by typing:

    ```
    service saslauthd start
    ```

11. We shall now turn our attention to deal with unwanted e-mail by activating the Postfix header and body checks. To do this, open the main configuration by typing:

    ```
    vi /etc/postfix/header_checks
    ```

12. Now scroll to the bottom of this file and add the following new lines:

    ```
    /^From:.*<#.*@.*>/ REJECT
    /^Return-Path:.*<#.*@.*>/ REJECT
    /^Subject:.*unwantedkeyword1/ DISCARD
    /^Subject:.*unwantedkeyword2/ DISCARD
    /^Subject:.*unwantedkeyword3/ DISCARD
    /^Subject:.*unwantedkeyword4/ DISCARD
    ```

13. Remember to customize the unwantedkeyword value by adding as many entries as you need, and when you have finished, simply save and close your work in the usual way before creating the body_checks file in the following way:

    ```
    vi /etc/postfix/body_checks
    ```

14. Add the following line:

```
/^(|[^>].*)unwanteddomain1.com/ REJECT
/^(|[^>].*)unwanteddomain2.com/ REJECT
/^(|[^>].*)unwanteddomain3.com/ REJECT
```

15. Again, remember to customize the `unwanteddomain` value by adding as many additional entries as you need, and when you have finished, simply save and close your work in the usual way before opening the main Postfix configuration file and uncommenting the following line:

```
#header_checks = regexp:/etc/postfix/header_checks
```

16. Then add the following line (underneath):

```
body_checks = regexp:/etc/postfix/body_checks
```

17. Scroll down further and find the following lines:

```
#smtpd_banner = $myhostname ESMTP $mail_name
#smtpd_banner = $myhostname ESMTP $mail_name ($mail_version)
```

18. Leave the previous lines commented out and add the following line:

```
smtpd_banner = $myhostname ESMTP
```

At this point and as an option you can also include additional restrictions based on limiting the actual e-mail size and the size of a mailbox. To do this, add the following lines:
```
message_size_limit = (value expressed in KB)
mailbox_size_limit = (value expressed in KB)
```

19. When you have finished, save and close your work before restarting the Postfix and Dovecot service in order for you new settings to take effect:

```
service postfix restart && service dovecot restart
```

How it works...

Dealing with the risk of spam is a high priority for any mail server. Of course, there is also more that can be done and additional packages that can be used, but by completing this recipe you now have a better understanding of how to close the open mail relay and harden your server against unwanted e-mails.

So what did we learn from this experience?

Knowing that the default user and group is `Postfix`, we started the recipe by configuring the `unix_listener` with required user/group based settings:

```
# Postfix smtp-auth
  unix_listener /var/spool/postfix/private/auth {
    mode = 0666
    user = postfix
    group = postfix
  }
```

We then proceeded to confirm the required login mechanisms with a caveat for certain e-mail clients that may have issues to log on even though you may have confirmed that My Server Requires Authentication:

```
disable_plaintext_auth = no
auth_mechanisms = plain login
```

Finally, after confirming that we will only trust `localhost` to send e-mails outside of the network:

```
mynetworks = 127.0.0.0/8
```

The recipe activated `sasl` and applied the relevant `sasl` common settings, protocols, and keys in the following way:

```
smtpd_sasl_type = dovecot
smtpd_sasl_path = private/auth
smtpd_sasl_auth_enable = yes
smtpd_recipient_restrictions = permit_mynetworks, permit_sasl_
authenticated, reject_unath_destination
broken_sasl_auth_clients = yes
```

Having done this we then activated `sasl` at boot:

```
chkconfig saslauthd on
```

Before restarting our mail servers services:

```
service saslauthd start
service postfix restart
service dovecot restart
```

After completing the previous steps, we then proceeded by opening the Postfix header file and added the following code:

```
/^From:.*<#.*@.*>/ REJECT
/^Return-Path:.*<#.*@.*>/ REJECT
/^Subject:.*unwantedkeyword1/ DISCARD
/^Subject:.*unwantedkeyword2/ DISCARD
/^Subject:.*unwantedkeyword3/ DISCARD
/^Subject:.*unwantedkeyword4/ DISCARD
```

Our intention at this stage was to set up a few basic rules that Postfix would follow in order to reject or discard unwanted header based content, and in the previous case, if the unwantedkeyword value appears in the subject line, then the e-mail will be discarded.

You had the opportunity to include as many additional statements as required by simply substituting X with a sequential value and repeating the following line:

```
/^Subject:.*unwantedkeywordX/ DISCARD
```

Similarly, with regards to body_checks we then created the relevant file by typing vi /etc/postfix/body_checks and adding code that would deny access to our mail server if a particular domain was found:

```
/^(|[^>].*)unwanteddomain1.com/ REJECT
/^(|[^>].*)unwanteddomain2.com/ REJECT
/^(|[^>].*)unwanteddomain3.com/ REJECT
```

Again, you were given the opportunity to include as many additional statements as required by simply substituting XXXXXXXXXXXX with a domain value and repeating the following line:

```
/^(|[^>].*)XXXXXXXXXXXX.com/ REJECT
```

Having done this we then opened the main Postfix configuration file, activated our new header and body check settings before providing a relative value for the SMTP banner as follows:

```
smtpd_banner = $myhostname ESMTP
```

The previous instruction is used to inform Postfix that system name is used in headers of any received mail.

Finally, having made the configuration changes, we then restarted the required services:

```
service postfix restart && service dovecot restart
```

If you do happen to encounter any errors you should always refer to the log file located at /var/log/maillog.

So as it can be seen, while SMTP provides an access control mechanism which will enable you to relay e-mails, the necessary activation of a `sasl` will serve to close the open relay and reduce the amount of unwanted attention your mail server may attract. Moreover, having initiated the header and body checks, you are now able to control the type of content received and from where the content can be issued, and for this reason you will always stay in control of how it all works and who of your users can e-mail.

There's more...

Having completed the previous recipe you can now test your mail relay settings by running the following Telnet session:

```
telnet <your_server_name>
```

When you are connected, type the following:

```
ehlo localhost
```

Then follow this by initiating the process to create a simple e-mail:

```
mail from:<your_username_here>
```

Specify a third party (non-local) e-mail address as the recipient as follows:

```
rcpt to:<username@some_external_domain.com>
```

If your configuration is correct you should see the following response:

```
Relay access denied
```

When complete, type `quit` to exit the Telnet session and remember, if you do happen to encounter any errors you should always refer to the `log` file located at `/var/log/maillog`.

Setting up e-mail software with SMTP authentication

Naturally, you will want to put the previous recipe in action straight away but before you do, remember that you will need to make a simple modification to the e-mail clients of your users.

The e-mail address format will remain unchanged:

```
system_username@servername.lan
```

However, due to the changes implied by the previous recipe the outgoing SMTP settings will require user based authentication as follows:

```
#Outgoing SMTP settings:
mail. domain-name.home
Port 25
```

```
Username: system_username
```

Connection Security: None

Authentication: Password (based on the username and password)

You will be glad to know that the original incoming e-mail settings will require no further attention and you can continue to follow these principles:

```
#Incoming POP3 settings:
mail. domain-name.home
Port 110
```

Username: system_username

Connection Security: None

Authentication: Password/None

See also

- ▸ Postfix Project Home page: `http://www.postfix.org`
- ▸ *Configuring SASL to use saslauthd*: `http://postfix.state-of-mind.de/patrick.koetter/smtpauth/sasl_configuration.html`
- ▸ *Basic Postfix configuration and preparation for SMTP AUTH*: `http://postfix.state-of-mind.de/patrick.koetter/smtpauth/postfix_configuration.html`
- ▸ *SMTP Authentication for Mail clients*: `http://postfix.state-of-mind.de/patrick.koetter/smtpauth/smtp_auth_mailclients.html`
- ▸ Dovecot Project Homepage: `http://www.dovecot.org/`
- ▸ CentOS Project Postfix, HowTo: `http://wiki.centos.org/HowTos/Postfix`
- ▸ Postfix Project, Header Checks Reference: `http://www.postfix.org/header_checks.5.html`

Using Postfix and Dovecot to serve e-mails across virtual domains

In this recipe we will learn how to configure Postfix and Dovecot to serve e-mails across virtual domains.

It is not unusual to find a single mail server serving one or more domains. In fact you could say it is common place and it is the purpose of this recipe to show you how to set up and configure virtual domains for your existing users in order to enhance the functionality of your local mail server.

Getting ready

To complete this recipe you will require a working installation of the CentOS 6 operating system with root privileges and a console based text editor of your choice. It is expected that your server will be using a static IP address running both Postfix and Dovecot with SASL, that maintains one or more system user accounts; and all the virtual domains are supported by a working DNS configuration. It is also assumed that you are working through this chapter, recipe by recipe in the order that they appear.

If you are running a firewall, you will need to confirm that the firewall has been disabled, removed, or the appropriate ports are open. Similarly, if you are running SELinux, then you should confirm that it has been disabled or it is now running in permissive mode.

How to do it...

There are many ways to add virtual domains to your mail server and this represents just one of them. No additional software packages are required and depending on the capability of your server you will be able to manage an unlimited number of users:

1. To begin, log in as root and open the following file with your preferred text editor:

   ```
   vi /etc/postfix/main.cf
   ```

2. Scroll down to the bottom of this file and by substituting the value `<virtual-domain-name>` with something more suitable to your own needs, add the following lines:

   ```
   virtual_alias_domains = <virtual-domain-name>
   virtual_alias_maps = hash:/etc/postfix/virtual
   ```

3. When you have finished, simply save and close the file in the usual way before proceeding to open the following file:

   ```
   vi /etc/postfix/virtual
   ```

4. Now create a virtual address for your virtual domain by replacing the value `virtual-username@virtual-domain.tld` with your virtual e-mail address and the value `<system-user>` with the name of the actual system user you want the e-mail to be received by:

   ```
   <virtual-username>@<virtual-domain> <system-user>
   ```

5. Repeat the previous steps as required for all users by listing them in the following way:

   ```
   <virtual-username>@<virtual-domain> <system-user>
   <virtual-username>@<virtual-domain> <system-user>
   <virtual-username>@<virtual-domain> <system-user>
   ```

6. When you have finished, simply save and close the file before proceeding to consolidate the file in the following way:

```
postmap /etc/postfix/virtual
```

7. Finally, restart the Postfix service to enable your new settings:

```
service postfix reload
```

How it works...

The ability for any particular user to have more than one e-mail address is common place in today's networking environment and the previous recipe has served to show you how to provide multiple domain support without using any additional packages. This approach may not suit everyone's needs, and this approach is only one of many, but it serves to provide you with an excellent starting point on which you can develop a more complex array of features.

So what did we learn from this experience?

Postfix allows you to store virtual alias maps in a basic text file. This instruction tells postfix how to route virtual e-mail addresses to actual or real users on the system; so we started by opening the main Postfix configuration file at `/etc/postfix/main.cf` and adding a few additional parameters that informed the system that such a virtual configuration was required and where it would find the map (database) file:

```
virtual_alias_domains = <virtual-domain-name>
virtual_alias_maps = hash:/etc/postfix/virtual
```

We then created the map file by typing:

```
vi /etc/postfix/virtual
```

You then opened the `virtual` text file and added your settings as follows:

```
<virtual-username>@<virtual-domain> <system-user>
<virtual-username>@<virtual-domain> <system-user>
<virtual-username>@<virtual-domain> <system-user>
```

On the other hand, instead of using a system user value you could use an e-mail address as follows:

```
<virtual-username>@<virtual-domain> <email-address>
<virtual-username>@<virtual-domain> <email-address>
<virtual-username>@<virtual-domain> <email-address>
```

Alternatively, you could use a mixture of both such as:

```
<virtual-username>@<virtual-domain> <system-user>

<virtual-username>@<virtual-domain> <system-user>

<virtual-username>@<virtual-domain> <email-address>

<virtual-username>@<virtual-domain> <email-address>
```

Of course, the list of virtual e-mail addresses can be as long or as short as you need but it is important to keep the correct formatting, as any white spaces in the wrong place will result in error messages.

Having done this you were then asked to run the Postfix command in order that the system can read the new configuration file:

```
postmap /etc/postfix/virtual
```

Finally, you were asked to reload Postfix in order that the new settings would come in to effect:

```
service postfix reload
```

If you encounter any errors you should always refer to the `log` file located at `/var/log/maillog`.

So having completed this recipe your users can now take advantage of using a virtual domain.

There's more...

If you wanted to add additional virtual domains then you would be required to make a few changes to the previous recipe.

To begin, open the main configuration file in your favorite text editor by typing:

```
vi /etc/postfix/main.cf
```

Scroll down to the bottom of this file and locate the following line:

```
virtual_alias_domains = <virtual-domain-name>
```

To support unlimited domains you will need to replace the value `<virtual-domain-name>` with a path to a map file as follows:

```
virtual_alias_domains = hash:/etc/postfix/virtual_domain_alias
```

When you have finished, simply save and close the file before proceeding to create the map file in the following way:

```
vi /etc/postfix/virtual_domain_alias
```

Now create a list of domain names in the following way:

```
<virtual-domain>     YYYYMMDD
<virtual-domain>     YYYYMMDD
<virtual-domain>     YYYYMMDD
```

 Separate each column with the *Tab* key. The date value will be ignored, but the map file must hold two columns of data. Remember, your virtual domains must be supported by a working DNS.

In this way, your file may look like this:

```
domain1.com          20120601
domain2.com          20120701
domain3.com          20120801
```

When you have finished, simply run the following Postfix command to consolidate the file:

```
postmap hash:/etc/postfix/virtual_domain_alias
```

Finally, you will need to restart Postfix in order that the new settings will take effect:

```
service postfix reload
```

Setting up a catch-all e-mail address for a virtual domain

Establishing unique e-mail addresses for your virtual domain can lead to some outstanding issues namely, what if someone tries an e-mail address that has no specific user assigned to it. E-mail is often subject to incorrect spelling, so if you wanted to create a catch-all e-mail address for your new domain then simply follows these steps:

1. Open the following file in your favorite text editor:

   ```
   vi /etc/postfix/virtual
   ```

2. At the start of your e-mail address list, add the following new line:

   ```
   @<virtual-domain> <system-user>
   ```

3. Remember to customize the values shown. In this way, you new file may look like this:

   ```
   @<virtual-domain> <system-user>
   <virtual-username>@<virtual-domain> <system-user>
   <virtual-username>@<virtual-domain> <system-user>
   <virtual-username>@<virtual-domain> <system-user>
   ```

4. When you have finished, simply save and close the file in the usual way before issuing the Postfix command like so:

```
postmap /etc/postfix/virtual
```

5. Now restart Postfix in order that your new settings take effect:

```
service postfix reload
```

6. Having done this, you now have a catch-all e-mail address for your virtual domain and you should never miss another e-mail again.

See also

- ▶ Postfix Project Homepage: `http://www.postfix.org`
- ▶ *Postfix Configuration Parameters*: `http://www.postfix.org/postconf.5.html`

10
Working with Apache

In this chapter, we will cover:

- ► Installing the Apache web server with CGI/Perl, PHP, configuring `mod_perl`, and preparing `httpd` for a production environment
- ► Adding a secure connection to the Apache web server by creating a self-signed SSL certificate using OpenSSL
- ► Hosting peers by enabling user directories on the Apache web server and troubleshooting suexec
- ► Configuring Apache name-based virtual hosting
- ► Working with publishing directories, `vhosts.d`, error documents, directives, and the rewrite rule for virtual hosting with the Apache web server

Introduction

This chapter is a collection of recipes that provides the guidance you need to start for running a web server and serving web pages by addressing the need to consider installing the Apache web server with CGI/Perl, PHP, configuring `mod_perl`, and preparing `httpd` for a production environment; adding a secure connection to the Apache web server by creating a self-signed SSL certificate using OpenSSL; hosting peers by enabling user directories on the Apache web server and troubleshooting suexec; configuring Apache name-based virtual hosting; and working with publishing directories, `vhosts.d`, error documents, directives, and the rewrite rule for virtual hosting with the Apache web server.

Installing the Apache web server with CGI/Perl, PHP, configuring mod_perl, and preparing httpd for a production environment

In this recipe we will learn how to install the Apache web server to enable dynamic pages and configure httpd in readiness for a production environment.

Apache is one of the world's most popular web servers and it can be used to serve both static and dynamic web pages. Commonly referred to as httpd, Apache is an open source that supports an extensive range of features, but it is the purpose of this recipe to show you how easily it can be installed using the Yum package manager in order that you can maintain your server with the latest security updates.

Getting ready

To complete this recipe you will require a working installation of the CentOS 6 operating system with root privileges, a console based text editor of your choice, and a connection to the Internet in order to facilitate the download of additional packages. It is expected that your server will be using a static IP address, a hostname, and that the option to use DNS is supported either locally or on external third-party server.

If you are running a firewall, you will need to confirm that the firewall has been disabled, removed, or the appropriate ports are open. Similarly, if you are running SELinux, then you should confirm that it has been disabled or it is now running in permissive mode.

How to do it...

Apache is not installed by default and for this reason we will begin by installing the necessary packages using the Yum package manager:

1. To do this, log in as root and type the following command:

   ```
   yum -y install httpd mod_perl
   ```

    mod_perl is not a requirement of this recipe, but it has been included for those individuals who wish to run CGI/Perl files.

2. Create a home page by typing:

   ```
   vi /var/www/html/index.html
   ```

3. Now add the required HTML. You can use the following code as a starting point but it is expected that you will want to modify it to suit your own needs:

```
<!DOCTYPE html>

<html lang="en">

<head>

<meta charset="utf-8">

<title>Welcome to my new web server</title>

</head>

<body>

<h1>Welcome to my new web server</h1>

<p>Lorem ipsum dolor sit amet, consectetur adipiscing
elit.<br>Phasellus et purus id ante ultricies consectetur et vel
libero. Cras ac nisl nisl.<br>Proin sed eros nibh. Etiam nec
elementum ipsum.</p>

</body>

</html>
```

 Remember, if you intend to use images, media files, or other assets for the server's home page, simply upload the relevant files to /var/www/html and reference them using the appropriate code.

4. When you have finished, simply save the file in the usual way before proceeding to remove the noindex error page by typing the following command:

```
rm -f /var/www/error/noindex.html
```

5. You can now remove the Apache 2 Test Page with the following command:

```
rm -f /etc/httpd/conf.d/welcome.conf
```

6. Now create a link for Perl by typing:

```
ln -s /usr/bin/perl /usr/local/bin/perl
```

7. Having completed these steps, we will now consider the need to configure the httpd service for improved performance, security, and a few extra features. To do this, open the httpd configuration file in your favorite text editor by typing:

```
vi /etc/httpd/conf/httpd.conf
```

8. Scroll down and find the following line:

```
ServerTokens OS
```

9. We do not want our server to relay any important information through the header so change this line to read:

```
ServerTokens Prod
```

10. Now scroll down and find the following line:

```
KeepAlive Off
```

11. In order to enable a persistent connection we should change this line to read:

```
KeepAlive On
```

12. Now scroll down to find the following line:

```
ServerAdmin root@localhost
```

13. The traditional approach to set this value is based on the use of the webmaster identity, so simply modify the e-mail address to reflect something more relevant to your own needs. For example, if your server's domain name was www.henry.home then your entry will look similar to this:

```
ServerAdmin webmaster@henry.home
```

14. Now scroll down a few more lines to find the ServerName directive as follows:

```
#ServerName www.example.com:80
```

15. Uncomment this line and replace the value www.example.com with something more appropriate to your own needs. For example, if your server's domain name was www.henry.home then your entry will look as follows:

```
ServerName www.henry.home:80
```

16. Now scroll down to find the following section:

```
# The Options directive is both complicated and important.  Please
see
# http://httpd.apache.org/docs/2.2/mod/core.html#options
# for more information
#
        Options Indexes FollowSymLinks
```

17. Change this to disable Indexes and enable CGI by making it as follows:

```
Options FollowSymLinks ExecCGI
```

 If you would like to keep Indexes, simply modify the previous instruction in the following way:

Options Indexes FollowSymLinks ExecCGI

18. Now find the following section:

    ```
    # AllowOverride controls what directives may be placed in
    .htaccess files.
    # It can be "All", "None", or any combination of the keywords:
    #    Options FileInfo AuthConfig Limit
    #

        AllowOverride None
    ```

19. Change this to read as follows:

    ```
    AllowOverride All
    ```

20. Now scroll down to find the following line:

    ```
    DirectoryIndex index.html index.html.var
    ```

21. Include a reference for CGI pages by making it as follows:

    ```
    DirectoryIndex index.html index.htm index.cgi
    ```

 You can use this opportunity to reorganize the order in a way that pages are called and add new home page variations to suit your own needs. For example, you could write the following:

    ```
    index.html index.cgi welcome.html welcome.cgi
    ```

22. Now scroll down to find the following lines:

    ```
    #CustomLog logs/access_log common
    #CustomLog logs/referer_log referrer
    #CustomLog logs/agent_log agent
    ```

23. To enable additional logging, simply uncomment them as follows:

    ```
    CustomLog logs/access_log common
    CustomLog logs/referer_log referrer
    CustomLog logs/agent_log agent
    ```

 For future reference, all `log` files for the `httpd` service can be found at `/var/log/httpd`.

24. Now find the following line:

    ```
    ServerSignature On
    ```

25. For reasons of security we do not want to expose the server's signature, so change this to read as follows:

    ```
    ServerSignature Off
    ```

26. Now scroll down to find the following line:

    `AddDefaultCharset UTF-8`

27. We want the character set to be determined by the values used in our web pages, so comment out this line in the following way:

    `#AddDefaultCharset UTF-8`

28. Now scroll down to find the following line:

    `#AddHandler cgi-script .cgi`

29. Uncomment this line to enable CGI and include a file reference for any other related CGI-based extensions as follows:

    `AddHandler cgi-script .cgi .pl`

30. Having done this, simply save and close the file in the usual way before proceeding to set the `httpd` service to start at boot by typing:

    `chkconfig httpd on`

31. Now start the `httpd` service by typing the following command:

    `service httpd start`

32. You can now test `httpd` by pointing your browser at the following URL by replacing `XXX.XXX.XXX.XXX` with the IP address of your server in order to see the **Apache 2 Test Page** at `http://XXX.XXX.XXX.XXX`.

33. Having done this you can now monitor the status of your web server by simply typing the following command at any time:

    `service httpd status`

How it works...

Apache is a software package that enables you to publish and serve web pages. More commonly known as `httpd`, it was the purpose of this recipe to show you how easily CentOS enables you to get started with your very first website.

So what did we learn from this experience?

We began the recipe by installing the Apache with `mod_perl` using the following command:

`yum -y install httpd mod_perl`

As it was stated in the main recipe, `mod_perl` is not a requirement for installing the Apache web server. However, should you wish to complete the recipe as shown then to run CGI files you will need `mod_perl`.

Having done this, our first task was to create a suitable home page by typing:

```
vi /var/www/html/index.html
```

It is expected that you would like to customize the look and feel of this page, but the following sample code was provided to get you started:

```
<!DOCTYPE html>
<html lang="en">
<head>
<meta charset="utf-8">
<title>Welcome to my new web server</title>
</head>
<body>
<h1>Welcome to my new web server</h1>
<p>Lorem ipsum dolor sit amet, consectetur adipiscing elit.<br>Phasellus
et purus id ante ultricies consectetur et vel libero. Cras ac nisl
nisl.<br>Proin sed eros nibh. Etiam nec elementum ipsum.</p>
</body>
</html>
```

Having created your `index` page we then proceeded to remove the `noindex` error page as it would not be needed. We did this by typing the following command:

```
rm -f /var/www/error/noindex.html
```

Following this, we then removed the **Apache 2 Test Page** by typing the following command:

```
rm -f /etc/httpd/conf.d/welcome.conf
```

Before enabling a link for Perl by typing the following command:

```
ln -s /usr/bin/perl /usr/local/bin/perl
```

Following this, the next stage was to open the `httpd` configuration file in your favorite text editor using the following command:

```
vi /etc/httpd/conf/httpd.conf
```

We began with a review of our basic security settings. When the Apache `httpd` web server generates either a web page or error page, valuable information regarding the server can be found in the header, so in order to stop this from happening we simply set the `ServerTokens` and `ServerSignature` as follows:

```
ServerTokens OS
ServerSignature Off
```

We then enabled support for persistent connections and defined the server's e-mail address and server name with the following configuration changes:

```
KeepAlive On
ServerAdmin root@localhost
ServerName www.example.com:80
```

 The ServerAdmin directive is used to confirm the e-mail address of the web server administrator. It often appears in error messages on server-generated web pages and for this reason it should reflect your domain name.

For the purpose of the main recipe, the following example was used, but you should change these values to something that is more appropriate to your own needs:

```
ServerAdmin webmaster@henry.home
ServerName www.henry.home:80
```

After this, we then determined the correct way in that we want to manage our server's Directives and Options as follows:

```
Options FollowSymLinks ExecCGI
AllowOverride All
```

Of course, the previous has only served to scratch the surface of this extensive topic but having established the basic principles we then moved towards defining the order of what type of web page will be served and in what order:

```
DirectoryIndex index.html index.htm index.cgi
```

Then, by simply uncommenting the following lines it was possible to enable additional logging features:

```
CustomLog logs/access_log common
CustomLog logs/referer_log referrer
CustomLog logs/agent_log agent
```

The server's signature was disabled for reasons of security while commenting out the default character would enable the web page to determine the character set used:

```
ServerSignature Off
#AddDefaultCharset UTF-8
```

Moving on from this we then added handlers for our CGI/Perl based pages thereby enabling you to create dynamic pages using the `.cgi` or `.pl` suffix:

```
AddHandler cgi-script .cgi .pl
```

Finally, we saved and closed the `httpd` configuration file in the usual way before proceeding to enable the `httpd` service to start at boot by typing:

```
chkconfig httpd on
```

We then started the `httpd` service by typing:

```
service httpd start
```

Having completed these steps it was simply a matter of opening your browser and electing a method of viewing the Apache 2 Test Page. For those of you who do not have a working hostname the default option is to use your server's IP address in the following way:

```
http://XXX.XXX.XXX.XXX
```

Whereas those with hostname support can use the following approach:

```
http://<hostname>
```

For example, if the server's IP address was `192.168.1.100` then you could use the following method:

```
http://192.168.1.100
```

Similarly, if the server's hostname was `henry` and your local network supports its identification then you could use the following URL:

```
http://henry
```

Finally, you were shown how to monitor the status of your web server by typing the following command:

```
service httpd status
```

So as you can see, the Apache configuration file is quite extensive and in simple terms this recipe has provided you with a starting point on which you can build a server that will suit your exact needs. The overall intention was to introduce Apache and enable it to serve static HTML from `/var/www/html`. Apache is a big subject and we cannot cover every nuance, but over the coming recipes we will continue to expose additional functionality that will enable you to build a web server of choice.

There's more...

PHP represents a must-have feature for any Apache web server. It is not installed by default and for this reason we will begin by installing the whole host of packages using the Yum package manager.

To do this, log in as root and type the following command:

```
yum install php
```

Having completed the installation the next task is to open the `php.ini` file in order to configure your date settings. To do this, type the following command using your favorite text editor:

```
vi /etc/php.ini
```

Scroll down to find the following line:

```
;date.timezone =
```

Uncomment this line and replace the location value with something more appropriate to your own needs:

```
date.timezone = "Europe/London"
```

For example, if your server was located in, near, or around London you would use:

```
date.timezone = "Europe/London"
```

When you have finished, simply save and close the file in the usual way before proceeding to adjust the directory index of the Apache configuration in order to account for the new page type. To do this, type the following command using your favorite editor:

```
vi /etc/httpd/conf/httpd.conf
```

Now scroll down to find the line that begins with the following:

```
DirectoryIndex index.html index.html.var
```

Include a reference for PHP by making it read as follows:

```
DirectoryIndex index.html index.htm index.php index.cgi
```

When you have finished, simply save and close the file in the usual way before proceeding to create a `phpinfo` file for your website. To do this, type the following command using your favorite editor:

```
vi /var/www/html/phpinfo.php
```

Add the following code:

```
<?php phpinfo(); ?>
```

Now save and close the file before restarting the Apache web server by typing:

```
service httpd restart
```

Where XXX.XXX.XXX.XXX is the IP address of your server, you can visit the following URL to view the PHP output:

```
http://XXX.XXX.XXX.XXX/php.php
```

The purpose of this file is to list the installed packages and inform you that PHP is working correctly. Naturally, you may want to delete this file at a later date but for the purpose of this recipe it was felt that your initial experience of installing PHP should be be far more rewarding and informative.

Running a CGI/Perl script

Running your first CGI/Perl script can be a tricky business, but having configured your server using the previous recipe you are now in a position to get started.

To begin, simply create a new file in your favorite text editor as follows:

```
vi /var/www/html/<my_script_name>.cgi
```

Now add the following code:

```
#!/usr/local/bin/perl
print "Content-type: text/html\n\n";
print "<html>\n<body>\n";
print "<div style=\"width: 80%; font-size: 50px; font-weight: bold; text-align: center;\">\n";
print "My Test Page";
print "\n</div>\n";
print "</body>\n</html>\n";
```

Having done this, unlike HTML or PHP files you will need to assign the correct permissions. To do this, simply type the following command by replacing the <my_script_name> value with something more appropriate to your own needs:

```
chmod 705 /var/www/html/<my_script_name>.cgi
```

Activating ModPerl::PerlRun

Having successfully completed the previous recipe you may want to consider activating the PerlRun mode in order to maximize the benefits of using `mod_perl`.

To do this, log in as root and open the following configuration file:

```
vi /etc/httpd/conf.d/perl.conf
```

Scroll down and uncomment the following line to enable global warnings:

```
PerlSwitches -w
```

(Optionally) scroll down to uncomment the following line:

```
PerlSwitches -T
```

 This feature will enable global taint checking. However, as not all the Perl modules enable this taint checking then for a production environment you should consider this to be optional.

Following this, scroll down towards the end of the file and make the following changes by replacing XXX.XXX.XXX.XXX/XX with your IP address:

```
Alias /perl /var/www/perl
<Directory /var/www/perl>
    SetHandler perl-script
    PerlResponseHandler ModPerl::PerlRun
    PerlOptions +ParseHeaders
    Options +ExecCGI
</Directory>
<Location /perl-status>
    SetHandler perl-script
    PerlResponseHandler Apache2::Status
    Order deny,allow
   Deny from all
    Allow from XXX.XXX.XXX.XXX/XX
</Location>
```

When you have finished, restart the Apache web server by typing the following command:

```
service httpd restart
```

Having done this, you should now be able to view the status of `mod_perl` by visiting the following URL:

```
http://XXX.XXX.XXX.XXX/perl-status
```

However, if you are in a production environment and you prefer to disable the previous URL then simply comment the following lines before restarting the Apache web server:

```
#<Location /perl-status>
#    SetHandler perl-script
#    PerlResponseHandler Apache2::Status
#    Order deny,allow
#  Deny from all
#    Allow from XXX.XXX.XXX.XXX/XX
#</Location>
```

See also

> ▸ Apache HTTP Server Project Home page: `http://httpd.apache.org`
>
> ▸ Apache Project, Documentation, *ModPerl::PerlRun - Run unaltered CGI scripts under mod_perl*: `http://perl.apache.org/docs/2.0/api/ModPerl/PerlRun.html`

Adding a secure connection to the Apache web server by creating a self-signed SSL certificate using OpenSSL

In this recipe we will learn how to add a secure connection to the Apache web server by creating a self-signed SSL certificate using OpenSSL.

In a previous recipe you were shown how to install the Apache web server, and with the growing demand for secure connections, it is the purpose of this recipe to show you how to enhance your current server configuration by showing you how to extend the features of the Apache web server.

Getting ready

To complete this recipe you will require a working installation of the CentOS 6 operating system with root privileges, a console based text editor of your choice, and a connection to the Internet in order to facilitate the download of additional packages. It is expected that Apache web server has been installed and that it is currently running.

Generally speaking, if you are intending to use an SSL Certificate on a production server you will probably want to purchase an SSL Certificate from a trusted Certificate Authority. There are many options open to you regarding as what certificate best suits your requirements and your budget, but for the purpose of this recipe we will confine our discussion to a self-signed certificate that is more than adequate for any development server or internal network.

How to do it...

mod_ssl is not installed by default and for this reason we will begin by installing the necessary packages using the Yum package manager:

1. To begin, log in as root and type the following command:

    ```
    yum install mod_ssl
    ```

    By doing this you will automatically install the openssl package.

2. We are now required to create the following directory in order that we can store our intended certificate and server key. To do this, type the following command:

    ```
    mkdir /etc/httpd/ssl
    ```

3. Having done this, we are now ready to begin creating a server certificate that will last for 365 days by typing the following command:

    ```
    openssl req -x509 -nodes -days 365 -newkey rsa:2048 -keyout /etc/httpd/ssl/apache.key -out /etc/httpd/ssl/apache.crt
    ```

4. You will then be asked a series of questions to which you should respond with the appropriate values:

    ```
    Country Name (2 letter code) [XX]:
    State or Province Name (full name) []:
    Locality Name (eg, city) [Default City]:
    Organization Name (eg, company) [Default Company Ltd]:
    Organizational Unit Name (eg, section) []:
    Common Name (eg, your name or your server's hostname) []:
    Email Address []:
    ```

Complete all the required details by paying special attention to the `Common Name` value. This value should reflect the domain name of your server or your IP address. For example, you may type:

`mylocaldomainname.home`

5. When the process of creating your certificate is complete we will proceed by opening main Apache SSL configuration in the following way:

    `vi /etc/httpd/conf.d/ssl.conf`

6. Scroll down to the section that begins with `<VirtualHost _default_:443>` and locate the following line:

    `#ServerName www.example.com:443`

7. Uncomment this line and modify the value shown to match the `Common Name` value used during the creation of your certificate as follows:

    `ServerName www.mylocaldomain.home:443`

8. Now make sure the following line reads as follows:

    `SSLEngine on`

9. Following this, scroll down and find the line that looks as follows:

    `SSLCertificateFile /etc/pki/tls/certs/localhost.crt`

10. Modify this line to reflect the location of your certificate as follows:

    `SSLCertificateFile /etc/httpd/ssl/apache.crt`

11. Now scroll down and locate the following line:

    `SSLCertificateKeyFile /etc/pki/tls/private/localhost.key`

12. Again, modify this line to reflect the location of your server key as follows:

    `SSLCertificateKeyFile /etc/httpd/ssl/apache.key`

13. When you have finished, simply save and close the file in the usual way before protecting your files with the following command:

    `chmod 400 apache.*`

14. Now restart the Apache `httpd` service:

    `service httpd restart`

15. Well done, you can now visit your server with a secure connection by visiting the `https://www.myserverdomain.lan`.

How it works...

The purpose of recipe was to show you how to create a self-signed server certificate using the OpenSSL encryption and add `mod_ssl` to the Apache web server. By doing this your web server now utilizes the HTTPS protocol and provides a secure connection.

So what did we learn from this experience?

We began the recipe by installing both the `mod_ssl` and the OpenSSL package in the following way:

```
yum install mod_ssl
```

The next step was to then create a folder that would form the location of the intended server certificate and key file. We did this by typing:

```
mkdir /etc/httpd/ssl
```

For simplicity you have been directed to store the files in `/etc/httpd/ssl`. Of course, you can always choose a different directory location but if you do, remember to make this new location applicable to the recipe as a whole.

Following this, we then proceeded to create the server certificate by typing the following command:

```
openssl req -x509 -nodes -days 365 -newkey rsa:2048 -keyout /etc/httpd/ssl/apache.key -out /etc/httpd/ssl/apache.crt
```

This single-line command will now initiate the process of creating a server key (`apache.key`) and a self-signed certificate (`apache.crt`). The encryption strength is set at 2048 bits while we have taken care to specify that the certificate will be valid for 365 days.

Having done this, you will be asked to complete a series of questions:

```
Country Name (2 letter code) [XX]:
State or Province Name (full name) []:
Locality Name (eg, city) [Default City]:
Organization Name (eg, company) [Default Company Ltd]:
Organizational Unit Name (eg, section) []:
Common Name (eg, your name or your server's hostname) []:
Email Address []:
```

Complete the questions but pay special attention to the `Common Name`. As it was mentioned in the main recipe, this value should reflect either, the domain name of your server or your IP address.

When you have finished you will be able to view your new server key and certificate when you type the following command:

```
cd /etc/httpd/ssl
```

In the next phase you were required to open the following configuration file in your favorite text editor:

```
vi /etc/httpd/conf.d/ssl.conf
```

You were asked to scroll down and locate the following line:

```
#ServerName www.example.com:443
```

Having been told to uncomment this line you were expected to match the value used with the `Common Name` value used by your certificate as follows:

```
ServerName www.mylocaldomain.home:443
```

You are then required to enable the SSL Engine by making sure that the following line reads as follows:

```
SSLEngine on
```

Before modifying the path to reflect the location of your server certificate and key in the following way:

```
SSLCertificateFile /etc/httpd/ssl/apache.crt
SSLCertificateKeyFile /etc/httpd/ssl/apache.key
```

The last step was to protect your files with the following command:

```
chmod 400 apache.*
```

Finally, you were required to restart the Apache `httpd` service in the following way:

```
service httpd restart
```

Having completed these steps you can now enjoy the benefits of a secure connection using a self-signed server certificate. However, if you are intending to use an SSL Certificate on a production server for members of the public then your best option is to purchase an SSL Certificate from a trusted Certificate Authority.

See also

- ▶ Apache HTTP Server Project Home page: `http://httpd.apache.org`
- ▶ CentOS Wiki, *Setting up an SSL secured Webserver with CentOS*: `http://wiki.centos.org/HowTos/Https`

Hosting peers by enabling user directories on the Apache web server and troubleshooting suexec

In this recipe you will learn how to host your peers by enabling user directories on the Apache web server and troubleshoot suexec.

In a previous recipe you were shown how to install the Apache web server, and with the desire to provide hosting facilities for system users, it is the purpose of this recipe to show you how to enhance your current server configuration by showing you how to extend the features of the Apache web server.

Getting ready

To complete this recipe you will require a working installation of the CentOS 6 operating system with root privileges and a console based text editor of your choice. It is expected that your server will be using a static IP address that supports a hostname or domain name and that the Apache web server is already installed and currently running.

If you are running a firewall, you will need to confirm that the firewall has been disabled, removed, or the appropriate ports are open. Similarly, if you are running SELinux, then you should confirm that it has been disabled or it is now running in permissive mode.

How to do it...

To provide the functionality offered by this recipe no additional packages are required but we will need to make some modifications to the Apache configuration file:

1. To begin, log in as root and open the main Apache configuration file in your favorite text editor by typing the following command:

   ```
   vi /etc/httpd/conf/httpd.conf
   ```

2. Scroll down and find the following line:

   ```
   UserDir disabled
   ```

3. Comment out this line in the following way:

   ```
   #UserDir disabled
   ```

4. Now uncomment the following line:

   ```
   UserDir public_html
   ```

5. Scroll down and find the following group of lines:

   ```
   # Control access to UserDir directories.  The following is an
   example
   # for a site where these directories are restricted to read-only.
   #
   #<Directory /home/*/public_html>
   #    AllowOverride FileInfo AuthConfig Limit
   #    Options MultiViews Indexes SymLinksIfOwnerMatch
   IncludesNoExec
   #    <Limit GET POST OPTIONS>
   #        Order allow,deny
   #        Allow from all
   #    </Limit>
   #    <LimitExcept GET POST OPTIONS>
   #        Order deny,allow
   #        Deny from all
   #    </LimitExcept>
   #</Directory>
   ```

6. Uncomment these lines and make the following changes:

   ```
   # Control access to UserDir directories. The following is an
   example
   # for a site where these directories are restricted to read-only.
   #
   <Directory /home/*/public_html>
       AllowOverride All
       Options Indexes Includes FollowSymLinks ExecCGI
       Order allow,deny
       Allow from all
   </Directory>
   ```

7. Now modify the permissions of the home folders by typing:

   `chmod 0711 /home/<username>`

8. Create the home directory web folder:

   `mkdir /home/<username>/public_html`

9. Ensure ownership of the new folder is assigned to the user:

   `chown <username> /home/<username>/public_html`

10. Set the read/write permissions to `0755`:

    ```
    chmod 0755 /home/<username>/public_html
    ```

11. To complete this recipe, simply restart the `httpd` service by typing:

    ```
    service httpd restart
    ```

12. You can now test your installation by enabling your system users to visit at `http://<your-server>/~<username>` in any browser.

How it works...

The purpose of this recipe was to show you how Apache provides you with the option to allow a system user to host web pages within their home directory. This approach has been used by ISPs since the outset of web hosting and in many respects it continues to flourish due to its ability to avoid the more complex method of virtual hosting.

So what did we learn from this experience?

We began the recipe by making a few minor configuration changes to the Apache configuration file in order that we could activate the user directory support module.

To do this we opened the main configuration by typing:

```
vi /etc/httpd/conf/httpd.conf
```

We activated user host adjusting the following lines to read:

```
#UserDir disabled
UserDir public_html
```

Then we proceeded to modify the remaining instruction to reflect the following changes:

```
# Control access to UserDir directories. The following is an example
# for a site where these directories are restricted to read-only.
#
<Directory /home/*/public_html>
    AllowOverride All
    Options Indexes Includes FollowSymLinks ExecCGI
    Order allow,deny
    Allow from all
</Directory>
```

As a consequence of these actions, the full code listing would look as follows:

```
<IfModule mod_userdir.c>
    #
    # UserDir is disabled by default since it can confirm the presence
    # of a username on the system (depending on home directory
    # permissions).
    #
    #UserDir disabled
    #
    # To enable requests to /~user/ to serve the user's public_html
    # directory, remove the "UserDir disabled" line, and uncomment
    # the following line instead:
    #
    UserDir public_html
</IfModule>
#
# Control access to UserDir directories. The following is an example
# for a site where these directories are restricted to read-only.
#
<Directory /home/*/public_html>
    AllowOverride All
    Options Indexes Includes FollowSymLinks ExecCGI
    Order allow,deny
    Allow from all
</Directory>
```

Having saved our work, we then began to make various changes to the home directories by running the following commands:

```
#set the permissions for the users home folder
chmod 0711 /home/<username>


#create a publishing directory that will host the web pages.
mkdir /home/<username>/public_html


#as we are root, assign ownership of the new folder to the user
chown <username> /home/<username>/public_html
#set the correct permissions for the publishing directory
chmod 0755 /home/<username>/public_html
```

You should be aware that the previous process of managing the home directories should be repeated for each user. You will not have to restart Apache every time you enable a new system user, but having completed these steps for the first time it was simply a matter of restarting the httpd service to reflect the initial changes made to the configuration file:

```
service httpd restart
```

From this point on your local system users can now publish web pages using a unique URL based on their username. They can publish pages through a network connection and viewing can be arranged through a variety of methods (hostname, domain name, or IP address) as it is simply a matter of pointing their browser at http://<hostname-or-domainname-or-ipaddress>/~<username>.

There's more...

If you intend to run CGI scripts in a user directory and your server is running suexec, then it is possible that you may encounter difficulties.

Apache suexec allows you to run web processes as an alternative user and if you are experiencing difficulties running a particular CGI/Perl or SSI based script from a user directory then disabling it will ensure that all web processes are active under a single user.

You can confirm that suexec is running by typing the following command:

```
suexec -V
```

To disable suexec we must first locate suexec. So log in as the root user and type the following command:

```
whereis suexec
```

To that the server will respond in the following manner:

```
suexec: /usr/sbin/suexec /usr/share/man/man8/suexec.8.gz
```

This response confirms that suexec can be found at /usr/sbin/suexec and with this in mind, rather than just deleting it, we will simply rename it in order that it is not called on reboot.

To do this type:

```
mv /usr/sbin/suexec /usr/sbin/suexec_disabled
```

Having completed this task, you may now simply restart the httpd service:

```
service httpd restart
```

Having completed this process you may now discover that running CGI in a user directory is problem free.

Reinstating suexec

Disabling suexec implies that CGI and SSI programs will not have access to the root account or have root permissions so by completing the previous process you will be happy to know that we have not removed suexec.

Should you ever wish to reinstate suexec, simply reverse the file renaming command (mv) used previously, and then restart the `httpd` service as follows:

```
mv /usr/sbin/suexec_disabled /usr/sbin/suexec
```

Then restart the `httpd` service in the following way:

```
service httpd restart
```

See also

- Apache HTTP Server Project Home page: `http://httpd.apache.org`
- Apache Project, *suEXEC Support*:
  `http://httpd.apache.org/docs/current/suexec.html`

Configuring Apache name-based virtual hosting

In this recipe we will learn how to configure name-based virtual hosting on the Apache web server.

In a previous recipe you were shown how to install the Apache web server, and where there are enormous advantages to be gained from name-based virtual hosting, it is the purpose of this recipe to show you how to enhance your current server configuration by showing you how to extend the features of the Apache web server.

Getting ready

To complete this recipe you will require a working installation of the CentOS 6 operating system with root privileges and a console based text editor of your choice. It is expected that your server will be using a static IP address and Apache is installed and currently running, and that your server supports one or more domains or subdomains.

How to do it...

For the purpose of this recipe we will be building a virtual host for `web1.servername.lan` and `web2.servername.lan`. These names are interchangeable and it is expected that you will want to customize this recipe based on something more appropriate to your own needs and circumstances:

1. To begin, log in as root and open the main Apache configuration file in your favorite text editor by typing the following command:

   ```
   vi /etc/httpd/conf/httpd.conf
   ```

2. Scroll down and locate the line that reads as follows:

   ```
   #NameVirtualHost *:80
   ```

3. Uncomment this line like so:

   ```
   NameVirtualHost *:80
   ```

4. Now scroll to the bottom of the file and add the following instruction for your server's root customizing the values as required:

   ```
   <VirtualHost *:80>

        ServerAdmin webmaster@servername.lan

        ServerName  servername.lan

        ServerAlias www.servername.lan

        DirectoryIndex index.html index.php index.cgi

        DocumentRoot /var/www/html/

   </VirtualHost>
   ```

5. When you have finished, we shall proceed by adding the first virtual host. In this instance the virtual host will be identified as `http://web1.servername.lan`.

   ```
   <VirtualHost *:80>

        ServerAdmin webmaster@servername.lan

        ServerName  web1.servername.lan

        ServerAlias web1.servername.lan

        DirectoryIndex index.html index.php index.cgi

        DocumentRoot /var/www/web1/public_html/

   LogLevel warn

   ErrorLog  /var/www/web1/error.log

        CustomLog /var/www/web1/access.log combined

   </VirtualHost>
   ```

6. Following this, we will now add a second and final virtual host in order to fully illustrate how this recipe works. In this instance the virtual host will be identified as `http://web2.servername.lan`.

```
<VirtualHost *:80>
    ServerAdmin webmaster@servername.lan
    ServerName  web2.servername.lan
    ServerAlias web2.servername.lan
    DirectoryIndex index.html index.php index.cgi
    DocumentRoot /var/www/web2/public_html/
LogLevel warn
ErrorLog  /var/www/web2/error.log
    CustomLog /var/www/web2/access.log combined
</VirtualHost>
```

7. Now save and close the file in the usual way before proceeding to create the directories for the first virtual host by typing:

```
mkdir -p /var/www/web1/public_html
```

8. Now type the following command for the second virtual host:

```
mkdir -p /var/www/web2/public_html
```

9. Having done this we can now create a default index page for our new subdomains by using your favorite text editor as follows:

```
vi /var/www/web1/public_html/index.php
```

10. Add the following code:

```
<html><head></head><body><p>Welcome to Web1</p><p><?php phpinfo();
?></p></body></html>
```

 If you have not installed PHP you should remove that section of code from the sample.

11. Save and close the file before repeating this for an index page in our remaining subdomain like so:

```
vi /var/www/web2/public_html/index.php
```

12. Add the following code:

```
<html><head></head><body><p>Welcome to Web2</p><p><?php phpinfo();
?></p></body></html>
```

Again, if you have not installed PHP you should remove that section of code from the sample.

13. Again, save and close the file before reloading the Apache web server:

```
service httpd reload
```

How it works...

The purpose of this recipe was to show you how easy it is to implement name-based virtual hosting. This technique will boost your productivity and using this approach will give you unlimited opportunities as opposed to the more traditional view of restricting yourself to a specific range of IP addresses or enabling home directories.

So what did we learn from this experience?

We began by opening the Apache configuration file and activating the Virtual Host:

```
NameVirtualHost *:80
```

Following this we then proceeded to determine the relevant settings for our default server root:

```
<VirtualHost *:80>
    #Include a reference for your server's main email address:
        ServerAdmin webmaster@servername.lan
    #Declare the server's domain name:
        ServerName  servername.lan
    #Declare the server's default alias:
        ServerAlias www.servername.lan
    #Determine the directory index order of preference:
        DirectoryIndex index.html index.php index.cgi
    #Assign a document root where the files will be found:
        DocumentRoot /var/www/html/
</VirtualHost>
```

Of course, there are many more settings you can include, but the previous solution provides the basic building blocks that will enable you to use it as the perfect starting point.

The server's default root is important. This is because, it will act as the default website for any virtual host that is not currently configured in Apache.

For example, if the DNS maintained entries for `web1.servername.lan`, `web2.servername.lan`, and `web3.servername.lan` but having followed this recipe that did not account for the latter, then pointing your browser at `http://web3.servername.lan` will effectively show you the default root found at `/var/www/html`.

 If you have PHP installed, you can confirm this by reviewing the `DocumentRoot` entry in a `phpinfo` file used in the sample index pages for the subdomains listed previously.

The next step was to then create individual entries for our subdomains using the following approach:

```
<VirtualHost *:80>
    #Include a reference for your server's main email address:
ServerAdmin webmaster@servername.lan
#Declare the server's domain name:
    ServerName  web1.servername.lan
#Declare the server's default alias:
    ServerAlias web1.servername.lan
#Determine the directory index order of preference:
    DirectoryIndex index.html index.php index.cgi
#Assign a document root where the files will be found:
    DocumentRoot /var/www/web1/public_html/
#Add entries for custom logging:
LogLevel warn
ErrorLog   /var/www/web1/error.log
CustomLog /var/www/web1/access.log combined
</VirtualHost>
```

Based on this simple inclusion, you can see that each virtual host supports the typical Apache directives and can be customized to suit your needs. For example, if we take the settings for `web1.servername.lan` a little further you could extend it in the following way:

```
<VirtualHost *:80>
    ServerAdmin webmaster@servername.lan
    ServerName  web1.servername.lan
    ServerAlias web1.servername.lan
    DirectoryIndex index.html index.php index.cgi
    DocumentRoot /var/www/web1/public_html/
```

```
#Add entries for custom logging:
LogLevel warn
ErrorLog   /var/www/web1/error.log
CustomLog /var/www/web1/access.log combined

#Add references for custom error documents
# (remember to create these html pages):
ErrorDocument 400 400.html
ErrorDocument 401 401.html
ErrorDocument 403 403.html
ErrorDocument 404 404.html
ErrorDocument 500 500.html
#Disable the server signature:
ServerSignature Off
</VirtualHost>
```

This process was repeated for all our virtual hosts but on completion, we then proceeded to create the directories to hold the actual content:

```
mkdir -p /var/www/web1/public_html
mkdir -p /var/www/web2/public_html
```

In this example, the new content directories were added to /var/www. This is not to imply that you cannot create these new folders in another place. In fact most production servers will generally place these new directories in the home folder such as /home/<username>/ web1 or /home/<username>/www.mynewdomain.lan. However, if you do intend to take this approach, remember to modify the permissions and ownership of these new directories in order that they can be used as they were intended.

Finally, we created several index pages for each subdomain:

```
vi /var/www/web1/public_html/index.php
vi /var/www/web2/public_html/index.php
```

The content of each index.php was then added before we reloaded the Apache web service in order that our new settings would take immediate effect.

```
service httpd reload
```

Unlike in other recipes, the reload command was used in order that we did not simply stop and restart Apache. In this way, whenever you add a new subdomain or domain then you will not be interfering with a visitor on any existing website.

There's more...

Having followed the previous recipe we will now consider the task of creating subdomains in the web root.

To do this, log in as root and create a directory in `/var/www/html` as follows:

```
mkdir /var/www/html/web1
```

Now open the main Apache configuration file in your favorite text editor as follows:

```
vi /etc/httpd/conf/httpd.conf
```

Scroll down to locate the existing entry for `web1.servername.lan` and make the following adjustments to the directory root as shown below:

```
<VirtualHost *:80>

    ServerAdmin webmaster@servername.lan

    ServerName  web1.servername.lan

    ServerAlias web1.servername.lan

    DirectoryIndex index.html index.php index.cgi index.rb

    DocumentRoot /var/www/html/web1/

</VirtualHost>
```

Notice that for simplicity I have removed the custom error logs but do keep them if this is preferred.

Now before we finish, if anyone visits `http://www.servername.lan/web1` we actually want them to see `http://web1.servername.lan` so let's add a small rewrite rule to the default virtual host to ensure this happens:

```
<VirtualHost *:80>

    ServerAdmin webmaster@servername.lan

    ServerName  servername.lan

    ServerAlias www.servername.lan

    DirectoryIndex index.html index.php index.cgi index.rb

    DocumentRoot /var/www/html/


#Add a re-write rule here

RewriteEngine on

    RewriteCond %{HTTP_HOST} ^(www\.)?servername\.lan$

    RewriteRule ^/web1(/.*)?$ http://web1.servername.lan$1 [R=301,L]

</VirtualHost>
```

Finally, reload the Apache web service to ensure your settings take immediate effect:

```
service httpd reload
```

You can repeat this for any number of subdomains but remember, if you do encounter any difficulties check your log files for more details.

See also

▸ Apache HTTP Server Project Home page: `http://httpd.apache.org`

▸ Apache Project, *Apache Virtual Host Documentation*: `http://httpd.apache.org/docs/2.2/vhosts/`

Working with publishing directories, vhosts.d, error documents, directives, and the rewrite rule for virtual hosting with the Apache web server

In this recipe we will learn how to configure publishing directories, `vhosts.d`, error documents, directives, and the rewrite rule for virtual hosting with the Apache web server.

If you have followed the previous recipe you will now be in a position to take your virtual hosting one stage further. The management of virtual hosting can be daunting and it is the purpose of this recipe to show you how to maintain a publishing structure, explore the world of virtual hosting, and include as many directives as you need.

Getting ready

To complete this recipe you will require a working installation of the CentOS 6 operating system with root privileges and a console based text editor of your choice. It is expected that your server will be using a static IP address and Apache is installed and currently running, and that your server supports one or more domains or subdomains.

How to do it...

Before you begin it is assumed that you are already familiar with the term virtual host and that you know how to create them. Unlike other recipes, the purpose of the following instruction is to provide a basic blueprint for web directory structure:

1. To begin, log in as your chosen user and access your home directory as follows:

   ```
   cd /home/<username>
   ```

2. So let's start by creating our master website structure by typing:

   ```
   mkdir /home/<username>/websites
   ```

3. Now we will build our first domain hosting structure by typing:

   ```
   mkdir -p websites/<your_domain_name>/{public_html,private_
   html,log,backup}
   ```

4. Now change to the recently created `domainname.lan` folder as follows:

   ```
   cd websites/<your_domain_name>
   ```

5. To finalize this structure we will now run the following command:

   ```
   mkdir -p public_html/{cgi-bin,images,scripts} && mkdir -p private_
   html/{cgi-bin,images,scripts}
   ```

6. In the next step we will now create our basic error documents for the public directory as follows:

   ```
   cd /home/<username>/websites/<your_domain_name>/public_html &&
   touch 400.html 401.html 403.html 404.html 500.html
   ```

7. Similarly, we will now create our basic error documents for the private directory like so:

   ```
   cd /home/<username>/websites/<your_domain_name>/private_html &&
   touch 400.html 401.html 403.html 404.html 500.html
   ```

8. At this stage you may want to consider customizing the documents created. If not, then let's jump straight in and begin enhancing and simplifying our Apache virtual hosts. We will begin by creating a new directory that will contain all our virtual host data. However, to do this, you will need to log out as the current user and log in as the root user.

9. As the root user type:

   ```
   mkdir /etc/httpd/vhosts.d
   ```

10. Now open the main Apache configuration with your favorite text editor by typing:

    ```
    vi /etc/httpd/conf/httpd.conf
    ```

11. Scroll down towards the bottom of this file. Locate the **name-based virtual hosting** section and make it look as follows:

    ```
    #
    # Use name-based virtual hosting.
    #
    NameVirtualHost *:80
    #
    ```

```
# NOTE: NameVirtualHost cannot be used without a port specifier
# (for example. :80) if mod_ssl is being used, due to the nature
of the
# SSL protocol.
#


#
# VirtualHost example:
# Almost any Apache directive may go into a VirtualHost container.
# The first VirtualHost section is used for requests without a
known
# server name.
#
#<VirtualHost *:80>
#       ServerAdmin webmaster@dummy-host.example.com
#       DocumentRoot /www/docs/dummy-host.example.com
#       ServerName dummy-host.example.com
#       ErrorLog logs/dummy-host.example.com-error_log
#       CustomLog logs/dummy-host.example.com-access_log common
#</VirtualHost>
Include /etc/httpd/vhosts.d/*.conf
```

12. Now create a new file to contain your name-based virtual hosting information for your primary domain:

```
vi /etc/httpd/vhosts.d/<your_domain_name>.conf
```

13. Add the following code by replacing the appropriate values:

```
<VirtualHost *:80>
      ServerAdmin webmaster@<your_domain_name>
      ServerName  <your_domain_name>
      ServerAlias www.<your_domain_name>

      DirectoryIndex index.html index.php index.cgi index.rb

      DocumentRoot /home/<username>/websites/<your_domain_name>/
public_html/

      LogLevel warn
```

```
        ErrorLog   /home/<username>/websites/<your_domain_name>/
log/error.log

        CustomLog /home/<username>/websites/<your_domain_name>/
log/access.log combined


AccessFileName .myhtaccessfilename


    Alias /cgi-bin/ /home/<username>/websites/<your_domain_name>/
public_html/cgi-bin/

    <Location /cgi-bin>

        Options +ExecCGI

    </Location>


    <Directory /home/<username>/websites/<your_domain_name>/
public_html >

        Options Indexes Includes FollowSymLinks

        AllowOverride All


        <Files ~ "^\.myhtaccessfilename">

            Order allow,deny

            Deny from all

            Satisfy All

        </Files>


        Allow from all

        Order allow,deny

    </Directory>


    ErrorDocument 400 400.html

    ErrorDocument 401 401.html

    ErrorDocument 403 403.html

    ErrorDocument 404 404.html

    ErrorDocument 500 500.html


    ServerSignature Off

</VirtualHost>
```

14. We will now create our first subdomain directory within the main document route. To do this, log out as root, and log in as your chosen `<username>` value then type the following command:

```
mkdir -p /home/<username>/websites/<your_domain_name>/public_
html/<your_subdomain_name>
```

15. Having created the subdomain directory we now want to create the relevant error documents. So, remaining logged in as `<username>` type:

```
cd /home/<username>/websites/<your_domain_name>/public_html/<your_
subdomain_name>&& touch 400.html 401.html 403.html 404.html 500.
html
```

16. Now build the directory structure for your new subdomain:

```
cd /home/<username>/websites/<your_domain_name>/public_html&&mkdir
-p <your_subdomain_name>/{cgi-bin,images,scripts}
```

17. In this second and final phase of this recipe we will now create the necessary record for our subdomain. To do this, you will need to log out as the current user and log in as the root user. We will then make this easy on ourselves by copying the content of our previous file to a new file for further customization. To do this, as the root user type:

```
cp /etc/httpd/vhosts.d/<your_domain_name>.conf  /etc/httpd/
vhosts.d/<your_domain_name>-<your_subdomain_name>.conf
```

18. Now open the file with your favorite text editor as follows:

```
vi /etc/httpd/vhost.d/<your_domain_name>-<your_subdomain_name>.
conf
```

19. Then proceed to customize the values as follows:

```
<VirtualHost *:80>
        ServerAdmin webmaster@<your_domain_name>
        ServerName  <your_domain_name>
        ServerAlias www.<your_domain_name>
        DirectoryIndex index.html index.php index.cgi index.rb
        DocumentRoot /home/<username>/websites/<your_domain_name>/
public_html/<your_subdomain_name>


        LogLevel warn
        ErrorLog  /home/<username>/websites/<your_domain_name>/
log/<your_subdomain_name>-error.log
        CustomLog /home/<username>/websites/<your_domain_name>/
log/<your_subdomain_name>-access.log combined
```

```
AccessFileName .myhtaccessfilename


    Alias /cgi-bin/ /home/<username>/websites/<your_domain_name>/
public_html/<your_subdomain_name>/cgi-bin/
    <Location /cgi-bin>
        Options +ExecCGI
    </Location>


    <Directory /home/<username>/websites/<your_domain_name>/
public_html/<your_subdomain_name> >
        Options Indexes Includes FollowSymLinks
        AllowOverride All


        <Files ~ "^\.myhtaccessfilename">
            Order allow,deny
            Deny from all
            Satisfy All
        </Files>


        Allow from all
        Order allow,deny
    </Directory>


    ErrorDocument 400 400.html
    ErrorDocument 401 401.html
    ErrorDocument 403 403.html
    ErrorDocument 404 404.html
    ErrorDocument 500 500.html


    ServerSignature Off


RewriteEngine on
    RewriteCond %{HTTP_HOST} ^(www\.)?servername\.lan$
    RewriteRule ^/web1(/.*)?$ http://web1.servername.lan$1
[R=301,L]


</VirtualHost>
```

20. When you are ready, save and close the file to proceed, but to ensure that our subdomain is always shown in the browser we will need to make a quick adjustment to the original domain. So open the original domain configuration as follows:

```
vi /etc/httpd/vhosts.d/<your_domain_name>.conf
```

21. Scroll down to the bottom of the file and before the `</VirtualHost>` closing tag type:

```
RewriteEngine on

RewriteCond %{HTTP_HOST} ^(www\.)?<your_domain_name>\.lan$

RewriteRule ^/<your_subdomain_name>(/.*)?$ http://<your_subdomain_name>.<your_domain_name>$1 [R=301,L]
```

22. When you have finished, save and close the file before reloading the Apache web service as follows:

```
service httpd reload
```

How it works...

You could say that this recipe represented a simplified case study. Apache is without doubt a very powerful web server and within this recipe you have seen how you can quickly build an enterprise-based solution. Of course, due to the scope of what we were trying to achieve there is always more that can be done, but it did provide an excellent starting point.

So what did we learn from this experience?

We began by creating a hosting structure that consisted of the files and folders that were necessary to build our virtual host. A sample configuration was given and by using this approach you could simplify the building of many web based publishing directories.

By asking you to log in as both root and the chosen username the recipe was careful to approach the subject of setting the correct file and folder permissions. Of course, you could have done it all as the root user but it is often felt that switching users proves to be the easiest way to avoid errors.

Remember, once you have completed one working domain structure, it is very straightforward to apply the copy command to replicate your work.

In the second phase we not only created a new directory (in which we would store our virtual host data files), but we opened the Apache configuration and modified it to include the following line:

```
Include /etc/httpd/vhosts.d/*.conf
```

In this way, I hope you will find that over time, the process of Apache maintenance becomes much easier and a little less confusing. This is particularly so when you consider that the virtual host files will be named more appropriately:

```
vi /etc/httpd/vhosts.d/<your_domain_name>.conf
```

Having done this, we then applied a much more detailed approach to the Apache directives:

```
<VirtualHost *:80>
#Your server details:
    ServerAdmin webmaster@<your_domain_name>
    ServerName  <your_domain_name>
    ServerAlias>


#Prioritise your directory structure
    DirectoryIndex index.html index.php index.cgi index.rb


#Confirm the location of the actual files
    DocumentRoot /home/<username>/websites/<your_domain_name>/public_
html/


#Use custom logging
        LogLevel warn
        ErrorLog   /home/<username>/websites/<your_domain_name>/log/error.
log
        CustomLog /home/<username>/websites/<your_domain_name>/log/
access.log combined


#Use an alternate name for your .htaccess file for reasons of security
AccessFileName .myhtaccessfilename


#Enable CGI in the appropriate folder
    Alias /cgi-bin/ /home/<username>/websites/<your_domain_name>/public_
html/cgi-bin/
    <Location /cgi-bin>
        Options +ExecCGI
    </Location>


#Include special settings for the directory
```

```
<Directory /home/<username>/websites/<your_domain_name>/public_html >
    #Set the Options for the specified directory, these can be applied
on a per folder basis.
Options +Indexes +Includes +FollowSymLinks
#Enable htaccess support
        AllowOverride All
        #Protect htaccess from external sources
        <Files ~ "^\.myhtaccessfilename">
            Order allow,deny
            Deny from all
            Satisfy All
        </Files>

        Allow from all
        Order allow,deny
    </Directory>


#Enable custom error documents
    ErrorDocument 400 400.html
    ErrorDocument 401 401.html
    ErrorDocument 403 403.html
    ErrorDocument 404 404.html
    ErrorDocument 500 500.html


#Turn off the server signature to keep these details private
    ServerSignature Off
</VirtualHost>
```

Having completed this task, we then added an Apache rewrite rule to ensure that the visitor will always see the subdomain as it was intended to be shown:

```
RewriteEngine on
RewriteCond %{HTTP_HOST} ^(www\.)?<your_domain_name>\.lan$
RewriteRule ^/<your_subdomain_name>(/.*)?$ http://<your_subdomain_
name>.<your_domain_name>$1 [R=301,L]
```

This recipe has served to cover a lot of information, and it may take sometime before the actual extent of what you have achieved can be appreciated. Much of this blueprint may appear to be common sense, and there are always going to be variations on a theme, but by putting it down on paper this recipe has provided you with a process of web directory configuration that is frequently used by server administrators all over the world.

See also

- ▶ Apache Project Home page: `http://httpd.apache.org/`
- ▶ Apache Project, *Apache Virtual Host Documentation*: `http://httpd.apache.org/docs/2.2/vhosts/`

11
Working with FTP

In this chapter, we will cover:

- ▶ Building a basic FTP service by installing and configuring VSFTP
- ▶ Providing a secure connection to VSFTP with SSL/TLS using OpenSSL encryption
- ▶ Implementing virtual users and directories in standalone mode on VSFTP
- ▶ Providing an anonymous upload and download or download only FTP server with VSFTP

Introduction

This chapter is a collection of recipes that provides step-by-step instruction on how to start building a basic FTP service by installing and configuring VSFTP; providing a secure connection to VSFTP with SSL/TLS using OpenSSL encryption; implementing virtual users and directories in standalone mode on VSFTP; and providing an anonymous upload and download or download only FTP server with VSFTP.

Building a basic FTP service by installing and configuring VSFTP

In this recipe we will learn how to install and configure VSFTP.

Very Secure FTP Daemon (**VSFTP**) is a well known FTP server solution that supports a wide range of features and enables you to upload and distribute large files across a local network and the internet. It is the preferred solution for the security conscious and the purpose of this recipe is to demonstrate one of the many reasons as to why VSFTP represents the first choice for any administrator running a CentOS server.

Getting ready

To complete this recipe you will require a working installation of the CentOS 6 operating system with root privileges, a console based text editor of your choice, and a connection to the internet in order to facilitate the download of additional packages. It is expected that your server will be using a static IP address; and that it maintains one or more system user accounts.

If you are running a firewall, you will need to confirm that the firewall has been disabled, removed, or the appropriate ports are open. Similarly, if you are running SELinux, then you should confirm that it has been disabled or it is now running in permissive mode.

How to do it...

VSFTP is not installed by default and for this reason we must begin this recipe by installing the relevant package and associated dependencies.

1. To do this, log in as root and type the following command:

    ```
    yum install vsftpd
    ```

2. Now open the main configuration file in your favorite text editor as follows:

    ```
    vi /etc/vsftpd/vsftpd.conf
    ```

3. To disable anonymous users, scroll down and find the following line:

    ```
    anonymous_enable=YES
    ```

4. Make this line read as follows:

    ```
    anonymous_enable=NO
    ```

5. Scroll down and locate the following line:

    ```
    xferlog_std_format=YES
    ```

6. We want to enable an independent `log` file, so change this line to read as follows:

    ```
    xferlog_std_format=NO
    ```

7. Now scroll down to locate the following lines:

    ```
    #ascii_upload_enable=YES
    #ascii_download_enable=YES
    ```

8. Our intention to enable ASCII mode that is useful when transferring single-byte character based text files. To do this, uncomment these lines as follows:

    ```
    ascii_upload_enable=YES
    ascii_download_enable=YES
    ```

9. Now scroll down to find the following lines:

```
#chroot_local_user=YES
#chroot_list_enable=YES
# (default follows)
#chroot_list_file=/etc/vsftpd/chroot_list
```

10. Uncomment these lines to enable the chroot environment for increased security:

```
chroot_local_user=YES
chroot_list_enable=YES
# (default follows)
chroot_list_file=/etc/vsftpd/chroot_list
```

11. Finally, scroll down to the bottom of the file and add the following line:

```
use_localtime=YES
```

12. Having done this, the next stage requires us to create a new file in order that we can manage our chroot settings and restrict user access to their home directories. To do this, type the following command:

```
vi /etc/vsftpd/chroot_list
```

13. Now add your local user(s) in the following way:

```
username1
username2
username3
username4
```

14. Now save and close the file in the usual way before proceeding to enable VSFTP at boot:

```
chkconfig vsftpd on
```

15. To complete this recipe, type the following command to start the FTP service:

```
service vsftpd start
```

How it works...

VSFTP is widely recognized as a fast, lightweight, and reliable FTP server. Otherwise known as the Very Secure FTP Daemon, the purpose of this recipe was to show you how to build a basic FTP service that is not only secure, but one that is optimized to continue providing excellent performance for any number of valid system users.

So what did we learn from this experience?

We began the recipe by installing the necessary packages in the following way:

```
yum install vsftpd
```

We then opened the main configuration file located at /etc/vsftpd/vsftpd.conf to disable anonymous access and thereby secure our FTP service against unknown users:

```
anonymous_enable=NO
```

The next step was to modify the default logging conditions by changing the following line to read:

```
xferlog_std_format=NO
```

Of course, an advanced user may argue that this was an optional step, but for simplicity this modification ensures that a log file is created at /var/log/vsftp.log instead of using /var/log/xferlog.log.

Following this, we then proceeded to enable ASCII transfers with the intention to support single-byte character based text files:

```
#Enable ASCII
ascii_upload_enable=YES
ascii_download_enable=YES
```

We then restricted users to their home directory by enabling a chroot jail in the following way:

```
#Enable Chroot
chroot_local_user=YES
chroot_list_enable=YES
chroot_list_file=/etc/vsftpd/chroot_list
```

We then required VSFTP to use local time by adding the following line at the bottom of the configuration file:

```
use_localtime=YES
```

So having completed our configuration changes the next step was to finalize the chroot environment by creating a new file in the following way:

```
vi /etc/vsftpd/chroot_list
```

We then added a single or list of system users as follows:

```
username1
username2
username3
username4
```

The chroot jail represents an essential security feature, and having done this, all users will be restricted to access the files in their own home directory only.

Finally, having saved your work we then proceeded to enable VSFTPD at boot:

```
chkconfig vsftpd on
```

Before starting the VSFTP service as follows:

```
service vsftpd start
```

At this point VSFTP will now be operational and it can be tested with any regular FTP-based desktop software. Users can log in using a valid system username and password by connecting to your server's name, domain, or IP address (depending on your server's configuration).

You can confirm the status of your FTP service at any time by typing:

```
service vsftpd status
```

The purpose of this recipe was to show you that VSFTP is not a difficult package to install and configure. There is always more to do, but by following this simple introduction we have quickly enabled our server to run a very secure FTP service.

There's more...

Having installed and configured a basic FTP service you may wonder how to direct users to a specific folder within their home directory.

To do this, ensure the location exists and then open the main configuration file by typing:

```
vi /etc/vsftpd/vsftpd.conf
```

Scroll down to the bottom of the file and add the following line by substituting the value `<users_local_folder_name>` with something more applicable to your own needs:

```
local_root=<users_local_folder_name>
```

For example, if this is for serving web pages, you may have created a folder called `/home/<username>/public_html`, and for this reason you may have added the following reference to the bottom of your VSFTP configuration file:

```
local_root=public_html
```

When finished, save and close the configuration file before restarting the service as follows:

```
service vsftpd restart
```

Changing the default time-out

When dealing with a large number of users you may want to consider changing the values for a default time-out in order to improve the efficiency of your FTP service. To do this, open the main configuration file in your favorite text editor by typing:

```
vi /etc/vsftpd/vsftpd.conf
```

Now scroll down and find the following lines:

```
# You may change the default value for timing out an idle session.
#idle_session_timeout=600
#
# You may change the default value for timing out a data connection.
#data_connection_timeout=120
```

Uncomment these lines and substitute the numeric values as required:

```
# You may change the default value for timing out an idle session.
idle_session_timeout=600
#
# You may change the default value for timing out a data connection.
data_connection_timeout=120
```

Banning a user from the FTP service

By enabling a chroot jail you will be restricting a user's access to the home folder, but if you wanted to ban a specific user from using the FTP service as a whole, the user's name should be added to /etc/vsftpd/ftpusers.

To do this, log in as root and type the following command:

```
echo username >> /etc/vsftpd/ftpusers
```

Remember to replace username with a value more appropriate to your own needs, and if you ever need to re-enable the user at any time, simply reverse the previous process by removing the user concerned from /etc/vsftpd/ftpusers.

Customizing the banner

In most instances, the default values will suit most needs but in certain circumstances you may want to consider customizing your banner.

To do this, open the main configuration file in your favorite text editor by typing:

```
vi /etc/vsftpd/vsftpd.conf
```

Now scroll down and find the following line:

```
#ftpd_banner=Welcome to blah FTP service
```

Uncomment this line and alter the message as required For example, you could use:

```
ftpd_banner=Welcome to my new FTP server
```

Having done this, close any active connection and restart the VSFTPD service by typing:

```
service vsftpd restart
```

On the next successful login your users should see the following message:

```
Response:     220 Welcome to my new FTP server.
```

If you happen to encounter the 500 error then you must either disable SELinux or set the appropriate SELinux permissions.

See also

- ▸ VSFTP Project Homepage: `https://security.appspot.com/vsftpd.html`
- ▸ VSFTP Project FAQ: `https://security.appspot.com/vsftpd/FAQ.txt`
- ▸ VSFTP Project Documentation: `http://vsftpd.beasts.org/vsftpd_conf.html`
- ▸ VSFTP Project Configuration File List: `http://vsftpd.beasts.org/vsftpd_conf.html`

Providing a secure connection to VSFTP with SSL/TLS using OpenSSL encryption

In this recipe we will learn how to configure VSFTP with **Secure Sockets Layer /Transport Layer Security (SSL/TLS)** in order to provide a secure connection using OpenSSL.

Where security is concerned, the Very Secure FTP Daemon is known for its attention in detail, but during the lifetime of your server there may come a time when you express some concerns over the safety of your data transfers. It could be the case that you have already considered the need for SFTP, having expressed concerns about the risk of packet sniffing, malicious activity in general or the use of clear text credentials, and to this end, it is the purpose of this recipe to show you how to encrypt all traffic by providing a secure connection to VSFTP with SSL/TLS.

Getting ready

To complete this recipe you will require a working installation of the CentOS 6 operating system with root privileges and a console based text editor of your choice. It is expected that your server will be using a static IP address; that VSFTP and OpenSSL are already installed; and that your server maintains one or more system user accounts.

Having followed this recipe all clients attempting to use your FTP service should connect via SFTP and accept the server certificate. All other connection methods will fail.

How to do it...

For the purpose of this recipe we will be configuring VSFTP to use OpenSSL encryption in order that a user's credentials and data files remain encrypted during transfer.

1. To begin, log in as root and change to the VSFTP installation directory by typing:

   ```
   cd /etc/vsftpd/
   ```

2. The first task is to create a server certificate that will last for 365 days. To do this type the following single-line command:

   ```
   openssl req -x509 -nodes -days 365 -newkey rsa:1024 -keyout /etc/
   vsftpd/vsftpd.pem -out /etc/vsftpd/vsftpd.pem
   ```

3. You will then be asked a series of question to which you should respond with the appropriate values:

   ```
   Country Name (2 letter code) [XX]:

   State or Province Name (full name) []:

   Locality Name (eg, city) [Default City]:

   Organization Name (eg, company) [Default Company Ltd]:

   Organizational Unit Name (eg, section) []:

   Common Name (eg, your name or your server's hostname) []:

   Email Address []:
   ```

4. When the process of creating your certificate is complete we will proceed by changing the file permissions in order to ensure that it remains accessible to the root user only. To do this, type the following command:

   ```
   chmod 600 vsftpd.pem
   ```

5. We now want to make reference to the certificate in the VSFTP configuration. To do this open the main configuration with your favorite text editor in the following way:

   ```
   vi /etc/vsftpd/vsftpd.conf
   ```

6. The next step requires us to enable SSL, reference our certificate and to activate TLS due to its improved security as opposed to using SSL V2 and SSL V3. To do this, scroll down to the bottom of this file and add the following lines:

```
ssl_enable=YES
force_local_data_ssl=YES
force_local_logins_ssl=YES
ssl_tlsv1=YES
ssl_sslv2=NO
ssl_sslv3=NO
rsa_cert_file=/etc/vsftpd/vsftpd.pem
```

7. When complete, save and close the configuration file in the usual way before restarting the VSFTP service as follows:

```
service vsftpd restart
```

How it works...

We all know that a standard FTP service is inherently insecure. It suffers from the use of plain text usernames, passwords, and unencrypted data transfer the purpose of this recipe was to mitigate these issues through the use of OpenSSL encryption in order to provide a secure connection to VSFTP.

So what did we learn from this experience?

We began the recipe by changing to our default installation folder located at /etc/vsftpd and creating a server certificate using OpenSSL.

To do this, it was simply a matter of issuing the following command:

```
openssl req -x509 -nodes -days 365 -newkey rsa:1024 -keyout /etc/vsftpd/
vsftpd.pem -out /etc/vsftpd/vsftpd.pem
```

 It is important that this is a single-line command and it is expected that you may consider modifying the values shown.

In the example shown, we simply requested a 1024-bit RSA private key that remains valid for a period of 356 days; a process that is followed by a series of questions that will be incorporated in the certificate request.

The full process is as follows:

```
Generating a 1024 bit RSA private key
.................++++++
.++++++
writing new private key to '/etc/vsftpd/vsftpd.pem'
-----
You are about to be asked to enter information that will be incorporated
into your certificate request.
What you are about to enter is what is called a Distinguished Name or a
DN.
There are quite a few fields but you can leave some blank
For some fields there will be a default value,
If you enter '.', the field will be left blank.
-----
Country Name (2 letter code) [XX]:
State or Province Name (full name) []:
Locality Name (eg, city) [Default City]:
Organization Name (eg, company) [Default Company Ltd]:
Organizational Unit Name (eg, section) []:
Common Name (eg, your name or your server's hostname) []:
Email Address []:
```

Having created the certificate, the next step was to change its permissions in order that access is restricted to the root user. We achieved this by typing the following command:

```
chmod 600 vsftpd.pem
```

The next step required us to open the main VSFTP configuration in our favorite text editor with the intention to activate SSL.

We did this by typing:

```
vi /etc/vsftpd/vsftpd.conf
```

The first modification was to activate and enable SSL by adding the following line:

```
ssl_enable=YES
```

We were then required to ensure that the FTP service will only support clients that employ TLS/SSL support.

To do this we then added the following instructions:

```
# All non-anonymous logins are forced to use a
# secure SSL connection in order to send and
# receive data on data connections.
force_local_data_ssl=YES


# All non-anonymous logins are forced to use a secure
# SSL connection in order to send the password.
force_local_logins_ssl=YES
```

Based on the previous settings we are expecting all FTP clients to support AUTH TLS/SSL in order to connect. There is a wide range of both free and paid software that supports this type of connection but, it is possible to enable users to connect securely or insecurely depending on the type of FTP client available to them.

To do this, simply make the following alterations to the previous instruction:

```
# Enable the FTP client to determine as to
# whether the connection will be secure or insecure.
force_local_logins_ssl=NO
```

Having done this, and due to the preference for VSFTP to use TLS due to its improved security over SSL V2 and SSL V3 we then applied the following settings:

```
# Permit TLS v1 protocol connections.
ssl_tlsv1=YES


# Permit SSL v2 protocol connections. Only TLS v1 connections are
# preferred. From a security standpoint its use is strongly discouraged.
ssl_sslv2=NO


# permit SSL v3 protocol connections. Only TLS v1 connections are
# preferred.
ssl_sslv3=NO
```

Following this, we then included a reference to the certificate in order to ensure a secure connection.

We achieve this by adding the following line:

```
# Specify the location of the RSA certificate to use
# for SSL encrypted connections
rsa_cert_file=/etc/vsftpd/vsftpd.pem
```

Finally, having saved our work we then proceeded to restart the VSFTP service by typing the following command in order that the changes would take immediate effect:

```
service vsftpd restart
```

Remember, from now on, all your users should connect using SFTP or it will result in connection failures. Thereby implying that not only all usernames and passwords will be secure, but all data transfers will be encrypted for that additional peace of mind.

See also

> ▶ Wikipedia, *Transport Layer Security*:
> `http://en.wikipedia.org/wiki/Transport_Layer_Security`

Implementing virtual users and directories in standalone mode on VSFTP

In this recipe we will learn how to implement virtual users in order to break away from the restriction of using local system accounts, enable standalone mode for significant performance gains, and improve the overall security of VSFTP.

During the lifetime of your server there may be occasions when you wish to enable FTP authentication for a user that does not have a local system account. You may also want to consider implementing a solution that allows a particular individual to maintain more than one username password in order to allow access to different locations on your server. This type of configuration implies a certain degree of flexibility afforded by the use of virtual users and because you are not using a local system account it can be argued that this approach offers improved security.

Getting ready

To complete this recipe you will require a working installation of the CentOS 6 operating system with root privileges, a console based text editor of your choice, and a connection to the internet in order to facilitate the download of additional packages. It is expected that your server will be using a static IP address; and that VSFTP is already installed with a `chroot` jail and it is currently running.

How to do it...

To support virtual users you will be required to download and install the DB4-Utils package that will be used to create a database of users:

1. To begin, log in as root and type the following command:

   ```
   yum install db4-utils
   ```

2. The first step is to create a plain text file called `virtual-users` that serves to maintain a list usernames and passwords of the virtual users. To do this, type the following command:

   ```
   vi /opt/virtual-users.txt
   ```

3. Now add your usernames and passwords in the following way:

   ```
   virtual-username1
   password1
   virtual-username2
   password2
   virtual-username3
   password3
   virtual-username4
   password4
   ```

    Repeat this process as required, but for obvious reasons, maintain a good password policy and do not use the same virtual-username more than once.

4. When you have finished, simply save and close the file in the usual way before proceeding to build the database file by typing the following command:

   ```
   db_load -T -t hash -f /opt/virtual-users.txt /etc/vsftpd/virtual-users.db
   ```

5. Having done this, we will now create the PAM file that will use this database to validate your virtual users. To do this, type the following command:

   ```
   vi /etc/pam.d/vsftpd-virtual
   ```

6. Now add the following lines:

   ```
   auth required pam_userdb.so db=/etc/vsftpd/virtual-users
   account required pam_userdb.so db=/etc/vsftpd/virtual-users
   ```

7. When you have finished, save and close the file in the usual way before opening the main VSFTP configuration file in your favorite text editor as follows:

```
vi /etc/vsftpd/vsftpd.conf
```

8. Scroll down to the bottom of the file and add the following lines by customizing the value /path/to/virtual/folder/ to suit your own specific needs:

```
guest_enable=YES

virtual_use_local_privs=YES

write_enable=YES

pam_service_name=vsftpd-virtual

user_sub_token=$USER

local_root=/path/to/virtual/folder/$USER

chroot_local_user=YES

hide_ids=YES
```

9. When you have finished, simply save and close the file in the usual way before creating your primary directory in which the user's folders will be held. To do this simply replace /path/to/virtual/folder with the value set in the previous step and type:

```
mkdir /path/to/virtual/folder
```

10. Now create a folder for each virtual user within the previous directory but remember to delegate the ownership of this folder to an appropriate system user, system group, and define the relevant directory permissions:

```
mkdir /path/to/virtual/folder/<virtual-username>

chgrp <system-usergroup> /path/to/virtual/folder/<virtual-username>

chown <system-username> /path/to/virtual/folder/<virtual-username>
chmod <XXXX> /path/to/virtual/folder/<virtual-username>
```

11. Repeat the previous action for each virtual user before restarting the FTP service as follows:

```
service vsftpd restart
```

How it works...

Having followed the previous recipe you are now able to invite an unlimited number of virtual users the chance to access your FTP service. The configuration of VSFTP was very simple, your overall security has been improved and all access is restricted to a defined home directory of your choice.

So what did we learn from this experience?

We started the recipe by installing a new package called `db4-utils` in the following way:

```
yum install db4-utils
```

This package is used to create the necessary database of usernames and passwords; a process that began by creating the following text file:

```
vi /opt/virtual-users.txt
```

We then added the required usernames and passwords as follows:

```
virtual-username1
password1
virtual-username2
password2
virtual-username3
password3
virtual-username4
password4
```

Having done this for each of our virtual users we then saved and closed the file before proceeding to run the following command in order to build the required database file:

```
db_load -T -t hash -f /opt/virtual-users.txt /etc/vsftpd/virtual-users.db
```

Having completed this step, our next task was to create a PAM file at `/etc/pam.d/vsftpd-virtual` that would read the previous database file with the following instruction:

```
auth required pam_userdb.so db=/etc/vsftpd/virtual-users
account required pam_userdb.so db=/etc/vsftpd/virtual-users
```

We then opened the main VSFTP configuration file at `/etc/vsftpd/vsftpd.conf` in order to consolidate the steps so far:

```
# Activate the virtual users feature-set.
guest_enable=YES
# All virtual users are to use local privileges, not anonymous
privileges.
virtual_use_local_privs=YES
# Enable uploads and the creation of new directories
write_enable=YES
# Confirm the PAM file used to authenticate the virtual uses.
pam_service_name=vsftpd-virtual
# Confirm a home directory for each virtual user.
```

```
user_sub_token=$USER
```

```
local_root=/home/virtual/$USER
```

```
# Ensure the virtual user is restricted to the allocated directory.
```

```
chroot_local_user=YES
```

```
# Hide the server's details from user view.
```

```
hide_ids=YES
```

You were then prompted to create the relevant `virtual` hosting folder:

```
mkdir /path/to/virtual/folder
```

As an option, you could even assign this new folder to a particular system user and system group in the following way:

```
chgrp <system-group> /path/to/virtual/folder
```

```
chown <system-username> /path/to/virtual/folder
```

Having done this, you were then required to create a folder for each user by correctly identifying a specific system user to take full ownership of the files:

```
mkdir /path/to/virtual/folder/<virtual-username>
```

```
chgrp <system-usergroup> /path/to/virtual/folder/<virtual-username>
```

```
chown <system-username> /path/to/virtual/folder/<virtual-username>
```

```
chmod <XXXX> /path/to/virtual/folder/<virtual-username>
```

If you have a lot of users, this was probably the most time-consuming section of the entire recipe, but having finished, it was simply a matter of restarting the VSFTP service as follows:

```
service vsftpd restart
```

There's more...

If you intend to exercise the FTP service more readily, then it is better to run it in standalone mode in order to improve the performance of your server.

To do this, simply open the main VSFTP configuration file:

```
vi /etc/vsftpd/vsftpd.conf
```

Now scroll down to the bottom of the file and add the following line:

```
listen=YES
```

When you have finished, simply save and close the file before restarting your FTP service by typing the following command:

```
service vsftpd restart
```

By doing this, you will reduce the number of run-on-demand calls and consume less server resources. Ultimately this action will result in improved performance of the FTP service and a happy server.

Providing an anonymous upload and download or download only FTP server with VSFTP

In this recipe we will learn how to provide an anonymous FTP service using VSFTP.

VSFTP can be employed in a variety of ways in order to suit a range of different roles and it is the purpose of this recipe to show you how to install and configure an anonymous FTP server that will enable you to receive or distribute a range of files for public consumption without the need for credentials.

Getting ready

To complete this recipe you will require a working installation of the CentOS 6 operating system with root privileges, and a console based text editor of your choice. It is expected that your server will be using a static IP address; that you have at least one local system account who can assume the ownership of all anonymous uploads and that VSFTP is already running.

In your primary role as the server administrator you should be aware that by completing this recipe, anonymous FTP access will grant anyone the ability to access the FTP services with full read and write permissions. No access credentials will be required so you will need to consider the security aspects related to this type of service.

How to do it...

Having already installed and configured the VSFTP package no additional packages are required. It is simply a matter of reconfiguring and optimizing your existing FTP service:

1. To begin, log in as root and open the main VSFTP configuration file in your favorite editor by typing the following command:

    ```
    vi /etc/vsftpd/vsftpd.conf
    ```

2. Scroll down to find the following line:

    ```
    anonymous_enable=NO
    ```

3. In order to activate anonymous access change this line to read:

    ```
    anonymous_enable=YES
    ```

4. Now find the following line:

```
local_enable=YES
```

5. In order to deactivate local user access change this line to read:

```
local_enable=NO
```

6. Now scroll down to find the following lines:

```
#anon_upload_enable=YES
#anon_mkdir_write_enable=YES
```

7. In order to allow uploads and enable write permissions change these lines to read:

```
anon_upload_enable=YES
anon_mkdir_write_enable=YES
```

8. Now find the following lines:

```
#chown_uploads=YES
#chown_username=<system-user>
```

9. We will expect that the server will automatically change the ownership of all uploaded files to an appointed local system account. To do this, change these lines to read as follows by substituting `<system-user>` with a relevant system user account:

```
chown_uploads=YES
chown_username=<system-user>
```

 You can choose any valid user account, but whatever you do, always avoid the temptation of using the `root`.

10. Now find the following line:

```
ls_recurse_enable=YES
```

11. We want our FTP server to avoid using excessive resources, so change this line to read:

```
ls_recurse_enable=NO
```

12. At this stage, if you have not already done so, you may wish to configure your time-out settings. To do this, find each of the following lines and uncomment and/or adjust them as required:

```
idle_session_timeout=300
data_connection_timeout=120
```

13. Additionally, you should optimize your server to use one process per connection. To do this, scroll down to the bottom of the file and add:

```
one_process_model=YES
```

14. Further to this, you may also want to include the following instruction in order to define the maximum data transfer rate in bytes per second. Use the following value as an example and alter this as required:

```
anon_max_rate=2048000
```

15. To complete our customization, simply define a local directory to be used by the FTP service. The default folder can be found in /var/ftp/ but for the purpose of this recipe we will choose to use a different location. To do this, find the following line and make the relevant changes:

```
anon_root=/var/ftp
```

16. By substituting a relevant path based on your specific needs, make the line read as follows:

```
anon_root=</path/to/your/ftp-directory>
```

17. Finally, you may want to make sure the FTP service is running in standalone mode in order to obtain a significant increase in server performance. To do this, scroll down to the bottom of the file and add the following line:

```
listen=YES
```

18. Now save and close the file in the usual way before making sure that the chosen ftp directory exists. To do this, begin by customizing the following command:

```
mkdir </path/to/your/ftp-directory>
```

The default directory can be found in /var/ftp but if you are intending to allow uploads you will need to modify the folder permissions. To do this, change the permissions of this directory using the <system-username> and <system-username-group> value relevant to the credentials identified in this recipe:

```
chgrp <system-username-group> </path/to/your/ftp-
directory> && chown <system-username> </path/to/your/ftp-
directory>
```

Following this, remember to assign the relevant permissions as follows:

```
chmod XXXX </path/to/your/ftp-directory>
```

Remember, if you do intend to manage a large repository of files (with a particular emphasis on enabling large uploads) you should investigate the need to place the FTP directory on a separate hard disk or partition.

19. Finally, and when you are ready, restart the FTP service as follows:

```
service vsftpd restart
```

How it works...

Anonymous FTP represents a way for individuals to download or upload an asset without requiring the needs to identify themselves. It is very easy to implement and having followed this recipe your server is now fully capable of distributing and receiving one of more files for public consumption without the need for any access credentials.

So what did we learn from this experience?

We started the recipe by opening the main VSFTP configuration in your favorite text editor in the following way:

```
vi /etc/vsftpd/vsftpd.conf
```

Our first modification to this file was to enable anonymous access and to prevent local users from logging in:

```
anonymous_enable=YES
local_enable=NO
```

Followed by enabling support for anonymous uploads with full write permissions:

```
anon_upload_enable=YES
anon_mkdir_write_enable=YES
```

For reasons of security and auditing the next task was to ensure that the server will automatically change the ownership of all uploads to the identified account:

```
#change the ownership of all uploads
chown_uploads=YES


#change the ownership to a local system account
chown_username=<system-user>
```

Having completed this phase, the next step was to optimize the server with the following set of instructions:

```
# Do not use "ls -R" to avoid reduce resource consumption
ls_recurse_enable=YES


#confirm an appropriate timeout value for the session
idle_session_timeout=300
```

```
#confirm an appropriate value for the data connection timeout
data_connection_timeout=120


# We will use one process per connection in order to
# support large numbers of simultaneously connected users.
one_process_model=YES


#define the maximum transfer rate in bytes per second
anon_max_rate=2048000
```

Finally, we not only confirmed a full path to the local directory that will be used by the anonymous FTP service but we also required the server to run in standalone mode to obtain a significant increase in server performance:

```
#define the full path to your public ftp directory
anon_root=</path/to/<ftp-directory>
#ensure the FTP service is running in standalone
#mode for performance gains
listen=YES
```

So having saved the file in the usual way the next task was to confirm that the local `ftp` directory stated in your configuration file exists:

You can do this by typing:

```
mkdir </path/to/your/ftp-directory>
```

The default directory can be found in `/var/ftp`. However, regardless as to whether you decided on using the default directory or using a custom location, the recipe suggested that you will want to consider changing the ownership of this directory to the relevant user credentials used by the main configuration file.

You can do this by typing:

```
chgrp <system-username-group> </path/to/your/ftp-directory> && chown
<system-username> </path/to/your/ftp-directory>
```

You should complete this action by substituting xxxx with the appropriate read/write value (that is `0644` or `0770`) and typing the following command:

```
chmod XXXX /home/<ftp-directory>
```

At this point, the only remaining task was to restart VSFTP in order that your settings will take immediate effect:

```
service vsftpd restart
```

From now on, all anonymous users will be able to upload and download files from your server without the need for login credentials; and as long as you are careful and keep a close eye on all activity, this simple recipe will enable you to coordinate the file transfer needs of users all over the world.

> For whatever reason, should you ever need to stop the FTP service, simply log in as root and type the following:
>
> ```
> service vsftpd stop
> ```

However, if you do intend to manage a large repository of files (with a particular emphasis on enabling large uploads and maintaining adequate security controls) you should investigate the need to place your `log` files and the chosen FTP directory on separate hard disks or partition to root.

There's more...

Enabling anonymous access to your FTP service has its advantages but if you decide to restrict this to a download only service, then simply make the following changes to the main configuration file located at `/etc/vsftpd/vsftpd.conf`.

The changes you will need to make are as follows:

```
#enable anonymous uploads.
anon_upload_enable=NO
#enable anonymous write support
anon_mkdir_write_enable=NO
```

Having done this, simply save the file in the usual way before proceeding to restart the FTP service in the following way:

```
service vsftpd restart
```

By making these changes, you will not only improve the security of your server, but you will still be able to allow anonymous access to your FTP service. All attempts to upload a file will be greeted by the typical "Permission Denied" message.

Index

N

nameserver
configuring 220-223
Nano text editor 31
netinstall
about 7
running, over HTTP 19-22
netinstall-based approach
requisites 19
Netmask value
substituting, with prefix 56
Network Manager 53
network recycle bin
providing, for Samba 188-192
Network Time Protocol. *See* **NTP**
newaliases command 84
nslookup 31
NTP
about 45
used, for synchronizing multiple machines 49, 50
used, for synchronizing system clock 46-48
NTP query program (ntpq) 47

P

packages
finding, YUM used 131-136
installing, YUM used 122-125
removing, YUM used 127-130
Package Selection Groups 17
PAM 79
PEERDNS 55
Perl 31
ping 31
Pluggable Authentication Module. *See* **PAM**
POP3/SMTP server
building, with Postfix and Dovecot 270-272
e-mail software, setting up 273
Posix Time Format 42
Postfix
about 264
configuring, as domain-wide MTA 264
Postfix and Dovecot
used, for serving e-mail across virtual domains 281

Postfix header
activating 276
Postfix Project documentation
URL 270
Postfix Project homepage
URL 274
PostgreSQL
about 254, 255
connecting to 257
database, accessing using psql 258
database copy, creating 259
database, creating 255
installing 254
remote access, configuring 259-262
user, adding 255
working 255, 256
PostgreSQL Project Homepage
URL 262
prefix
about 56
Netmask value, substituting with 56
Python 31

R

reflective synchronization 51
remote access, to PostgreSQL
configuring 259-262
repository 115
Rescue Mode 28
reverse DNS lookup 219
rsync
about 88
used, for synchronizing directories 88-93
used, for synchronizing files 88-93
runlevel
about 35, 36
changing 35, 36

S

Samba
about 178, 185
accesses, managing 186, 187
configuring, as standalone server 175-177
custom share folder, creating for specific user or group of users 195-199

About Packt Publishing

Packt, pronounced 'packed', published its first book "*Mastering phpMyAdmin for Effective MySQL Management*" in April 2004 and subsequently continued to specialize in publishing highly focused books on specific technologies and solutions.

Our books and publications share the experiences of your fellow IT professionals in adapting and customizing today's systems, applications, and frameworks. Our solution based books give you the knowledge and power to customize the software and technologies you're using to get the job done. Packt books are more specific and less general than the IT books you have seen in the past. Our unique business model allows us to bring you more focused information, giving you more of what you need to know, and less of what you don't.

Packt is a modern, yet unique publishing company, which focuses on producing quality, cutting-edge books for communities of developers, administrators, and newbies alike. For more information, please visit our website: www.packtpub.com.

About Packt Open Source

In 2010, Packt launched two new brands, Packt Open Source and Packt Enterprise, in order to continue its focus on specialization. This book is part of the Packt Open Source brand, home to books published on software built around Open Source licences, and offering information to anybody from advanced developers to budding web designers. The Open Source brand also runs Packt's Open Source Royalty Scheme, by which Packt gives a royalty to each Open Source project about whose software a book is sold.

Writing for Packt

We welcome all inquiries from people who are interested in authoring. Book proposals should be sent to author@packtpub.com. If your book idea is still at an early stage and you would like to discuss it first before writing a formal book proposal, contact us; one of our commissioning editors will get in touch with you.

We're not just looking for published authors; if you have strong technical skills but no writing experience, our experienced editors can help you develop a writing career, or simply get some additional reward for your expertise.

Game Maker 8 Cookbook

ISBN: 978-1-84969-062-1   Paperback: 346 pages

Over 100 recipes for quickly enhancing your games

1. Enhance the complexity of your games using the Game Maker Language

2. Apply these recipes to virtually any type of game, including 3D and online games!

3. Simple, well explained recipes designed for game maker enthusiasts at all levels

HTML5 Game Development with GameMaker

ISBN: 978-1-84969-410-0   Paperback: 250 pages

Experience a captivating journey that will take you from creating your first social web browser game to a full on shoot 'em up

1. Build browser-based games and share them with the world

2. Master the GameMaker Language with easy to follow examples

3. Every game comes with original art and audio, including additional assets to build upon each lesson

Please check **www.PacktPub.com** for information on our titles

Android NDK Beginner's Guide

ISBN: 978-1-84969-152-9   Paperback: 436 pages

Discover the native side of Android and inject the power of C/C++ in your applications

1. Create high performance applications with C/C++ and integrate with Java

2. Exploit advanced Android features such as graphics, sound, input, and sensing

3. Port and re-use your own or third-party libraries from the prolific C/C++ ecosystem

Drupal 7 Development by Example Beginner's Guide

ISBN: 978-1-84951-680-8   Paperback: 366 pages

Follow the creating of a Drupal website to learn, by example, the key concepts of Drupal 7 development and HTML5

1. A hands-on, example-driven guide to programming Drupal websites

2. Discover a number of new features for Drupal 7 through practical and interesting examples while building a fully functional recipe sharing website

3. Learn about web content management, multi-media integration, and e-commerce in Drupal 7

Please check **www.PacktPub.com** for information on our titles